CHILDFREE AND HAPPY

CHILDFREE AND HAPPY

Transforming the Rhetoric of Women's Reproductive Choices

COURTNEY ADAMS WOOTEN

UTAH STATE UNIVERSITY PRESS
Logan

Published by Utah State University Press
An imprint of University Press of Colorado
1624 Market Street, Suite 226
PMB 39883
Denver, Colorado 80202-1559

 The University Press of Colorado is a proud member of the Association of University Presses.

The University Press of Colorado is a cooperative publishing enterprise supported, in part, by Adams State University, Colorado State University, Fort Lewis College, Metropolitan State University of Denver, University of Alaska Fairbanks, University of Colorado, University of Denver, University of Northern Colorado, University of Wyoming, Utah State University, and Western Colorado University.

∞ This paper meets the requirements of the ANSI/NISO Z39.48-1992 (Permanence of Paper).

ISBN: 978-1-64642-437-5 (hardcover)
ISBN: 978-1-64642-438-2 (paperback)
ISBN: 978-1-64642-439-9 (ebook)
https://doi.org/10.7330/9781646424399

Library of Congress Cataloging-in-Publication Data

Names: Wooten, Courtney Adams, author.
Title: Childfree and happy : transforming the rhetoric of women's reproductive choices / Courtney Adams Wooten.
Description: Logan : Utah State University Press, [2023] | Includes bibliographical references and index. | Summary: "Childfree and Happy examines how millennia of reproductive beliefs have positioned women who choose not to have children as deviant. Considering affect and emotion alongside the lived experiences of women who have chosen not to have children, Wooten offers a new lens to feminist scholars' examinations of reproductive rhetorics"— Provided by publisher.
Identifiers: LCCN 2023012094 (print) | LCCN 2023012095 (ebook) | ISBN 9781646424375 (hardcover) | ISBN 9781646424382 (paperback) | ISBN 9781646424399 (ebook)
Subjects: LCSH: Childfree choice—Social aspects. | Childlessness—Social aspects. | Happiness—Social aspects. | Women—Identity—Social aspects. | Feminism and rhetoric.
Classification: LCC HQ755.8 .W677 2023 (print) | LCC HQ755.8 (ebook) | DDC 306.87—dc23/eng/20230411
LC record available at https://lccn.loc.gov/2023012094
LC ebook record available at https://lccn.loc.gov/2023012095

Cover art: © Veng Photography/iStock

CONTENTS

ACKNOWLEDGMENTS

Writing acknowledgments is a strange exercise that can only attempt to make visible the huge amount of mostly invisible labor many people in my life have willingly put forth to bring this book to fruition. While I attempt to do so here, I am undoubtedly missing others who have contributed to this book project, and I recognize acknowledgments themselves are a poor attempt at making visible the labor and support provided by everyone around me as I wrote this book.

First, I must start by wholeheartedly thanking all my interviewees for being willing to talk with me about their experiences as childfree women. As should be abundantly clear, this book would not have been possible without the trust they gave me—a childfree woman who was often merely a stranger or acquaintance—trust that made it possible for them to open up to me about their experiences and allow me the honor of representing them here. I feel as if I have come to know each of them through this work while also feeling keenly my inability to fully represent in this work their lives as childfree women. I hope this book does justice to their time and willingness to talk with me.

I have been thankful for the mentors I have had throughout my educational experience who have supported me and shown me there is space for me and my ideas in the field. Brooke McLaughlin Mitchell mentored me as an undergraduate at Wingate University and convinced me, a first-generation college student, that I could go to graduate school when I had never even considered this option. Kelly Ritter, my mentor and friend, has been a faithful supporter since I was in my doctoral program, and I truly do not think I would be here today if it weren't for her demonstrating what being a working-class woman academic can look like. Risa Applegarth provided sound wisdom and advice in my time as a doctoral student, and I continue to pass on her advice to others.

Several of my colleagues gave up so much time to reading many, many drafts of this project, providing feedback, and supporting me through times I wanted to quit writing. Annie Mendenhall has been with me from the beginning and read many terrible drafts of this project, encouraging me to keep writing and revising and celebrating along the way. Roxanne Aftanas, Patricia Fancher, and Brian Ray all read parts of the project at various points and provided feedback I needed to understand how to keep refining ideas and framing this work. Finally, my colleague Heidi Lawrence kept me from giving up on this project multiple times and gave me strategies for moving forward when I wasn't sure I could. The amount of collective labor this group graciously gave me made this project possible.

At Utah State University Press, Rachael Levay believed in this project and encouraged me to continue working on it even when it hit roadblocks. I am grateful to the anonymous reviewers who also gave their time, especially during the tragedies and difficulties experienced from 2020 to 2022, and made this project the best it can possibly be. Their feedback was encouraging yet critical, and I know this book would not be the same without their thoughtfulness in approaching this work. I also must thank Kate Epstein, whose editorial work helped push me through the last stages of book revisions that would have taken me much longer to manage on my own. An article based on a subset of interview data from this book was published in *College English* (" 'I Get Some Discrimination They Don't Get, They Get Discrimination I Don't Get': Childfree Reproductive Experiences in English Studies," 2021), and I thank editor Melissa Ianetta and anonymous reviewers of that piece for their feedback on it.

Both institutions I have been at while writing this book provided me research support. Stephen F. Austin State University gave me research release time in Spring 2017 that helped me draft the initial version of this project. George Mason University provided me with a full semester of research leave in Fall 2021 that gave me time to finish the final version of this book. I must stop here to express my deep thanks to my entire writing program administration team, who stepped in and took on additional responsibilities during my semester of research leave to make my finishing this project possible: Lourdes Fernandez (who stepped in as interim director in my place), Anna Habib, Lisa Lister, Jessica Matthews, and Jennifer Messier, along with our graduate WPA Ron'ada Hewitt. I am appreciative to all of you for your support. Finally, Lauren Hoerath, a graduate student in a theory and practice of editing class at George Mason University, worked on editing my references, which helped me complete this project.

As should be obvious, I have been honored to have a strong group of colleagues and friends who have supported me throughout writing this book. To these, I would like to add the support of my best friend Alison Johnson, who read very early versions of this project and never doubted I would publish it even when I did doubt it. Jacob Babb, my friend and colleague from graduate school, similarly encouraged me at every step, even when I was discouraged. Ansley Adams, my sister-in-law, has been an encouraging friend for many years, supporting me through graduate school and two academic jobs. My grandparents, parents, and siblings have also been sources of support, for which I am grateful.

Finally, my partner Mikell has unfailingly been by my side for over fifteen years, putting up with moving across the country twice for my dreams and fitting his own career around mine. He has celebrated my successes and pulled me through failures at every step, and without his support this book most certainly would not exist. He and I both determined we would be childfree around the same time thankfully, and we have enjoyed being cat and dog parents, an uncle and aunt, workout buddies, and drinking buddies together. My dog Dottie was part of my initial inspiration for thinking about being childfree, and her passing in Summer 2021 reinforced for me the need to enjoy every second I have with those I love.

Throughout the process of writing this book, I have grown as a person, and I have come to embrace my childfree identity even more than I did before while recognizing the privileges that have allowed me to be childfree. I hope this book opens up more conversations about child-freedom and shows more people that childfree women lead full, rich, happy lives and that we don't need anyone else to tell us we will change our minds later, regret our choices, or have no one to take care of us when we're old, thank you very much. I also hope readers, regardless of their own reproductive experiences, will take this book as an opportunity to reflect on the reproductive options available to different folx, including themselves, and find ways to advocate for reproductive justice wherever they are.

CHILDFREE AND HAPPY

Introduction

NORMALIZING CHILDFREEDOM
Affect, Reproductive Doxae, and Childfree Rhetorics

"Falling Birthrates: The Threat and the Dilemma"
—*Reuters*, December 7, 2012

"The U.S. Fertility Rate Just Hit an All-Time Low. Why Some Demographers are Freaking Out"
—*Washington Post*, June 30, 2017

"A Surprising Reason to Worry about Low Birth Rates: They're Linked to an Increase in Populist Sentiments"
—*Atlantic*, May 26, 2018

"Birth Rates Are at an All-Time Low in the U.S., and Experts Fear It Could Turn the Country Into a 'Demographic Time Bomb'"
—*Insider*, August 1, 2019

"U.S. Birthrate Falls to Its Lowest Level in Decades in Wake of Pandemic"
—*Washington Post*, May 5, 2021

"Why American Women Everywhere Are Delaying Motherhood"
—*New York Times*, June 16, 2021

It's been clear for a long time, at least from the headlines, that some people—notably women—aren't performing their reproductive duties by producing tax-paying citizens. Even articles that present a balanced look at falling birth rates, such as the ones above from the *Washington Post* and the *New York Times*, have clickbait headlines that predict sociopolitical failure. These headlines are inserted into a United States sociopolitical environment of heightened anxiety around reproductive

https://doi.org/10.7330/9781646424399.c000

rights, LGBTQIA+ rights, racial equity, and immigration in the midst of threats of environmental catastrophe and global war, highlighted in part by the murders of Trayvon Martin, Michael Brown, Eric Garner, Breanna Taylor, Ahmaud Arbery, Tony McDade, and many other Black Americans that spurred the ongoing Black Lives Matter protests in the late 2010s and early 2020s; the COVID-19 pandemic and resulting rise in unemployment, loss of childcare, and schools shifting online that affected many women in particular; the devastating effects of the United States abruptly removing military forces from Afghanistan in 2021; new laws in Texas, Florida, and other states banning the recognition of queer identities (colloquially known as "Don't Say Gay" laws); Russia's 2022 invasion of Ukraine; and the Syrian, Afghan, and Ukrainian refugee crises that have highlighted the effects of global war on the displacement and relocation of people around the world. For some, living through these times has made it even more likely they would choose not to have children, even as there has continued to be sociocultural backlash against those who make this decision.

On the surface, concerns over falling birth rates are largely tied to decreasing tax-generated government funds, in particular to support the Baby Boomer generation, and fewer workers, and graying countries in Asia and Western Europe have already been grappling with these problems. The *Atlantic* headline suggests readers should also fear cultural shifts from declining birth rates, which increase the prevalence of racist and nationalist ideologies. Indeed, as activist and reproductive justice scholar Loretta J. Ross (2006) claims, reproductive politics shape entire communities "by controlling how, when, and how many children a woman can have and keep" (61). As those women[1] seen as productive citizens—mostly white middle- and upper-class women—have fewer children, tensions about who will inherit the country surface. Journalist Olga Khazan (2018) argues in the *Atlantic* article that such tensions contributed to populist sentiments that fueled the election of leaders such as Donald Trump. Indeed, immigration resistance, a core feature of Trumpism, is common in times of falling birth rates even though immigration might solve some of the economic problems of population decline (Zavodny 2021).

While at least some might prefer to avoid both the economic complications of an aging population and increasing nationalism and racism, in a country that tries to define itself around "liberty and justice for all," ideological tensions quickly arise in matters of reproductive choice. *Childfree women*, a term I deliberately use throughout this project to point to the personal and political implications of choosing not to have children (see later discussion of the term *childfree* in this chapter for a more nuanced analysis of this term and similar terms), names a fairly homogeneous group that is typically white, college educated, and middle to upper class (Dykstra and Hagestad 2007; Gillespie 2000; Hayden 2010; Park 2005). These are privileged positions that provide them with the affordances to make choices about their reproductive lives despite common beliefs about reproduction—or reproductive *doxae*—in circulation. Yet when childfree women make decisions they view as largely personal (such as the decision not to have children), such personal choices quickly become linked to discourses of nationalism, race, class, and so on that complicate the idea of personal reproductive freedom, as they highlight systemic social problems with declining birth rates, particularly as the childfree group has grown in number and has increasingly become visible in the past several decades. Arguments about childfreedom become increasingly complex as public claims about particular women becoming mothers—which are tied to rhetorical articulations of selflessness, care, and happiness—are connected with arguments about capitalist structures, citizenship, and immigration. These arguments make visible often-hidden doxae about reproductive expectations for some women, as they intersect with doxae about nationalism, citizenship, and xenophobia.[2]

Because motherhood has been inscribed as the natural and preferred—or happy—state of womanhood, contributing heavily to gendered happiness scripts in the United States, those women who choose not to have children are viewed as deviant or outside typical gender constructions. Although childfree women do not embrace motherhood, they still identify with womanhood; these identities are hard to separate in a society that ties women's gender to reproductive functions. Since the mid-twentieth century, "postwar Americans approached patriotic parenthood as a major source of joy and satisfaction in life. Happy families became synonymous with the 'American way of life'" (May 1995, 134). Not having children was associated, and continues to be associated, with unhappiness. Work by other scholars further explains how the childless, particularly childless women, are ostracized in different parts of the world. In a study of five childless women in Australia, Stephanie Rich Ann Taket, Melissa Graham, and Julia Shelley (2011) concluded that "the reproductive status of women is still made to be relevant to how women are perceived, defined and valued, in contemporary Australian society. Importantly, lived experiences of childless women revealed in this research of feeling discredited and undervalued, and being perceived as unnatural and unwomanly, demonstrate that misconceptions and negative stereotypes about childlessness continue to pervade" (244). Studies with larger samples in other geographical locations have had similar results (Gillespie 2000; Kopper and Smith 2001; Mueller and Yoder 1999).

More recently, a study by Leslie Ashburn-Nardo (2017) asked 197 undergraduates at a midwestern US university about their perceptions of childfree people. She found this group perceived childfree people "as leading less fulfilling lives than do people who had chosen to have children. Moreover, their decision to forgo parenthood, arguably individuals' most personal choice, evoked moral outrage—anger, disgust, and disapproval. Moral outrage in turn served as a mechanism by which targets' parenthood status affected their perceived psychological fulfillment" (398). While Ashburn-Nardo, like Rich et al. (2011) and others, have focused on particular groups' perceptions of childfree people, a growing amount of research suggests that, at least in some places, childfree women (and people more generally) are negatively perceived and have often been seen, as sociologists Pearl A. Dykstra and Gunhild O. Hagestad (2007) put it, as deviants. Because their disidentification as mothers works against doxae about women's reproductive lives as reflected in gendered happiness scripts, society casts childfree women as unhappy in order to reinforce gendered doxae and to marginalize them.

At an individual level, childfree women can struggle to articulate why they do not want children to family, friends, colleagues, and even strangers in rhetorically effective ways. The ideological threads wrapped up in why some women are encouraged to become mothers and others are not (see Fixmer-Oraiz 2019; Harper 2020), as well as the sociocultural baggage that attends becoming a mother, constrain what arguments others will hear and respond positively to. Childfree women's careful rhetorical positioning of their decision in such a complex sociocultural milieu provides one avenue for rhetorical scholars to explore how a particular group of women is speaking back to *doxic* understandings of reproduction as underpinned by hegemonic mothering ideologies.

Drawing on interviews with thirty-four childfree women and analyses of texts about childfree women, this book examines the ways childfree women's rhetorics are constrained and opened up by affectual circulations of reproductive doxae. In so doing, this book shows how feminist rhetorical scholars can use affect theory frameworks, which draw attention to the often-invisible threads that bind our actions and reactions, to interrogate how reproductive doxae affect the discourses that construct, support, and reject particular women's identities. I argue that childfree women's rhetorical interventions into these doxae demonstrate the difficulty of contesting and shifting these beliefs about their reproductive decisions. Ultimately, I claim that reproductive doxae limit the rhetorics available to childfree women so they feel forced to work with these threads even as they weave them in different patterns. These restrictions constrain the ways various people and groups, including childfree women themselves, rhetorically construct childfree women's identities and call for new theorizations of their identities that move away from or complicate the binds of motherhood, selflessness, and care. This approach also demonstrates how feminist rhetorical scholars can use affect theory frameworks to make doxae about gender visible for critique as they operate on rhetorics used by and about women.

DOXAE AND AFFECT IN REPRODUCTIVE RHETORICS

Although much of the work in feminist rhetorics deals with doxae about women and their bodies, explicit focus on gendered doxae and how they affect women's rhetorics has been rare. This may be, in part, because doxae can be tricky to analyze; in his well-known work *Outline of a Theory of Practice*, Pierre Bourdieu (1977) suggests why: doxae typically operate at an undiscussed or undisputed level, often affecting our lives without our even being aware of them. Doxae about women's reproductive lives and the pressures for women to become mothers operate in this unseen space, making it sometimes difficult to pinpoint particular affordances and constraints on childfree women's rhetorics. What I offer here is an attention to the affectual circulations of gendered reproductive doxae; this type of attention to affect and doxae can demonstrate the binding power of doxae and, therefore, make them more available for analysis and critique.

Several central tenets about doxae underscore the kinds of constraints and affordances seen in discourses by, about, and around childfree women. First, echoing Bourdieu, scholars such as Karen LeFevre (1986), Thomas B. Farrell (1993), Dana Anderson (2007), and Caddie Alford (2016) draw attention to the often unspoken and unexamined nature of doxae. Anderson (2007) claims that doxae are "those ideas we think *with* rather than think *about*" (8), and Alford (2016) claims they are "the discursive glue that both roots and insulates a community." Common assumptions made about childfree women's lives form part of this glue that makes them feel separated from others and that limits their rhetorics.

Second, many scholars (Bourdieu 1977; Crowley 2006; Farrell 1993; Holiday 2009; LeFevre 1986; Richards 2017; Ritivoi 2006; Thimsen

2015) claim doxae reflect a community's social understandings of ideas and knowledge, forming an epistemological web that unconsciously or subconsciously supports what those in a community do and think. For example, LeFevre (1986) claims that "the inventing 'self' is socially influenced, even socially constituted" (33), such that doxae influence what people say, do, write, and so forth. Doxae can form not only what epistemologies a community accepts but also obscure those it does not (Richards 2017), sometimes forcing them outside the realm of possibility. Even people not explicitly opposed to women choosing not to have children may repeat or at least fail to notice or object to discourses about women's lives that presume they will choose to have children.

Third, doxae are often circulated by people with power who are reluctant to make them visible (Bourdieu 1977; Crowley 2006; Thompson 1999; Thimsen 2015; Richards 2017). Equating doxae with commonly held beliefs as I and other scholars do, Sharon Crowley (2006) argues "that beliefs are views or attitudes or assessments about nature (including human nature) that serve the interests of the believer and/or some other person, group, or institution" (68). As operations of social systems, doxae often carry forward epistemologies that serve those in power and, as such, are better for those in power when doxae are less available for critique. Any attempt at making doxae visible, such as resisting and publicly questioning gender roles, must be countered because this forces doxae into the open and makes them susceptible to change, change that can harm existing social structures.

Fourth, although making doxae visible can be difficult, doxae do shift and evolve across different places and times whether made explicit or not (Richards 2017). However, some scholars (Hariman 1986; Muckelbauer 2008; Ritivoi 2006; Thimsen 2015) argue that the concept of doxae also speaks to the collective reputation needed to change doxae. John Muckelbauer (2008), for instance, claims doxa can mean both "a sense of subjective conviction" and "an objective quality similar to that indicated by the word 'reputation' (and also similar to the concept of ethos)" (150). A. Freya Thimsen (2015) echoes Muckelbauer's understanding. What is at stake for childfree women, then, is whether and how they can gain enough collective reputation to shape and change doxae about women's reproductive lives.

These four central ideas about doxae can be found moving through some feminist rhetorical scholarship, although doxae are not often directly analyzed through this lens. In the next section, I trace how reproductive doxae have been taken up in feminist rhetorical scholarship and made way for further work into how such doxae circulate and operate on and through women's rhetorics. I then draw on Sara Ahmed's theory of happiness scripts to develop a framework for analyzing how reproductive doxae are both affectually and discursively circulated through childfree rhetorics.

Circulations of Reproductive Doxae in Studies of Feminist Rhetorics

Feminist rhetorical scholars have already explored the affordances and constraints different women or groups of women have experienced as rhetors, particularly in inventing new or different platforms and spaces, positions, and rhetorical strategies for themselves. Scholars such as Karlyn Kohrs Campbell (1989), Andrea Lunsford (1995), Cheryl Glenn (1997), Wendy Sharer (2004), and Lindal Buchanan (2005) have analyzed many platforms and spaces in which women rhetors have found an audience. However, the types of platforms and spaces granted to women rhetors can depend greatly on their positions and intersectional identities, which feminist rhetorical scholars have also examined (Logan 1999; Royster 2000; Gold 2020). In response to the constraints women rhetors experience because of the platforms and spaces available or unavailable to them and their perceived authority as rhetors based on their positions and identities, different individual women and groups of women have developed a broad variety of rhetorical strategies to influence the discourses around and about them, such as silence (Glenn 2004), rhetorical listening (Ratcliffe 2006), and rhetorical impatience (Cary 2020).

Feminist rhetorical scholars have also built rhetorical approaches out of feminist principles that reshape how rhetoric is viewed and open up for further analysis the rhetorical practices of everyone, including invitational rhetorics (Griffin and Foss 2020). In all these contributions, feminist rhetorical scholars have developed new methodologies for studying rhetoric, expanding what researchers can examine and how they can account for their own personal investment in their research (Booher and Jung 2018; Glenn 2018; Jarratt 2009; Restaino 2019; Royster and Kirsch 2012; Schell and Rawson 2010). Collectively, this body of scholarship reflects a deep attention to the ways women rhetors have individually and collectively found platforms and spaces where they could speak, acknowledge, and leverage how their identities shape their discursive practices, and to the ways they have developed unique strategies for talking with others. Throughout these texts, scholars show how women rhetors have constantly had to respond to, speak back against, and work with evolving doxae about their gendered identities as women. This work also shows how women rhetors have been active in shaping and reshaping the discourses at work around them about gender, race, sexuality, medicine, politics, and so on. In other words, women rhetors have found ways to resist doxae even as they understand the need to negotiate them in speaking with others.

Within this body of work, a growing number of feminist rhetorical scholars in writing studies, as well as related fields such as communications, have specifically studied the constraints and affordances reproduction (pregnancy, motherhood, infertility, etc.) presents to women rhetors. Like much of the work of other feminist rhetorical scholars, such studies often relate to specific platforms and spaces, positions, and rhetorical strategies women use, examining how women navigate their own and others' reproductive lives, as well as the reproductive rhetorics that circulate around them. This growing area of research—exemplified by Maria Novotny, Lori Beth De Hertogh, and Erin Frost's *Reflections* special issue in Fall/Winter 2020 about reproductive justice and Hannah Taylor's (2021) *College English* book review "Complicating Reproductive Agents: Material Feminist Challenges to Reproductive Rhetorics"—has brought together scholars from rhetorical studies who have focused on feminist rhetorics, digital rhetorics, and the rhetorics of health and medicine in the pursuit of a better understanding of how women rhetors are shaped by and themselves shape reproductive rhetorics and, as a result, their own and other women's reproductive experiences. Feminist rhetorical scholars' attention to reproductive rhetorics has paved the way for more scholars such as myself to examine the ways reproduction works on, around, and through women's rhetorics. Thus far, however, these studies do not explicitly theorize how doxae affectually circulate through women's rhetorics, particularly when examining their reproductive experiences, such as the case of childfree women. Jacqueline Jones Royster and Gesa E. Kirsch (2012), in *Feminist Rhetorical Practices*, call for examinations of "social circulation," which refers to "the social networks in which women connect and interact with others and use language with intention" (101). Here, I trace how existing scholarship about reproductive rhetorics—specifically women's reproductive capacities, pregnancy and childbirth, motherhood, and infertility—intersects with reproductive doxae, even though these studies do not typically theorize or analyze doxae in these ways.

Several texts examine how reproductive doxae are circulated in arguments about women's bodies' reproductive capacities and how some women have created alternative platforms, positions, and tools to undermine such doxae. Only one text explicitly examines circulations of reproductive doxae: Kristin Marie Bivens, Kristi Cole, and

Amy Koerber's (2019) work "Activism by Accuracy: Women's Health and Hormonal Birth Control." This book chapter traces how doxae about hormonal birth control (HBC) are used to "control and sanitize women's bodies (and hormones)" by repressing information about how hormonal birth control actually works (163–64). They claim that some of the doxae circulated through twenty-first-century advertisements for HBC emphasize its ability to not only effortlessly prevent pregnancy but to also " 'cure' acne, take away the menstrual period, reduce menstrual pain, and even prevent certain kinds of cancer" while blocking "women from accessing accurate health information" (164) that would help women understand how HBC works and, as a result, what physiological side effects they might experience when using it. Altogether this doxa "prioritizes expediency and effectiveness of preventing pregnancy over hormonal, physiological health" (164). Alternatively, Bivens, Cole, and Koerber analyze how some "alternative medical and naturopathic arguments and texts provide a powerful counterdiscourse capable of productively disrupting the *doxa* about HBC; this accurate information on hormonal health might empower patients by providing them with increased and more accurate information about the bodies and the potential consequences of taking HBC" (164). Their work demonstrates how studies of reproductive doxae can make visible the constraints operating on women's lives and how some women have recognized and spoken back to these, which this book takes up.

Bivens, Cole, and Koerber's work picks up themes from Koerber's (2018) book *From Hysteria to Hormones: A Rhetorical History*, although this book does not directly theorize circulations of reproductive doxae. It's clear, though, that Koerber's exploration of the evolution of understandings of women's bodies that shifted from discourses of hysteria to discourses of hormones is about the ongoing circulation of doxae about women's bodies. The doxa she traces is the belief—underpinning early understandings of hysteria and transferring to more contemporary diagnoses of hormones—"that women are motivated by something inside themselves that they cannot control, whereas men control themselves through rationality and the male brain" (xiv). In short, Koerber argues that this doxa has not changed for millennia, but the ways this doxa is explained, particularly by the modern scientific community, has. The result is that "today's experts remain committed to a belief that the hormone-brain relationship in women's bodies is more difficult to control and understand than it is in men's bodies" (xvi–xvii). Lydia M. McDermott's (2019) *Liminal Bodies, Reproductive Health, and Feminist Rhetoric: Searching the Negative Spaces in Histories of Rhetoric* links the ways women's bodies are pathologized with a feminist disability rhetoric framework, identifying the womb as a bodily space used to pathologize women: "Both the wandering womb narrative and ultrasound technology used as a routine aspect of prenatal care are meant to discipline the female reproductive body. As a medical theory, the wandering womb punished the woman who was not reproducing. As a surveillance technology, the ultrasound searches inside the reproducing woman to monitor her creation of a fetus" (15). Like Koerber, McDermott traces the ways women's bodies—whether "hysterical from lack of children, or insanely driven by desire from pregnancy"—are contrasted with supposedly "well-formed, clearly bounded, able to be touched and seen" men's bodies (145). McDermott primarily examines historical texts, but reproductive doxae continue to circulate these ideas, as Koerber's book examines. Koerber's (2018) and McDermott's (2019) books highlight a masculine fear of a lack of control over women's bodies that circulates through reproductive doxae. In chapter 1, I take up my own analysis of the ways theories of the wandering womb and hysteria have contributed to the pathologization of women without children by reinforcing the doxae that women's bodies naturally need to experience reproduction in order to be healthy and normal.

When women become pregnant and go through childbirth, their bodies are often marked differently from women who are not pregnant, and they can face increased scrutiny and interference from others, often men who purport to be experts despite having never experienced pregnancy or childbirth themselves. Marika Seigel's (2014) *The Rhetoric of Pregnancy* analyzes how pregnancy manuals such as *What to Expect When You're Expecting* describe pregnant women's bodies as systems that must be cared for through the rhetoric of risk management. Seigel identifies three assumptions, or what I call aspects of reproductive doxae, that underlie the structure of prenatal care.

> The first is that what we as a society consider to be the "work" of pregnancy has the potential to have an impact on the bodies and practices of not only pregnant women but also potentially pregnant women and that pregnant bodies can become the sites through which social, political, and environmental risks are managed. Second, there is a supposition that in cases where the pregnant woman is seen not to be adequately working to discipline her own body and practices, the role of doctors, employers, law enforcement officials, fathers, and other "enforcers" of prenatal care practices is to impose such discipline. Finally, the telos, or goal, of the work of pregnancy as informed by the medical-technological system of prenatal care is assumed to be not only a healthy fetus (or a healthy mother) but also a normal fetus. (13)

Such doxae affect the types of care available to pregnant women and how they and their fetuses are positioned in a medicalized environment focused on producing a normal fetus, not on supporting a woman through her pregnancy. Seigel concludes with ways pregnant women can push against such doxae and construct pregnancy and birth experiences that are woman centered and that complement the baby's health (143). Taking up this question of agency, and in some ways picking up where Seigel's book ends, Kim Hensley Owens's (2015) *Writing Childbirth: Women's Rhetorical Agency in Labor and Online* recounts how women assert agency over childbirth through their written birth plans and online birth narratives. She claims these written texts are a way for women to speak back to a medical field that often undervalues their desires, as Seigel's book also demonstrates. Much as my own project examines how childfree women negotiate childfree rhetorics, Owens's book "explores *how women accept, negotiate, and/or resist various subject positions* in and through their birth writing" (14). Chapter 1 of Owens's book explores what she calls the "commonplaces of modern American childbirth advice" (18), or what I see as reproductive doxae circulating through childbirth advice. The central commonplace or belief is that "childbirth was exceedingly and inherently life-threatening for women and that it is safer now only because of the advent of modern obstetric technologies and methods" despite evidence showing childbirth is safer now due to "improved sanitation, improved access to food, and improved understanding of germs" (19). This belief that childbirth is dangerous has led to a host of shifts in childbirth practices (such as changes from midwives to mostly male physicians, from home births to hospital births) and innovations (such as fetal heart monitoring) that have not necessarily improved childbirth outcomes for mothers or babies. Seigel's (2014) and Owens's (2015) work demonstrate how reproductive doxae construct and constrain women's bodily experiences and how some women have tried to resist such doxae and assert agency over their bodies.

Pregnant women in particular workplaces or professions can grapple with specific types of reproductive doxae that circulate even in spite of policies that ostensibly should make those workplaces more amenable to pregnancy and childbirth. Megan D. MacFarlane's (2021) *Militarized Maternity: Experiencing Pregnancy in the U.S. Armed Forces* draws attention to the dichotomy between the policies in the US military intended to support pregnant members of the armed forces and the actual reproductive doxae that circulate about pregnant servicewomen. She argues that this dichotomy is a result of a disjuncture between policies and culture—which I see as underscored by doxae—that reinforce "responsibilization," or the need for individuals to make choices that support themselves and others without consideration of the material constraints on those "choices." In the US military, servicewomen "become cocreateors in what [McFarlane calls] the circuit of discipline in which responsibilization is institutionalized, communicated, and performed by systems and individuals in the military" (17), such that doxae about what makes good military members and good pregnant women come into conflict and are unresolved by policies. MacFarlane's work demonstrates some of the limits of policy when reproductive doxae remain unchanged.

Once mothers, women continue to grapple with the ways reproductive doxae inform who they are as women and how they can leverage this role to build their own ethos in public spheres. Several scholars have examined how motherhood has circulated through women's rhetorics and has both constrained and offered opportunities to women rhetors. Nan Johnson's (2002) *Gender and Rhetorical Space in American Life, 1866–1910* examines how some women who were public speakers in the late 1800s took on a "mother-of-the-nation" role as a way to legitimize their presence in public. This role allowed them to claim that they "were watching over the affairs of the nation as they would their own households" (113) and that their public engagement was not inappropriate or out of line with their positions as women. Such moves countered doxae about women's roles as confined to private, domestic spaces and opened up ways for them to legitimate their participation in public spaces. Similarly, Lindal Buchanan (2013), in *Rhetorics of Motherhood*, analyzes how various women speakers, including Margaret Sanger, Diane Nash, and Michelle Obama, use motherhood rhetorics, and to what effect, whether beneficial or detrimental to the arguments they are making. Although in some cases using motherhood rhetorics can contribute to the ethos of the woman speaking, these rhetorics also are built on gendered doxae about women's roles, as with the women speakers Johnson discusses. Lisa Mastrangelo (2017) similarly takes up the affordances and constraints of ideographs of motherhood for American women during World War I. She claims that ideographs reflect cultural beliefs, or what I call *doxae*, one of which is that women are the "inherently morally superior sex, responsible for education and defense of the home" (217). Ultimately, she concludes, like Buchanan, that the motherhood rhetorics used during this time did not ultimately empower women; instead, women "were increasingly silenced and disempowered overall" (229). Johnson's, Buchanan's, and Mastrangelo's work demonstrates how reproductive doxae circulate through and around women's rhetorics, offering both opportunities and limitations on how women are positioned and what kinds of agency they have in their own and others' lives.

More recently, scholarship has examined how different reproductive doxae can circulate through motherhood rhetorics depending on women's intersectional identities. Three pieces in particular examine women's race and ethnicity in relation to reproduction: Natalie Fixmer-Oraiz's (2019) *Homeland Maternity: US Security Culture and the New Reproductive Regime*, Kimberly Harper's (2020) *The Ethos of Black Motherhood in America: Only White Women Get Pregnant*, and Lori Beth De Hertogh's (2020) "Interrogating Race-Based Health Disparities in the Online Community Black Women Do Breastfeed." Tying together US nationalism with motherhood, Fixmer-Oraiz (2019) argues that in a post-9/11 landscape, motherhood has been linked to what she calls "homeland security culture" by specifying "how *national security is tethered to securing the domestic and reproductive body*" (4). The reproductive doxa she traces through several discursive sites is "that white, heteronuclear domesticity remains central to the flourishing of the nation, that reproduction and mothering outside of these contexts are constituted as a public threat" (145). This text takes up how this reproductive doxa circulates around different women's bodies, most notably stratified by race and socioeconomic class, and influences our understandings of motherhood as tied to US nationalism. Examining Black mothers' experiences in particular, Harper's (2020) book analyzes how reproductive discourses revolve around concerns for white women's bodies and babies, eliding Black mothers in an erasure of their humanity, continuing an erasure embedded in US history. Part of the reproductive doxae circulating among researchers who have studied the health disparities facing Black mothers in the past is the belief "that the high rate of infant mortality could be attributed to the choices of poor, less educated Black women. It was assumed they were not taking care of themselves or their newborn" (xv). More recently, researchers have become more critical of this doxa and have found that "Black women, regardless of education or class, are not exempt from the dangers of receiving poor maternal healthcare" (xvi). Harper analyzes how reproductive doxae about Black mothers have positioned them as "bad" in contrast with white mothers who are "good" (55), drawing on characterizations of Black women as breeders, mammies, matriarchs, welfare queens, and crack mothers that span hundreds of years to trace how such doxae has circulated. She also points to the work of activists such as the Black Maternal Health Momnibus as offering counterdiscourses that can change health outcomes for Black mothers (and all mothers).

De Hertogh's (2020) chapter similarly points to the work done on social media platforms "to create activist health texts that challenge and rewrite race-based health disparities rooted in sociocultural and medical epistemologies that pathologize breastfeeding among Black women" (188). Such pathologies are built on doxae such as "Blacks have a higher pain tolerance than whites" (194) and on historical contexts such as the forcing of enslaved women to act as wet nurses to their white slave-owner's children. De Hertogh's examination of what she calls "counter-activist" and "parallel activist" health texts demonstrates different ways women try to speak back to these beliefs even as they are also limited by the platforms on which they speak and the ways they position various choices women may (have to) make about breastfeeding or using formula. These texts force attention to the ways reproductive doxae circulate differently through women's lives depending on their own positionalities and identities.

Studies of reproductive rhetorics have also extended to those women who struggle to become pregnant due to infertility, whether their own or their partner's. This work demonstrates how reproductive doxae circulate through all women's lives, regardless of their reproductive experiences. An early work in this vein is Elizabeth C. Britt's (2001) *Conceiving Normalcy: Rhetoric, Law, and the Double Binds of Infertility*. In this text, Britt argues that the "normalization" of fertility is communicated through the double bind of fertility and infertility women who seek out fertility treatments must navigate; the normality of having children is reified through the argument that all women should be able to go through fertility treatments so they can have children (as seen in arguments in Massachusetts for fertility treatments to be covered through insurance). Such arguments circulate doxae that all women should have the opportunity to become mothers and, in fact, that women have a right to have children even if medical intervention is required. As Britt (2001) claims, these arguments further ingrain doxae about women's reproductive experiences even as they recognize the method by which infertile women become mothers is not "natural" (144). Building on Britt's work, Karen Throsby (2004) analyzes how reproductive "normality" becomes vexed in situations in which reproductive technologies are used by women who operate outside reproductive norms (such as queer women, women of color, and poor women) and when women choose to stop fertility treatments because they have not led to pregnancy. Although some of the women Throsby interviewed eventually identified as childfree, most found "themselves occupying an ambiguous liminal space between social conformity and transgression: they have tried to conceive but have been unable to; they desire children, but are no longer actively pursuing that desire; they have brought technology into the 'natural' process of reproduction, but without the counterbalancing 'natural' outcome of a baby" (9). Throsby's examination of those in this liminal space points to some of the gaps that emerge when people try to conform to but ultimately cannot align with doxae, which puts them outside social norms they want to embody. Extending the work of Britt and Throsby, Kristin J. Wilson's (2014) *Not Trying: Infertility, Childlessness, and Ambivalence* further explores the liminal positions of socially marginalized women who experience infertility. Unlike women in other studies of infertility or in my own study of childfree women, women in Wilson's book do not definitively identify as "infertile" or "childfree," instead living in a more liminal space in which not having children operates against social norms but is a positionality to which they more flexibly identify. Wilson's book points out sociocultural commonplaces about infertility—such as that it is a "yuppie disease" (3) and that it is a "life crisis" (6)—and the normalization of motherhood, pushing against such straightforward and simplistic views of women's reproductive experiences.

More recently, work on infertility by feminist rhetorical scholars has analyzed how beliefs about reproduction point to biomedical technologies as a way for any woman to experience motherhood. Robin E. Jensen's (2016) *Infertility: Tracing the History of a Transformative Term* traces rhetorics of infertility and how they have evolved over time to establish what infertility means and to rhetorically constrain how people use the term *infertile*. By examining how the medicalization of infertility overlaps with moralizing about it, Jensen demonstrates how reproductive doxae circulating through infertility rhetorics "[situate] subjects as both responsible for their health and yet inherently incapable of meeting that responsibility on their own" (4). Much as I contend in chapter 1 and as Koerber (2018) posits in her book, Jensen also argues that "old ideas and arguments do not disappear when their chronological time . . . has passed but, instead, percolate at subsequent, often seemingly disconnected moments to combine and contend with newer arguments, appeals, and narratives" (5). Grounded in assumptions about gender and reproduction, reproductive doxae perniciously circle back around time and again, albeit in new forms, to constrain women's lives. Some of the newer forms of reproductive doxae that have circulated include women's ability to significantly delay when they conceive and have children due to technologies such as egg freezing. However, as Kylie Baldwin (2019) examines in her book *Egg Freezing, Fertility, and Reproductive Choice: Negotiating Responsibility, Hope and Modern*

Motherhood, such doxae, while seemingly empowering women to make their own reproductive choices, minimize the significant possibility women older than age thirty-five will be unable to have children even with the assistance of biomedical interventions such as egg freezing. The interactions of personal and biomedical form new types of reproductive doxae that circulate through women's lives and shape their experiences with reproduction and infertility. Indeed, in the twentieth and twenty-first centuries, reproductive technologies have become an even larger part of sociocultural beliefs about reproduction. Maria Novotny and Elizabeth Horn-Walker (2020) argue that one central reproductive doxa is that "infertility is a disease that can and must be beaten [through medical procedures] so as to fulfill one's desire to become a mother/parent" (45), a doxa that contributes to the stigmatization of infertility and the silence and isolation those who are infertile often experience (46). Novotny and Horn-Walker discuss a traveling art exhibit they created called *The ART of Infertility* that seeks to act "as a disruptive discourse expanding cultural assumptions of infertility . . . calling attention to the gendered pathology of infertility and reproductive loss" (46). Similar to some of the counternarratives and counteractivist texts discussed by other scholars focused on reproductive rhetorics, this art exhibit holds the potential to help "the general public . . . revise common beliefs and become more culturally sensitive to the stigmatization of infertility" (59). The stigmatization of those experiencing infertility also points to reproductive doxae about the normality of women's lives as mothers that speak to the stigmatization childfree women often experience as well, although of course the reasons for this stigmatization and the effects on women differ because of their personal desires to become or not become mothers.

These scholars have collectively examined the reproductive doxae circulating through women's lives in the United States in particular and have examined how some women have tried to speak back to the ways such doxae constrain their reproductive experiences. However, besides Bivens, Cole, and Koerber's (2019) article, this work has not explicitly theorized the question of how reproductive doxae circulate through women's lives and affect the ways they interact with others about and define for themselves their reproductive experiences. By extending this work to analyze how reproductive doxae circulate through the affective as well as discursive experiences of childfree women, I offer a framework for better understanding how doxae circulate through women's lives and how women negotiate these doxae both privately and publicly.

Happiness Scripts as Affectual Interpellations of Gendered Doxa

Feminist rhetorical scholars' glimpses into how reproductive doxae circulate paves the way for further attention to how these doxae work in childfree rhetorics. However, this work does not fully account for the invisibility of doxae and how childfree women bring doxae about women's reproductive decisions to light. In order for rhetorical scholars to do this work, we must understand doxae through an affectual lens. As affect scholars such as Brian Massumi (2002), Eve Kosofsky Sedgwick (2003), Adam Frank (2007a, 2007b), John Protevi (2009, 2013), Lauren Berlant (2011), Sara Ahmed (2006, 2010), and Lauren Berlant and Kathleen Stewart (2019) theorize, building on work by Silvan Tomkins (1962) and Gilles Deleuze and Felix Guattari (1987), among others, affect involves attention to the body and its ways of belonging to the world, including through relational capacities between bodies and objects that lead to motion of some kind. Affect, as Melissa Gregg and Gregory J. Seigworth (2010) define it, "arises in the midst of *in-between-ness*: in the capacities to act and be acted upon" that "is found in those intensities that pass body to body (human, nonhuman, part-body, and otherwise), in those reso- nances that circulate about, between, and sometimes stick to bodies and worlds, *and* in the very passages or variations between these intensities and resonances themselves" (1). Affect forces our attention as rhetori- cal scholars to the things not easily identified or seen that influence the discourses around us.

The invisible yet weighty force of affect aligns in some ways with schol- arly conceptions of doxae; both are unseen forces on the ways we think and both are often socially circulated. However, affect is one way doxae are circulated in minute, often imperceptible exchanges among bodies, spaces, surfaces, objects, and so forth. Those exchanges in accretion can affect rhetorics, actions, emotions, and so on. As Gregg and Seigworth (2010) claim, "Cast forward by its open-ended in-between-ness, affect is integral to a body's perpetual *becoming* (always becoming otherwise, however subtly, than what it already is), pulled beyond its seeming surface-boundedness by way of its relation to, indeed its composition through, the forces of encounter" (3). Affect thus is one vehicle that often invisibly circulates doxae through childfree women's lives, con- straining the rhetorics they use to think and talk about their decision not to have children.

Affect theorists commonly argue that once affect rises to the level of consciousness, it transforms into something else. At this point, affect can become rhetoric; in other words, at this point, the imperceptible exchanges occurring between, within, and around people can become visible through discourse. Although affect theorists may view these affects as having been transformed when this occurs, rhetorical scholars make some common connections between rhetoric and affect (see, for example, Blankenship 2019; Gross 2007; Marinelli 2016; Pruchnic 2017). One of the most recent studies of affect and rhetoric is Lisa Blankenship's (2019) *Changing the Subject.* In this book, she reframes pathos as "rhetorical empathy" that often powerfully leads to "persuasion and change" (5). This framing offers rhetorical scholars a way to focus on emotions and empathy as rhetorical, in the case of empathy whether experienced "on a deliberate, strategic, conscious level or on an affective level influenced by experience" that is "encompassed, created, and expressed within and through language and cultural codes" (10). Blankenship's attention to the links between affect, or the unexpressed, and rhetoric opens up the productive connections that can be made in this work and paves the way for my own explications of doxae through affect.

Other scholars have made connections between affect and doxae that also inform this project. Peter Simonson (2014) argues that the attention to "arguments, words, and cognitions" when examining invention ignores its connection to "affects, things, and bodily sensations" (312). These affects can make doxae more or less persuasive to others. Crowley (2006) makes this case in asserting that "rhetorical effect is achieved by means of affect: the beliefs and behavior of audiences are altered not only by the provision of proofs but by establishment of ethical, evaluative, and emotional climates in which such changes can occur. . . . While persuasion can of course be effected by means of reasoned argument, I posit that ideology, fantasy, and emotion are primary motivators of belief and action" (58–59). Affect thus does have a strong influence on the rhetorical strategies used by rhetors, even though this effect is often minimized or unaccounted for.

Although some affect theorists such as Massumi (2002) claim ideologies do not influence affect, others, including Frantz Fanon (2005) and Claudia Garcia-Rojas (2017), emphasize that the translation of affect through language ties it to cultures, ideologies, and subjectivities. Following this argument, Phil Bratta (2018) argues that ideology and affect are connected and that rhetoric offers one of the best ways to see this connection: "Identifying the connection between affect and ideology can often best be located in various arguments, hence making rhetoric—in its common definition of the study and use of persuasion—a promising object of analysis for studying both affect and ideology" (93). I argue here that, like affect, doxae, as one reflection of ideologies at work in a sociocultural milieu, can be made more visible and available for critique through a study of rhetoric. Since childfree women's reproductive decisions still come out of the doxae at work in a society and the gendered ideologies informing these doxae, examining affect and doxae in tandem with their rhetorical strategies brings to light often hidden constraints and affordances at work in the ways childfree women position their decision not to have children. This type of analysis offers one framework for rhetorical scholars to study the ways affect and doxae influence and circulate through each other and inform the rhetorics used by different rhetors. While other scholars have explored gender and shame specifically (Fischer 2018; Monagle 2020), the most useful theory of gender and affect I have found in my building of theory about reproductive doxae and affect in childfree women's rhetorics is Sara Ahmed's (2010) theorization of happiness and happiness scripts in *The Promise of Happiness*. Here, I briefly explain her theory and how it interacts with doxae to bring to the forefront the constraints operating on rhetorics by and about childfree women.

Ahmed's (2010) book presents a queer theory of happiness and its sociocultural role in constraining individuals. She argues that happiness is not a state of being but the way social norms are seen as good and goods (11). Those people who create happiness by submitting to and illustrating happiness according to social standards (or doxae) are then viewed as "good" people with "good taste" (34) who contribute to the common good. In other words, they conform to doxae and are rewarded by those in power, both literally (through systemic support) and figuratively (through the labeling of "happy" and "good"). Happiness is framed as a responsibility in that everyone is supposed to want to be happy, and being unhappy or not fitting other's people's definitions of happiness is seen as selfish (9).

Objects, positions, and actions such as cars, jobs, houses, marriage, children, and so forth acquire value as they point to happiness, not because people view them as happy in their own right. Instead, people associate these things and choices with happiness because they directly relate to our society's ideas about who someone should want to be or become, often in keeping with doxae. According to Ahmed (2010), we desire the objects, positions, actions, and so forth that we do because we think some objects will bring happiness (203), whether those objects are two children or a Porsche. Connecting happiness with gender, Ahmed posits that what she calls "happiness scripts" govern happiness for individuals based on their gendered identities. In her view, these scripts "[provide] a set of instructions for what women and men must do in order to be happy, whereby happiness is what follows being natural or good. Going along with happiness scripts is how we get along: to get along is to be willing and able to express happiness in proximity to the right things" (59). Such happiness scripts can vary depending on particular sociocultural beliefs or doxae about what is "natural or good" for different genders. In other words, gendered happiness scripts are not universal and can vary by location, community, and even from family to family.

Those who do not conform to gendered happiness scripts (or doxic gender identities) are frequently portrayed as unhappy and deviant[3] (or heterodoxic). Ahmed (2010) posits that because gendered happiness scripts are linked with ideologies about gendered subjectivities, they can be extremely limiting: "Happiness scripts could be thought of as straightening devices, ways of aligning bodies with what is already lined up. . . . To deviate from the line is to be threatened with unhappiness. . . . In this way, the scripts speak a certain truth: deviation can involve unhappiness. Happiness scripts encourage us to avoid the unhappy consequences of deviation by making those consequences explicit" (91). To think of this in another way, happiness scripts reinforce doxae, further pushing those who don't conform to gendered doxae to the margins by presenting those without heteronormative gender identities as deviant or unhappy. Although there are happiness scripts that link motherhood with womanhood (Buchanan 2013), women's intersectional identities shape how these scripts are written on different women's lives (Collins 2000; Fixmer-Oraiz 2019; Harper 2020; Solinger 2005). Ahmed (2010) claims that "ideas of happiness involve social as well as moral distinctions insofar as they rest on ideas of who is worthy as well as capable of being happy 'in the right way' " (13). Happiness therefore is contextual, relying on sociocultural ideas about individual bodies, whether these bodies should be happy, and whether they can be happy in ways society approves of. Happiness scripts about motherhood not only reflect doxae about women's reproductive lives but also doxae speaking to women's intersectional identities in ways that overlap with race, class, sexuality, (dis)ability, and so on. While this project focuses on childfree women, other conclusions about how happiness scripts and doxae are interpellated would necessarily result from analyzing different women's rhetorics.

In short, through doxae about families in the United States, children are typically viewed as the ultimate "good" that bring happiness not only to oneself but to others, including family, friends, communities, and even the government, which wants tax-paying citizens. Children also hold the promise of future happiness and make current unhappiness palatable for parents: "Parents can live with the failure of happiness to deliver its promise by placing their hope for happiness in their children" (Ahmed 2010, 33), a form of "expectant" (181) or anticipatory happiness. As a necessary part of the childbearing and child-rearing process, women's lives are tied to motherhood because their becoming mothers contributes a good to society that brings happiness to others. Becoming a mother, then, is the ultimate selfless act society says will bring them and many others happiness. Happiness scripts for women reinforce the necessity for them to become mothers and the unhappiness that can result from not assuming this role; women without children are selfish, will regret their decision later, will leave no legacy, and will die alone.[4] In order for doxae about motherhood to maintain their power, society must constantly reinforce, through affectual circulations of these doxae, the messages that women's happiness revolves around motherhood and that there are sociocultural consequences for deviating from this script.

Because childfree women voice their arguments against the ideology of compulsory motherhood, unique doxae have circulated about their reproductive decisions. While many women experience constraints on their reproductive decisions (see Harper 2020), childfree women have recently gained enough collective voice to be recognized in contemporary media channels. The privilege that adheres to women with the power to make the choice not to have children provides them with physical and virtual platforms other women with less reproductive choice may not be able to access, and these platforms have created growing communities of childfree women that further strengthen their identification as women without children. Their rhetorical strategies for eliding, countering, or appeasing others' expectations about their reproductive decisions offer rhetorical scholars an opportunity to study the often-hidden constraints these women must work around or with as they articulate their decision to be childfree to themselves and others.

AFFECTUAL AND DOXIC ARTICULATIONS OF REPRODUCTION

Childfree women often recognize the gendered happiness scripts working on them and try to use these scripts or push against them as a way to discursively disrupt doxae, even as they are caught up in the affects surrounding reproductive doxae. Up to this point historically, however, childfree women have not had the collective power or ethos themselves to change doxae about gender and reproduction. Given the emergence of a collective identity for childfree women evidenced through websites such as The Not Mom (n.d.), local meetup groups for childfree people, and social media groups such as The Childfree Choice, this may be changing. Childfree people—and childfree women in particular—are becoming more outspoken and more active in working against the happiness scripts that seek to constrain them.

Childfree women as a group have frequently been erased from both popular and academic view. As Tasha N. Dubriwny (2013) claims, "this group, as well as women who are not fully engaged in the heterosexual matrix," is "at the edge of discourse, invisible, next to the equally invisible ranks of poor women and women of color" (141). The research on childfree women is likewise thin. Indeed, at this point, little data is available in the United States that accurately pinpoints the number of women who are childfree in the sense that they chose not to have children. The United States Census generally lumps all women without children together without regard for the reasons. As seen in table 0.1, the US Census Bureau (2017) in 2016 found that a high number of women in the United States do not have children, and the number of twenty-five- to twenty-nine-year-old women without children was the highest in history. The only national survey that separates the reasons women do not have children, and therefore the best source of this information for now, is the National Survey of Family Growth by the CDC (Centers for Disease Control n.d.). From 2015 to 2017, through in-person interviews with a national probability sample of 5,554 women, this survey found that 41.9 percent of women ages fifteen through forty-nine were childless; of those, 31 percent were temporarily childless and expected to have at least one child in the future, 3.3 percent were involuntarily childless because they were physically unable to have children, and 7.6 percent were voluntarily childless or childfree.

Despite the growing prevalence of childless and childfree women, articulations that connect gendered ideologies about women with reproduction and mothering persist. Crowley (2006) claims that articulations are "the form of the connection that can make a unity of two different elements, under certain conditions" (60), such as between religion and politics. She claims that completely new articulations "are relatively rare" (60) but that "rearticulation and disarticulation of common elements occur all the time within a given community, and these processes constitute rhetorical lines of force" (61). As Harper (2020) argues, articulations between women and motherhood shift depending on the positionality of the women being discussed, including race/ethnicity, class, sexual orientation, gender identification, (dis)ability, and so on. The US Census Bureau in 2016 found that 44.9 percent of white women,

Table 0.1. Number of women without children in the United States (US Census Bureau 2017)

Age	Percentage without children
15–19 years old	96.2
20–24 years old	75.8
25–29 years old	53.8
30–34 years old	30.8
35–39 years old	18.5
40–44 years old[5]	14.4
45–50 years old	17.1
15–50 years old (total)	43.4

40.6 percent of Black women, 38.8 percent of Hispanic women, and 47.6 percent of Asian women did not have children by choice, chance, or circumstance.[6] However, a study of voluntarily childless US women suggests white women are more likely to consider themselves childfree by choice; this study found 72 percent of childfree women were white, 11.1 percent were Black, 8.8 percent were Hispanic,[7] and 3.3 percent were Asian, even though the groups represent approximately 60 percent, 13 percent, 18 percent, and 6 percent of the US population (Martinez, Daniels, and Chandra 2012).[8] No research has broken down the data respecting women without children by other identity markers such as class or sexual orientation, thus shedding no light on the intersectional identities represented among childfree women. However, particular women's experiences can vary broadly depending on the power dynamics at work upon them that differ according to their subject positions, reflecting intersectional lived experiences.[9]

Challenging reproductive doxae and making them visible is a difficult task because they are so embedded in US culture through a complex web of articulations. Multiple strands of ideological thought bind together to construct motherhood, including selflessness, care, and happiness, and these strands become part of the reproductive doxae in a community through their repetitive use. Childfree women's rhetorics undertake a process of rearticulation and disarticulation in deconstructing the ties among womanhood, motherhood, selflessness, care, and happiness.

Throughout this book, I use the metaphor of weaving to explain how childfree women rearticulate and disarticulate different threads of ideological thought about womanhood in order to create tapestries—or ideologies that are "connections made between and among moments (positions) that occur or are taken up within ideology" (Crowley

2006, 60)—about their lives that make sense to themselves and others. Weaving is a tactile experience, speaking to the embodied and lived experiences that influence how childfree women make and interpret arguments about childfreedom. Despite the ways language imperfectly mediates these embodied and lived experiences, it is an important way for childfree women to construct identities that are legible and acceptable within the confinement of the articulations they are entangled with. Childfree women's rhetorics thus are tied to rhetorical threads about gender and motherhood that attach to and adhere to their own, including rhetorics of happiness, selfishness, and care. I call these the weavings of childfree women's discourse, involving threads in many ways entangled, interwoven, and inescapable. Our temptation may be to try to pull apart these strands, but they cannot be disentangled or examined separately because they constantly and continuously twist and weave around each other when childfree women try to enact discursive identity work. Other articulations function similarly; for example, T J Geiger (2013) identifies "the intersection of religious and sexual discourses" as saturating "ideological formations" (249) in his work on pedagogical approaches to these discourses. Rhetorical scholars may more productively seek to examine the entanglements of these rhetorics and their relationships with affect and doxae to better understand how these rhetorics present constraints and affordances to those using them.

Some of the articulations or weavings childfree women contend with revolve around rhetorics of care. As Joan C. Tronto (2013) argues in *Caring Democracy*, care work, including care for children, is much more often "ascribed to women and people of lower class and status" (99). Because men are released from shouldering their share of care work, women's identities are much more readily tied to care, specifically of children, and motherhood is the ultimate symbol of care and selflessness. The interweaving of these creates an ideology that reinforces the passive status of women without disrupting the status quo, which allows childfree women the possibility of rearticulating or reweaving these threads in a recognizable way while simultaneously downplaying their power to create new articulations or ideologies in making doxae visible. Another way childfree women try to present their identities is by disarticulating and creating new strands (similar to but slightly different from the old, much like someone might combine different strands of thread when weaving) that push at narrow definitions of care to include self-care, placing themselves rather than others at the center of their identities, and by constructing supportive communities around themselves. These new strands support childfree women by working against negative discourses in circulation about falling birth rates and population issues, discourses that blame systemic social problems on women's individual reproductive decisions—decisions sometimes influenced by a lack of adequate systemic support for mothering—instead of critiquing the oppressive power operating on some women's reproductive lives.

For some childfree women, the affectual and doxic links between motherhood and selflessness, care, adulthood, duty, and morality create hegemonic ideologies, or an intricately woven tapestry of constraints, in which they struggle to assert their own agency. These constraints can vary by the intersectional identities of these women, although childfree women are often perceived as broken, physically and even psychologically or emotionally incapable of motherhood. Dykstra and Hagestad (2007), in their introduction to a special issue of the *Journal of Family Issues* about childless older adults, discuss how the childless are often "viewed as deviants. Overwhelmingly, they are perceived in a negative light, as problem cases. Moreover, the childless are seen as being disadvantaged" (1284). The normalcy of motherhood casts childfree women into a binary that works against them, reinforcing their deviancy and putting the onus on them to explain why they have failed to follow expected life patterns (1277). It also supports discourses in "a society that often equates adulthood with parenthood" and places the childless outside "the adult norm" (May 1995, 222).

Women with different intersectional identities can experience different affectual, doxic understandings of their childlessness.[10] For poor Black women after enslavement and other women of color, reproduction has historically been used as a racist, weaponized power to control their communities (Collins 2000; Davidson 2017; Solinger 2005; Taylor 2011). Choosing whether or not to have children in this context could open a woman up to criticism from her own communities about this choice (Davidson 2017; Martinez and Andreatta 2015). Queer women's reproductive decisions are differently complicated. Charlotte J. Patterson and Rachel G. Riskind (2010) claim, "Parenthood has long been seen as a formative aspect of adult development, and this is increasingly the case for gay and lesbian as well as heterosexual adults" (336). However, other scholars point out the ideological tensions at work when weaving the discursive threads of "lesbian" and "mother" (Ryan-Flood 2009; Thompson 2002), opening up queer women's mothering to interrogation. Poor white women's reproductive decisions have also been scrutinized in different ways (Guglielmo 2013). They are often criticized for raising their children rather than relinquishing them to wealthier people to parent through adoption (Collins 2006). What these examples show is how articulations about childfreedom and, as a consequence, the affectual, doxic web constraining childfree women's rhetorics, vary depending on a childfree woman's intersectional identity. This book cannot account for all these differences as they work on individual women's lives. Instead, it focuses on one group of thirty-four childfree women to examine how these articulations affect the rhetorics they use to talk about their childfreedom to others and themselves and to explain how they contend with the affectual, doxic understandings of motherhood at work on their rhetorics.

In its examination of this group of childfree women, this book extends the ways feminist rhetorical scholars view doxae by connecting them with the affectual theory of happiness scripts. My examination of childfree women's rhetorics through this lens demonstrates how this theoretical approach makes doxae about women's lives visible and more readily available for analysis and critique. In doing this work, it asks,

- How embedded in doxae are gendered happiness scripts and how do these scripts constrain or open up women's rhetorical practices?
- When rhetors are embedded in happiness scripts, what must happen in order for them to challenge or even change the doxae underlying these scripts?

This book also calls on rhetorical scholars more broadly to explore how affect adds to our understandings of the doxae at work on individuals and groups in particular sociocultural contexts. Affect underpins doxae and circulates often invisibly, but, as seen in this book, it has profound effects on the ways people construct rhetorics about their lives. Ultimately, this study asks how possible it is to shape or change doxae that circulate in part through often-invisible affect and what must rhetors do in order to make such shifts possible.

INTERVIEWEES' INTERSECTIONAL CHILDFREE IDENTITIES

The ways childfree women experience privilege and power affect their experiences with systemic issues such as access to healthcare and childcare, economic resources and working conditions, and so on that affect the reproductive choices available to them. Some childfree women, such as childfree women of color, may see deciding not to have children as resistance to the oppressive power that has historically operated on their reproductive decisions (Collins 2000; Harris 2015; hooks 1990). Other childfree women may view their decision not to have children as a radical resistance to reproductive doxae because they are supposed to supply children to the nation (Fixmer-Oraiz 2019). Here, I highlight the lived experiences of four interviewees to illustrate the diverse backgrounds they come from and how reproductive doxae broadly circulate through their lives.

Grace,[11] fifty-four, identifies as a Black woman whose family is from the Caribbean. Her family moved from England to New York City when she was a child. She told me that she did not "really [understand] a lot of American things" and that she felt like an outsider socially at school. Her British accent marked her as different to her Brooklyn classmates, which led to her being "singled out." Later her family moved to Miami, but she moved back to New York by herself when she was nineteen. She described her extended family as "huge," encompassing both "blood family" and "the mystery family"—people who had been "adopted into the family" for so long "nobody remembers how they got there." Her family seemed to assume for a long time that she would have children, but they had moved on from that assumption: "After thirty went by, and forty went by, I think they were like, 'I think it's a wrap with this one.'" Being childfree was not the only reason she felt out of place in her family, as she considered herself an introvert and her family to be comprised of extroverts. She said, "There's still kind of that energy of, 'You're odd, you were an odd child and you're an odd adult.'" She said this perception of her manifested as not exactly tension but a sense of strangeness: "You're unfamiliar to me, I'm unfamiliar to you no matter how long we've been related. So I feel like there's a little gulf there that we can't lose." This sense led her family to assume she is a lesbian, which she is not. Grace also mentioned strangers tend to assume she is a mother, something she attributes in part to race. Her experiences show how being a childfree woman, and how someone's identity, whether race, sexual orientation, sociality, and so on, can shape the ways others interact with someone and influence their perception of that person's positionality as a childfree person.

Another interviewee, Shanna, was a first-generation college student who earned a PhD and has been teaching in a university for eight years. She has what appears to be a solidly middle-class lifestyle, although she is the first in her family to go beyond high school, and her family was working class. Her maternal grandfather was Native American, and her family has largely worked in blue-collar jobs. She said that being from "a very enclave community" and being a first-generation college student made her "experience different from some of [her] other friends' experiences." The gender dynamics in this community were quite traditional, as Shanna recounts: "Most of the women in my family were stay-at-home mothers and didn't . . . there was a prevailing attitude that women didn't work outside the home. The men worked in blue-collar jobs . . . and the women when they had jobs, they were these sort of little stop-gap jobs, like a couple of months at JC Penney, or my sister worked at a doctor's office for a couple of months." These gender dynamics influenced how she thought about the expected scripts people follow in their lives. Shanna said she was unusual in her extended family in that she had left her community of origin and that she felt "banished" with little connection to her family because she left: "My mother's father grew up on a reservation, he was Cherokee. And so that absolutely rooted them to place, and it kept them sort of in the area. And then also the industries, the extractive industries, kept them in the area. So, as far as family background, very rooted to place, and the people who moved away was sort of, it was sort of seen as, 'Why would you ever want to leave this place?'" Shanna's rejection of a central aspect of the gender dynamics at work in her community—motherhood—alongside her physical distance from this community influenced the sense of separation she felt from this community and highlighted the sense of difference she felt in being childfree.

Sarah is a white woman who knew she didn't want kids from the age of fifteen. One of two interviewees who did not identify as heterosexual, she aligned her childfree identity with her sexual identities: "Like I said, I [am] bisexual, polyamorous. We should just add childfree on there. . . . It's the biggest part of my life and my personality." She views her childfree status as a central thread in her identity, one that works upon many other parts of her life. Sarah had also been a stepmother while in a long-term relationship, which she said was "very difficult." She had joined a childfree stepmoms' group "because no one else was really in my situation. I had other friends who were stepmoms, but none who didn't want kids and then had ended up with one, someone else's. So that was kind of a unique situation that I found myself in, and I really found that I needed some support because even other stepmoms who have kids or who want kids can't understand what it's really like. So that group was very, very helpful for me." Her experiences illustrate some of the complicated threads that can become snarled for childfree women and how she navigates through these as she maintains a childfree identity.

Finally, Claudia is a Latina woman whose family immigrated to the United States from Panama when she was a child. She described her leadership role in a Christian Reformed Church and how it interweaves with her childfreedom.

So I felt called into ministry as a freshman in high school. And I remember, I felt that all the women that I knew that were in ministry, once they had children they left ministry. They left work and really focused on staying at home and raising their children. And I just felt very strongly that . . . not necessarily that I didn't want children but that I didn't want to give up the thing that I felt that was what I was meant to be doing. And for me at that time there were no examples of women in ministry that weren't leaving work in order to raise their children at home, and so I really struggled with that.

Claudia felt that the more fundamentalist "strands of Christianity" she had known in her past "viewed the world of women" in a traditional way and said this view "really shaped just [her] desire in some ways to push against that, to challenge that." Claudia had found a church where she felt her choice was accepted, but she remembered being asked in a job interview at a previous church, "What's gonna happen when [you] become pregnant?" She recalled, "I just said to him that when my husband and I had made our decision about family planning I'd be sure to let him know, and that ended the conversation." This interviewer seemed to think her reproductive choices were their business and assumed she would have children. Claudia has also experienced these types of assumptions at work from congregants in church who have told her she was not faithful to God because "God expects husbands and wives to multiply." She noted that it was unlikely anyone would say something similar to her husband and that such comments were painful as well as making her feel defensive. On the other hand, she was optimistic: "I think that has changed. I think it changes where you are in terms of the type of church you're going to, and where they are culturally. And I think that it is—that has been less of the case where I work now." Claudia's experiences illustrate how religious affiliation constructs yet another set of beliefs that affects how childfree women interact with others around their decision not to have children.

These four snapshots illustrate the many different threads at work in childfree women's lives; their childfree decisions take on different meanings for them as they reflect on their backgrounds and as they interact with those around them. Although it is impossible to fully account for the ways childfree women's intersectional identities affect childfree rhetorics, these snapshots provide a road map for complicating some of the ways we think about reproductive doxae and the rhetorics childfree women use as they talk about childfreedom in the rest of the book. Women who are expected to have children—typically white middle- and upper-class women—and who have chosen not to have children fail to reach this important benchmark for women's adulthood and are often isolated and stigmatized through rhetoric that reinforces their marginal status in society. Such marginalization can be seen in the lack of representation of childfree women in popular culture and in studies that describe the negative judgments women without children face (Bute et al. 2010; Morell 2000; Park 2005). Alternatively, for women who have less privileged positionalities, including women of color, poor women, queer women, and so on, motherhood represents a vexed identity, one they are alternatively forced into and denied as power structures work to constrain their reproductive freedom (Harper 2020; Solinger 2005).

This book takes up how doxae can constrain childfree women because they face a complex web of socioculturally bound expectations, which are further complicated through intersectionality and the expectations differently layered on them through doxae about their lives depending on their race, sexual orientation, class, (dis)ability, and other facets of their identities. I then triangulate these expectations with doxae about women's gender roles and the affects that circulate these doxae through sociocultural expectations and women's lives. By examining the affects and discursive acts that circulate doxae about motherhood and childfree women's rhetorical resistance to these doxae, this book demonstrates how affect and doxae can work coterminously to constrain women's lives and how women can make affect and doxae visible and available for critique. Rhetorical scholars can use this type of analysis to study the ways this group—and other groups—make affect and doxae visible to explain whether and how rhetorical interventions in doxae in small communities have the potential to lead to the evolution of similar rhetorical interventions on a broader scale.

AFFECTUAL AND DOXIC CIRCULATIONS OF CHILDFREE WOMEN'S RHETORICS

Through analysis of interview material from thirty-four childfree women located in the United States, Canada, and Britain, historical analysis of moments when childless women became objects of scrutiny, and brief textual analysis of work by or about childfree women, this book examines the reproductive doxae circulating by and around childfree women and offers happiness scripts as a way to understand the constraints and affordances reproductive doxae place on these women's rhetorical practices. I trace how reproductive doxae about childless/childfree women have contributed to understandings of their positions, particularly in relation to mothers. I demonstrate how childfree women are rhetorically strategic in their positioning of their decision and how they pick up different rhetorical threads to try to make their decision legible to themselves and others. Finally, I argue contemporary childfree women are gathering force as a group, calling into question reproductive doxae and offering potential changes to common beliefs about reproduction.

To further build my theorization of reproductive doxae through happiness scripts and to analyze the rhetorics of childfree women, I start with a brief historical examination of moments throughout the last two thousand years when reproductive doxae became more visible. Chapter 1, "Hegemonic Mothering Ideologies and Gendered Happiness Scripts," explains how articulations of happiness, selflessness, care, and motherhood bind together to form a hegemonic construction of womanhood/motherhood that is not often explicitly recognized but that has a near-exclusive hold on how women's lives are viewed. It then examines two sets of ideological beliefs about reproduction that continue to circulate in the twenty-first century and constrain how childfree women are situated in a Western sociocultural context. Chapter 2, "Reproductive Commonplaces and Rhetorical Roadblocks," builds on chapter 1 to introduce my interview methodology and data and to explore what commonplaces about motherhood and childfreedom are contemporarily circulated that reinforce the hegemonic constructions of women's identities explored in chapter 1. These two chapters demonstrate how millennia of reproductive doxae have created a hegemonic view of women's reproductive lives and continue to influence how childfreedom is viewed.

Following this understanding of reproductive doxae, chapter 3, "Reproductive Arguments and Identity Work," explores how childfree women take their recognition of the reproductive doxae circulating around them and negotiate what this circulation means for their identities as childfree women of different races, socioeconomic classes, religions, and geographical areas and cultures. This chapter also asks what happens when a person's choices rewrite happiness scripts not only for themselves but also for others by examining grandparenting as a happiness script interrupted by childfree women. Taken together, the chapter demonstrates how childfreedom threatens the hegemonic construction of women's reproductive lives, breaking open the many values and emotions that come along with these beliefs. Chapters 4 and 5 then examine how reproductive doxae influence childfree women's rhetorical practices through the happiness scripts explicitly and implicitly imposed on them and their rhetorical strategies in negotiating and speaking back to these scripts. Chapter 4, "The Limits of Rearticulating Hegemonic Reproductive Beliefs," claims that one strategy childfree women use to negotiate reproductive doxae is built on their attempts at rearticulating care as something all women, even those without children, can exhibit. This chapter focuses on how happiness scripts shape interviewees' interactions with others about their reproductive decisions and their attempts to work against negative rhetorics about childfreedom while also working with some of the rhetorical articulations of motherhood.

Moving beyond constraints into some of the affordances of happiness scripts, chapter 5, "New Articulations of Childfree Women's Identities," claims there are some relationships or even communities in which childfree women can speak back to and challenge reproductive doxae and create identifications with others that may lead to new articulations of women's lives apart from motherhood in these smaller networks. Interviewees discuss using humor, directness, and strategic explanations to try to speak back to happiness scripts that limit other people's views of the interviewees' reproductive decisions. They also formed positive communities that circulated new rhetorics about reproductive choices that could support broader changes in doxae about childfreedom and motherhood. As the conclusion, "No Regrets? Happiness and Reproductive Doxae," examines, the question remains concerning to what extent it is possible for a particular group to reshape doxae and how we can reconceive of rhetorics invoking happiness and regret. It also asks feminist rhetorical scholars to continue to connect theories of reproductive doxae and affect in order to make some of the invisible beliefs circulating around us visible and to give us the opportunity to examine the ways these close down and open up the rhetorics people use.

In bridging the gaps between doxae and affect, this book claims these exist in an intricately connected, often-invisible relationship with each other. Because both affect and doxae typically circulate beneath the surface of consciousness, their effects on people's rhetorics can be hidden. However, as this book demonstrates, the interconnections between affect and doxae can be examined and made visible through careful attention to the discursive threads that constrain people's rhetorics. Through further attention to these threads, rhetorical scholars can dig beneath the surface of the rhetorics in circulation to consider the maelstrom of beliefs that underlie these and limit not just people's rhetorics but, in the process, the ways they present their identities and lives to each other and themselves. This work could open up new avenues for research in the field and calls on rhetorical scholars to develop new approaches for investigating and analyzing these connections.

REARTICULATING TERMINOLOGIES FOR CHILDFREE WOMEN

Many terms in popular and scholarly discourse describe people without children. Thus, choosing which term(s) to use and how is not a simple decision but, instead, one that has consequences for the ways people view women who choose not to have children. Childless people also develop their own vocabulary of terms for describing themselves, often with slightly different meanings, which makes assigning a name to this group difficult. Without such a label, however, it is difficult to discuss people who choose not to have children without overly belabored syntactical constructions that still cannot adequately account for the complexity of the identities of people without children.

Mardy Ireland (1993) was perhaps one of the first scholars to openly address the labels placed on or used by specifically women without children. She positions childless women into three categories: the childless who are infertile or cannot conceive due to health problems; the childfree and childless who delay making a decision about childbirth until it is too late; and the childfree who actively choose not to have children (15). Despite her use of these words, Ireland argues that "using 'child-free' or 'childless by choice' as words to categorize women is inadequate. 'Child*less*' or 'child-free' still focuses our attention on the identity of woman in terms of attachment to a child; they still define her in relation to mothering rather than as an individual and separate person making choices" (156). She claims that this "deficiency model" of naming womanhood must change in the future so women are described by "*what is* rather than *what is not*" (157). The importance of language in identity construction highlights Ireland's insistence that women without children be identified in other terms, although she does not offer such alternatives herself.

Other scholars have also taken up the difficulty of naming those people who choose not to have children, with almost every scholar who discusses this group explicitly talking through the term(s) used to describe them. Kristin Park (2005) notes, in "Choosing Childlessness," "A variety of terms are used by activists, scholars, and voluntarily childless individuals for the status of choosing not to parent. These terms include voluntarily childless, intentionally childless, childless by choice, and childfree. The choice of term may reflect scholarly conventions of objectivity, personal identity constructions, or political positions that proactively respond to pronatalism. For example, some researchers, activists, and nonparenting individuals prefer 'childfree' to emphasize a positive experience of choice rather than the sense of loss or deficiency that they believe 'childless' connotes. Others dislike 'childfree,' seeing it as artificial or reinforcing of stereotypes about dislike of children" (399). Any decision to use one term over another risks reinforcing some stereotypes and rejecting others. The term used can also offend certain groups; *childfree*, for instance, also seems to suggest people in general should want to be free from children.

Different members of the nonparent community have differently embraced terms such as childfree or childless that may have negative connotations for some. For example, the popular website The Not Mom (n.d.) uses "childfree" to describe all women without children but further explains the website sometimes uses "childfree," as I have been, to mean women who choose not to have children, whereas "childless" indicates being unable to have children. Like Ireland (1993), The Not Mom realizes language choices about nonparents matter. In writing this book, I have sought to use a term in this project that clearly labels the group of women who actively choose not to have children. Originally, I used the term *childless by choice* to frame the study, which some of my interviewees liked and others did not; later, I switched to using the term *childfree* because it seemed more commonly used across the literature and in popular sources to describe people who choose not to have children. Because the term *childfree* seems to be stabilizing as a term for those who specifically have chosen not to have children, I ultimately chose to use it throughout this text, although not all people who have chosen not to have children would use this term themselves. There are still problems with this term; as Ireland (1993) claims, it defines childfree people in terms of who they are not rather than in terms of who they are.

As a rhetorical scholar and a childfree woman, I yearn for a term that more accurately describes the identities of nonparents. But I recognize that, unfortunately, there is not yet a word for this group that does not rely on deficiency and that Gregory Coles's (2016) observation that minority groups infrequently have the power to eliminate words from the majority group's vocabulary means it would take widespread use for another term to persist. Until childfree individuals gain a more critical mass and their identities become more familiar, the language used to describe them will be largely defined through the terministic screen of parenthood familiar to our society. The term *childfree* thus, for me, does the work of indicating the group of interest. While this group includes many different women with different motives for not having children, these women reject society's insistence that their adulthood is tied to motherhood[12] and create deliberate and complex rhetorical strategies for making their identities legible.

PERSONAL AND POLITICAL INTERWEAVINGS OF CHILDFREEDOM

Finally, I must address my own investment in childfree rhetorics and how it informs this study. Catherine Molloy, Cristy Beemer, Jeffrey Bennett, Ann Green, Jenell Jonson, Molly Kessler, Maria Novotny, and Bryna Siegel-Finer's (2018) article "Dialogue on Possibilities for Embodied Methodologies in the Rhetoric of Health and Medicine" offers a heuristic for researchers working on topics in the rhetoric of health and medicine to which they have a personal connection. In this article, Maria Novotny, one of the coauthors, describes how it feels more natural for her to be open about her personal connections to her research on infertility: "I tend to examine infertility from an intersectional methodological perspective. By bringing in cultural and feminist rhetorical perspectives to my RHM [rhetoric of health and medicine] work, I find it difficult to not be upfront about my own positionality in terms of infertility. By not disclosing, I feel as if I am not practicing this intersectional methodology" (356). The heuristic offered helps researchers examine their personal connections and whether these can be used to productively advance a project's rhetorical aims; it also speaks to the need to be ethical in representations of our own and other's experiences and to consider the personal effects of researching these topics on those we work with and ourselves. In this closing section, I briefly recount my own experiences as a childfree woman to try to be transparent about my own life experiences and how these necessarily inform the work I do in this book.

My experiences as a childfree woman have necessarily informed my interest and ongoing investment in the ways those women who have chosen to be childless experience their identities. I made the decision not to have children in my midtwenties after a period of time during which my husband and I considered having children while I was in graduate school. We both came to the realization—perhaps belatedly–that having children was socioculturally expected, particularly given his family's close ties to the Christian faith that tells couples to "go forth and multiply" and my own parents' decision to have six children (of which I am the oldest). At the time, we also had close friends who were contemplating parenthood, were pregnant, or had recently had children, which reinforced the idea that having children at that time was normal and perhaps even expected. After close introspection, however, we knew having children was not something we ourselves wanted for a variety of reasons, including our intense desire to be able to focus on our relationships with each other and others in our lives (including children such as our niece and nephews), our desire to be able to move and travel at will without worrying about the effects of these travels on children, and our drive to maintain the rhythms of life we had already established and enjoyed.

At the time, perhaps because of my privileged position as a white woman who appears to be heterosexual (even though I'm bisexual) and thus does not often face social censure for many parts of my life, I did not realize how political this decision would be or how much scrutiny I would endure because of this decision. Naïvely, I thought telling people I didn't want children was not a big deal. But I found family and friends generally told me that I would "change my mind" or that I "wasn't old enough yet" to know what I wanted. Even acquaintances or strangers often asked when we were going to have children and expressed disbelief when we said we didn't want children. As I've grown older, those around me have increasingly scrutinized what I'm doing and why I might not want children. It appears they can hear my biological clock ticking even if I can't. Academia generally acts as an insulating bubble in which people are overall accepting and supportive of this decision; outside this bubble, however, people often struggle to understand this decision.

I recount my experiences here not to focus on my own life as an example of a childfree woman. Instead, I want it to be obvious that I do have a stake in the arguments circling around childfree women and that this project is what I consider an important step toward recognizing the rhetorical identity work childfree women are doing. Being part of this group of women may prevent me from being aware of some aspects of their lives, but it allows me to highlight those aspects of their identities' discursive constructions that remain ongoing concerns when childfree women attempt to make their lives legible to themselves and those around them. My hope is that other feminist rhetorical scholars will identify ways they can use affect as a lens through which to critique and identify how doxae present constraints and affordances on the rhetorical practices of women every day. I also hope to make childfree women as a group, and the rhetorical threads they use to construct their identities, more visible so scholars invested in reproductive rhetorics can continue to identify how these threads work on different groups of women in different ways.

1

HEGEMONIC MOTHERING IDEOLOGIES AND GENDERED HAPPINESS SCRIPTS

When Heather Heyer, a white childfree woman, was killed at Charlottesville, Virginia, on August 12, 2017, during a protest march against a Unite the Right rally, the neo-Nazi website *The Daily Stormer* published an article (since removed) written by founder Andrew Anglin that claimed, "A 32-year-old woman without children is a burden on society and has no value."

Anglin's article invoked the perennial interweaving of race with issues of reproduction, drawing attention to the conflicting sociocultural scripts circulating about motherhood for white, middle- and upper-class heterosexual women and, among others, women of color, queer women, immigrant women, and poor women. As Kaila Adia Story (2014) writes, "The dominant portrayal of what is, and what it means to be a 'mother,' . . . remains locked within a reductive and imaginary prism of white supremacy, heteronormativity, and sexism" (1). Anthropologist Ann Anagnost (2000) similarly argues that procreation for "white, middle-class subjects" increasingly signals "value, self-worth, and citizenship" that is necessary for "becoming a fully realized subject in American life" (392). This point is demonstrated more fully in Fixmer-Oraiz's (2019) examinations of motherhood as connected with US homeland-security culture, including rhetorics of choice and risk that differently position women's reproductive lives based on their identities in relation to the US nation-state. The white supremacy underlying this nation-state, Ross (2006) claims, determines and informs "what Americans [including both conservatives and liberals] think as a society about women of color and population control," which affects "the country's reproductive politics" (54). Consequently, while reproductive doxae can appear to similarly circulate through women's lives, often these doxae have different historical and sometimes contemporary shapes depending on who women are and how they are situated within US reproductive politics.

https://doi.org/10.7330/9781646424399.c001

My argument in this chapter is that the rhetorical web of motherhood—woven with the threads of happiness, selflessness, and care—forms a hegemony that has been used to control women's reproductive experiences, albeit in different ways. Although Anglin's suggestion that Heyer's childlessness justified murdering her are extreme, they point to the historically embedded belief that good (white) women are mothers and those women without children are suspect. For millennia and across cultures,[1] women's roles as mothers have defined them as good, and those who have not become mothers have been viewed as deviant, abnormal, or even immoral. My argument, therefore, is that the reproductive doxae contemporary women contend with have circulated for thousands of years, forming hegemonic views about women's lives difficult for childfree women to contest, as is seen in later chapters of this book.

However, I also open space in this chapter for us to consider the work feminist scholars have done to demonstrate how motherhood has been differently constructed and used as a tool of oppression against different groups of women. An examination of the historical circulations of reproductive doxae must take into account the ways women's reproductive experiences have been controlled differently depending on their identities. A woman's race and ethnicity, socioeconomic class, sexual orientation, immigration status, (dis)ability status, and so on affect what ideological beliefs have formed about her and constrain her reproductive life. I do not here attempt to provide a thorough recounting of the many ways women of color, poor women, queer women, immigrant women, and other women in historically minoritized subject positions have been kept from making their own reproductive choices (for detailed analysis, I highly recommend Collins [2000, 2006], Fixmer-Oraiz [2019], Roberts [2017], Ross and Solinger [2017], and Solinger [2005]). However, I do briefly analyze some of the key historical moments in US history when beliefs about Black, Indigenous, and Asian immigrant women's reproductive lives surfaced and how these beliefs feed into the capitalist, racist, patriarchal systems that continue to constrain women's lives in the twenty-first century. bell hooks (1989) argues, "By calling attention to interlocking systems of domination—sex, race, and class—black women and many other groups of women acknowledge the diversity and complexity of female experience, of our relationships to power and domination" (21). Childlessness has been forced on women of color and poor women in particular through sterilization, forced adoption, and, as Tiffany Taylor (2011) points out, by limitations on social welfare, particularly the 1996 welfare reform law (903), while being stigmatized for white women of means. The intersectionality of women's experiences demonstrates the often-conflicting efforts of women to challenge reproductive ideologies that work on them differently, especially because of race or ethnicity. In many of these instances, upper- and middle-class white women have been complicit in reinforcing particular ideologies about other groups of women even as they tried to resist the ideologies at work on their own lives.

Even given the differences in the ways reproductive doxae operate on women's lives, motherhood is definitive not just for childfree women but for most women, as Christine Battersby (1998) claims: "Whether or not a woman is lesbian, infertile, post-menopausal or childless, in modern western cultures she will be assigned a subject-position linked to a body that has perceived potentialities for birth" (16). This chapter is concerned with the struggles of childless women to resist and assume this subject position and the struggles of all women to assert control over their reproductive experiences, even as they were condemned, sometimes to death, if they did not follow the reproductive scripts laid out for them. Understanding how the silencing of childless women who resist following gendered happiness scripts reinforces hegemonic values about women's bodies illustrates the threats to patriarchal, sexist, homophobic, nationalist systems felt whenever these values are resisted. It also demonstrates how feminist rhetorical scholars can use affect theory to bring doxae to the forefront of our work so we can more closely examine how people try to contend with these ideological forces working on their lives. I do this work through the examination of two sets of ideological beliefs underpinning hegemonic values about childlessness and reproduction: the theories of the wandering womb as manifested in the pathologization of hysteria at the turn of the twentieth century and the racialization of reproduction through the laws and policies in the United States that in the twenty-first century revolved around eugenics and sterilization.

THE DEVELOPMENT OF REPRODUCTIVE DOXAE AS HAPPINESS SCRIPTS

Beliefs and values about womanhood are circulated through articulations that bind together womanhood with motherhood, care, selflessness, and happiness. As Harper (2020) points out, such articulations do not pertain equally to all women; instead, they are configured differently depending on a woman's intersectional identities. Connecting these articulations with Ahmed's (2010) theory of happiness scripts highlights the hegemonic ideologies about women's reproductive lives that have been in circulation for millennia and provides a window into how some childfree women try to contest these scripts. Here, I briefly trace the development of these hegemonic beliefs and values and how they support mothering ideologies that constrain women's lives and rhetorics. I then explain how connecting doxae and happiness scripts can make visible these often-invisible, affectual forces that affect childfree women's lives and the rhetorics they use to position their identities.

Hegemonic Mothering Ideologies and Women's Happiness

The ability to choose whether or not to have children and to determine how to care for one's children often intersects with other privileges based on race, class, sexuality, immigration status, (dis)ability, and so forth. While other scholars have traced how motherhood has been constructed for particular groups of women (Harper 2020; Hequembourg 2007; Solinger 2005), I focus here on hegemonic mothering ideologies that circulate about the reproductive choices that women are or are not expected to make and that childfree women typically must contend with.

Other scholars have examined hegemonic mothering ideologies about women's lives, ideologies predicated on white, middle- and upper-class heterosexual motherhood and against which other women's mothering capacities are measured. Following Crowley's (2006) definition of hegemony as "any set of signifiers and practices that achieves a powerful, near-exclusive hold on a community's beliefs and actions" (63), I use the term *hegemonic* to draw attention to the power of these ideologies in Western culture despite only reflecting a particular group of women. Taylor (2011) calls this set of ideologies "intensive mothering." As she writes, it "might be the hegemonic form of mothering . . . that may not be feasible for many, if not most, women to practice" (898). Philosopher and women's studies scholar Patrice DiQuinzio (1999) calls it "essential motherhood." DiQuinzio interrogates the concept of essential motherhood as it relates to feminist theory and theories of selfhood. She claims that "essential motherhood is an ideological formation that specifies the essential attributes of motherhood and articulates femininity in terms of motherhood so understood" (xiii). Essential motherhood, as she sees it, is based on the idea that being a mother is "natural" and "inevitable," requiring "women's exclusive and selfless attention to and care of children" (xiii). Because women are seen as biologically equipped for such work, the construct underscores the need for women to mother in order to develop psychologically and have emotional satisfaction (xiii).

DiQuinzio points out that this expectation has implications for the ways women without children are viewed: "Essential motherhood dictates that all women want to be and should be mothers and clearly implies that women who do not manifest the qualities required by mothering and/or refuse mothering are deviant or deficient as women" (xiii). Thus, essential motherhood reifies the belief that women must be dedicated to childcare and that they cannot opt out of it without facing social consequences.

Similarly, communications scholar Susan J. Douglas and philosopher Meredith W. Michaels (2004) call this phenomenon "new momism," a specific range of mothering practices, behaviors, and values viewed as normative. They point out how mothering ideologies are predicated on women's desire to have children and to devote their lives to their children, which informs some of the commonplaces about women's reproductive experiences discussed in the next chapter. Deconstructing the notion that motherhood is the perfect and natural outcome for women, Douglas and Michaels argue that the new momism is "the insistence that no woman is truly complete or fulfilled unless she has kids, that women remain the best primary caretakers of children, and that to be a remotely decent mother, a woman has to devote her entire physical, psychological, emotional, and intellectual being, 24/7, to her children" (4). This insistence suggests that mothers' happiness, as well as their claim to be "good" women who value the "right" things and produce "goods" (children), requires their unselfish and unending attention to their children. Douglas and Michaels explain the paradoxes at work in new momism, arguing that the "ideals, norms, and practices" that seem to "celebrate motherhood" actually "promulgate standards of perfection" beyond women's reach (5). They claim new momism seems to both draw from and repudiate feminism by insisting that women do have choices but that "the only truly enlightened choice to make as a woman, the one that proves, first, that you are a 'real' woman, and second, that you are a decent, worthy one, is to become a 'mom'" who is selfless and devoted to childrearing (5). Douglas and Michaels (2004) reference gender and culture studies scholar's Elspeth Probyn's (1993) concept of "choicoisie" (281): some women are told they have reproductive choice, but making the "wrong" choice to not have children may lead to sociopolitical repercussions.

Sara Hayden and D. Lynn O'Brien Hallstein (2010) explore the discourses of choice with more depth, arguing that neither of their own mothers was able to choose whether to become a mother and that "the centrality of maternity in their lives was paired with limited opportunities in the public sphere" (xvi). They list many of the ways women's reproductive choices are determined outside individual or personal choice, including "relationships with others, mental and physical health, race, sexual orientation, and economic status, public and workplace policies, developments in reproductive technology, and the social norms and messages communicated to women about the appropriateness of becoming mothers (or not)" (xvii). Their examination of choice highlights the many ways women are prevented from governing their reproductive lives, especially if they are part of a historically minoritized group.

Despite the prevalence of emphasis on reproductive choice as the main mechanism of women's freedom in US culture, the rhetoric of choice in relation to reproduction has largely served to put emphasis on certain groups of women making the "right" choices. US society encourages some women to choose when to have children and how many they want but ultimately censures them if they decide to be childfree. Others are denied the same choices. As Collins (2006) argues, "Affluent, married, White, and holding American citizenship, 'real' mothers are those who fit cultural criteria for idealized motherhood. Against these idealized 'real' mothers, other categories of women of the wrong social class, marital status, race, and citizenship status are judged to be less fit and less worthy to be mothers" (55). Collins points out that although intensive mothering, essential motherhood, and new momism are pervasive and construct the ways mothering in general is viewed, they do not reflect the articulations at work upon all women. Instead, these frameworks reflect the sociocultural ideologies that broadly construct motherhood for those women viewed as "legitimate" members of the nation-state.[2]

Although motherhood is a central thread in gendered happiness scripts, it is a role granted only to certain women who are allowed to be happy in certain ways. As sociologist Nancy J. Mezey (2008) argues in her book about lesbian mothering, reproductive choice is possible only for those privileged in some way: "The more privilege that structures of race, class, gender, and sexuality confer upon women, the fewer barriers they will face, and therefore the more intentional their mothering decisions will be" (152). For women with privilege, particularly race and/or class privilege, motherhood often becomes the definitive symbol of their adult identity, one of the few ways they can prove their value and assert their social agency. Given the oppressive nature of reproductive ideologies, the childfree choice is politically charged in different ways for those women who are expected to have children in order to fulfill ideas about happiness than for women who are not expected or even allowed to be "happy" in these ways.

Happiness, Selflessness, and Care in Articulations of Motherhood

Several articulations or weavings are connected with hegemonic beliefs about reproduction that construct a binary opposition of mother and woman. These associate women's happiness with selflessness and care for children, connections circulated through hegemonic discourses about motherhood. As Harper (2020) claims, these articulations operate differently on Black women and other women who are not white, heterosexual, and middle and upper class even as they have a strong sociopolitical influence on the ways all women's reproductive experiences are framed. Although scholars have interrogated the identities of mothers and women through the deconstruction of the binary between mother and woman, they do not focus on childfree women specifically. Instead, childfree women are linked with the category of woman because they are *not* mothers, a defining of their identities as lack.

Buchanan (2013), in *The Rhetoric of Motherhood*, most clearly lays out this binary by using Richard Weaver's concepts of "god terms" and "devil terms" to describe how "Woman" is used as a devil term that is repulsive and reproachful, whereas "Mother" is used as a god term that is acceptable and valued.[3] Here, then, Buchanan's focus is on women whose motherhood is held up as a desirable good, meaning childfree women can be differently judged depending on whether their subjectivities align them or not with those bodies seen as capable of embodying the good-mother identity. Describing rhetorics related to each of these terms, "woman" and "mother," Ireland (1993) claims that "the availability of these privileged and devalued positions for women creates a shorthand of sorts, enabling speakers to sketch immediately identifiable characters—the sainted mother or selfish career woman—with only a few strokes" (9).[4] As Buchanan (2013) explains, women who are not mothers are generally considered "selfish," including by themselves: "Empathy, altruism, and self-sacrifice" are associated with Mother whereas "self-centeredness and self-indulgence" are associated with Woman (8).[5] Ireland (1993) argues that these associated values create two common cultural myths about childless women: that they "do not value or are not as capable of sustaining personal relationships" and that they "are overinvested in career or work" (8). Both these myths underscore the selfishness of childless women by emphasizing their desire to fulfill personal goals rather than to care for others.

Selflessness is most readily displayed through women's care for children, although reproductive doxae circulate through the articulation of care and women in different contexts. Psychologist Carol Gilligan (1993) argues in her well-known book *In a Different Voice* that rather than view separation from others as the gold standard of psychological development, one that privileges men, we must "reframe women's psychological development as centering on a struggle for connection" (xv). In doing so, Gilligan refocuses women's psychological development around the need to care for others and the self, theorizing "an ethic of care [that] rests on the premise of nonviolence—that no one should be hurt" (174). In a discussion about abortion, Gilligan describes women who justify termination in terms of care for themselves and for their fetuses. However, she does not in this text confront the idea that viewing women through an ethic of care revolving around relationships, even if it acknowledges the importance of self-care, lifts up mothers, whose relationship with their children has been viewed as one of the deepest humans can have.

Even for those women with reproductive options, constructing adult women's identities outside motherhood is difficult since their lives position them into a counterhegemonic space. As Tronto (2013) argues, care is constructed as "women's work" to such an extent that men can "avoid having to take, or to think much about, the responsibilities for the caring tasks assigned to women" (68). The primary form of care most women assume is care for children, and those who don't are often cast as deviant. The resistance childfree women face illustrates the constraints women experience on their reproductive lives, especially when they make choices that do not align with this hegemony.

Revealing Reproductive Doxae

I claim that happiness, selflessness, and care form articulations that, when combined, create a rhetorical cloth or ideology of hegemonic motherhood that generally rests on racist, classist, and heteronormative assumptions. This cloth is not limited to common linguistic threads; instead, it can also be circulated via images, texts, videos, and other types of texts or symbols that support this discourse and contribute to these articulations surrounding motherhood. The proliferation of language, texts, symbols, and even scenes or spaces of motherhood bolster the belief that women should choose to become mothers who then act in particular ways as proof of their womanhood and their valuing of motherhood.

Some of these kinds of proof form the "happy objects" Ahmed (2010) describes and Julie Wilson and Emily Chivers Yochim (2015) identify in their article "Pinning Happiness" about the affective value of the social media platform Pinterest to mothers. Rather than focusing on language, Wilson and Yochim (2015) identify online spaces in which women visually proclaim their investment in hegemonic ideologies of motherhood through support of the articulations of happiness, selflessness, and care for their children. Wilson and Yochim claim Pinterest allows users to point "toward the possibility of happiness" through "happy scenes, good habits and best practices, fun activities, and thoughtful ruminations on the meaning of life" (234) that they virtually pin, thereby circulating them. Wilson and Yochim identify these happy objects on Pinterest as one of many ways contemporary mothers demonstrate their adherence to the hegemony. These mothers do so by tapping into the rhetorical weaving of happiness (through the happy objects and the illusion that family happiness is always possible), selflessness (through the time mothers give to create family happiness), and care (through the attention mothers give to their children in hopes they will become happy).

Childfree women's attempts at reweaving or rearticulating these ideological strands and contesting hegemony are constrained, and constrained in different ways depending upon their unique positionalities. At this point, it should be clear how happiness is reserved for particular groups of women—typically, white, middle- and upper-class heterosexual women—and has been so tightly woven that it is quite limited. Ultimately, women generally do not really have reproductive options that are all socially accepted and supported. Instead, they have options socioculturally sanctioned differently depending upon their intersectional identities. Focusing on happiness scripts as they play out in women's lives brings up the beliefs and values at work on them so these beliefs and values can be more closely examined and challenged. This chapter examines two sets of beliefs that collectively construct hegemonic ideologies about childless women and state-sanctioned reproductive control. In doing so, it traces how these beliefs about childless women have and have not shifted in response to sociohistorical contexts and centers the affectual circulation of these beliefs to demonstrate how feminist rhetorical scholars can make the affectual dimensions of doxae visible in analyzing texts and events.

HISTORICAL ARTICULATIONS OF HEGEMONIC MOTHERING IDEOLOGIES

Gendered beliefs about the roles of mothering in women's lives have lasted millennia, surviving into contemporary discourses about the reproductive choices women make, as the next chapter particularly examines. One of the oldest stories of a demonic woman who fails to live up to mothering standards comes from approximately 700 to 1000 CE. The Jewish myth of Lilith, using the name of a demoness from Sumerian mythology dating to around 2000 BCE (Gaines 2001), describes the first woman created by God. Unlike Eve, she is created from the earth, not Adam's rib. When Lilith and Adam argue about who will lie beneath the other during sex, Lilith recognizes they do not have an equal relationship and runs away. After Adam complains to God, God sends three angels to bring Lilith back; she refuses, and due to her disobedience, God requires her to sacrifice one hundred of her sons every day as a consequence. Lilith becomes a demon who curses human babies by stating she will weaken them upon their birth. Later mythology depicts her as the demonic cause of men's wet dreams. Ireland (1993) claims that "Lilith . . . manifests women's difference in equal terms instead of woman's difference being defined in opposite and lesser terms than man" (151). However, Lilith also represents a dangerous woman who does not care for her children and, instead, makes her needs primary even to the point of sacrificing her own children for those desires. Lilith's independence led to her being erased from biblical accounts of the creation of earth and demonstrates the silencing childless women—who are seen as selfish—can experience.

Across time and sociocultural milieus, the articulations that bind together motherhood with happiness, selflessness, and care have shifted but not drastically altered, creating a hegemony difficult to contest. I here examine two ways ideologies about childless women and control over women's reproduction rise to the surface to examine what they show about the affective circulation of reproductive doxae. In examining the hegemonic system at work on contemporary childfree women as seen in the rest of the book, it is clear the gendered beliefs that construct happiness scripts in European American nations today have many threads stretching back thousands of years that continue to shape childfree rhetorics. A full understanding of contemporary reproductive doxae is only possible if we take into account the ideologies that continue to be woven together, as I do here. The rest of this book then analyzes how this web continues to constrain contemporary childfree women's rhetorics and experiences.

The first set of beliefs I analyze is comprised of those first formulated in ancient Egypt and Greece thousands of years ago by the theory of the wandering womb, setting up male narratives about women's bodies that have persisted in different forms for millennia. This theory's binding of female sexuality and motherhood as an antidote to physical and mental illness contributed to early manifestations of the rhetorical crafting of hegemonic motherhood and set the stage for childless women to be viewed as unnatural and for women's voices to be left out of reproductive discourse about their own bodies. A more recent manifestation of this doxa is found in the pathologization of deviant women as hysterical; in order to explain how hysteria has framed childless women in particular, I analyze early psychological texts' diagnoses of the hysteria of white, middle- and upper-class childless women and the attending scrutiny of their sexual lives. The second set of beliefs I examine is about how reproduction has been racialized in the United States through early laws in the US colonies delineating race in relation to reproduction, subjecting enslaved women's reproductive experiences to the racist, sexist, capitalist violence of their white oppressors. I then examine how reproductive control predicated on racism alongside classism and nationalism surfaced in the early twentieth-century eugenics movement, with its laws about immigration and sterilization differentiating the reproductive control different women have in their own lives. These historical moments bring to light the reproductive hegemony that has controlled women's lives across time and point to its continued influence on childfree women's rhetorics.

A note: the term *childfree* does not fit into history before cheap, widely available, safe birth control and abortion, of course, as people could only choose not to have children through abstinence, potentially dangerous remedies and procedures, and unreliable methods such as withdrawal and the rhythm method. Although female sterilization was first performed in the late nineteenth century, it did not become more common and less invasive until the 1960s when the birth control pill was also becoming more available. As is discussed later in this chapter, female sterilization has been used as a weapon against some groups of women to prevent pregnancy without their consent and, as seen in the next chapter, doctors often refuse to perform this procedure on otherwise healthy, potentially fertile women whose reproductive capacities are seen as an asset to the nation-state. Thus, historical texts and contexts that mention women without children often reflect an assumption of infertility, perhaps caused by a woman's evil selfishness or sexual promiscuity that prevents pregnancy. When examining historical texts, then, I use the term *childless* in part because of the difficulty of distinguishing women who actively tried to prevent pregnancy from those who were celibate or infertile, although reproductive doxae operate differently on women who are infertile than on their counterparts, as I discuss in the introduction.

Wandering Wombs and Hysterical Women
at the Turn of the Twentieth Century

One of the earliest theories pathologizing women without children was that of the wandering womb.[6] This theory that the uterus must be anchored in a woman's body by sex with a man and/or impregnation clearly established motherhood as the normative state of a woman's body from which women should not deviate, else they would face bodily (physical and mental) consequences. The wandering-womb theory explicitly tied ideas about women's happiness to the reproductive activities occurring—or not occurring—in their bodies. In her exploration of the historical moments when the theory of the wandering womb was created, Lana Thompson (1999) traces the beginnings of this theory to the Egyptian Kahun gynecological papyrus from approximately 2100 to 1800 BCE. This text claims that "if not satisfied by sex or impregnation, the uterus was believed to leave its deep-seated place in the pelvis and search for that certain something somewhere else" (21). This became one of the first recorded texts explicitly tying childlessness to pathology, an idea picked up in other cultures and later labeled *hysteria.* The pathologization of women's sexual practices was the focus of the wandering womb and hysteria, often manifested through particular attention to childless women and their sexual practices. In the Kahun papyrus, typical cures for the wandering womb often involved a male element of some kind, including the burning of male excrement, due to beliefs that the "unhappy" womb desired something masculine to cure its need for men (33). These beliefs set up women's bodies as inadequate on their own, requiring something from men in order to be complete.

Ancient Greek culture similarly theorized the idea of the wandering womb in the pathological woman's body. In *Timaeus,* written around 360 BCE, Plato claims, "In females, what is called the womb or uterus is like a living thing, possessed of the desire to make children. . . . The womb is an animal which longs to generate children. When it remains barren too long after puberty, it is distressed and sorely disturbed, and straying about in the body and cutting off the passages of the breath, it impedes respiration and brings the sufferer into the extremest anguish and provokes all manner of disease besides" (quoted in Thompson 1999, 33–34). Hippocrates, the so-called father of medicine, concurred that barrenness, whether caused by infertility or the decision—forced or not—to remain childless, was the main cause of women's sickness of all types despite the reality that childbirth has historically been dangerous for women. Once labeled *dissatisfied* or a *hysteric,* women would not be taken seriously if they asserted their own points of view about their happiness.

Instead, male physicians' interpretations of the female body's need for sexual intercourse with men and pregnancy/childbirth were viewed as the authority over women's bodies. Galen, a Greek physician in the second century CE, expanded on the idea of the wandering womb, arguing that the uterus was an inverted scrotum and that if women went without sex for too long, "semen" would accumulate in their bodies and cause hysteria. He developed the idea of "hysterical suffocation" or "suffocation of the mother" that persisted for centuries, an idea predicated on the belief that women who had been pregnant and used to sexual intercourse but no longer experienced it regularly were particularly vulnerable to hysteria (Thompson 1999, 36). This belief system reinforced women's tying themselves to men through marriage and childbearing/childrearing in order to avoid their own physical and mental pain. Women's bodies were thus seen as inadequate and only curable through interaction with men's bodies, although men were not viewed as having responsibility for curing hysteria by having intercourse with women.

The theory of the wandering womb spread the belief that women who did not follow gendered scripts through marriage and reproduction would physically and mentally suffer as a result. The idea of hysterical suffocation created a patriarchal bind in which women were told they must have children in order to avoid hysteria but were given no remedy for infertility and were prohibited sex outside marriage. It also silenced childless women who might be suffering due to other causes, psychological or physical. Thus male physicians cast childless women's reactions against patriarchy as the bodily results of failing to accomplish their bodies' purpose, rather than a result of the oppressive cultures in which they lived.

Despite this set of beliefs about women's bodies persisting for centuries, around the turn of the twentieth century, white women in particular used their social leverage to argue they could choose when to have sex and bear children, leading to lower rates of marriage and motherhood. According to May (1995), 11 percent of women in the US born in the 1870s remained single and childless (51). As Angela Davis (1983) recounts, the late nineteenth century's movement for "voluntary motherhood," which called for women's right to abstinence even in marriage, resisted hegemonic beliefs about reproduction and husbands' entitlement to sex. In contrast to the many racist laws and practices that shaped Black, Indigenous, and Asian immigrant women's reproduction discussed later in this chapter, white women experienced generally more reproductive freedom: "Prescriptively, and in distinction to the African American mother, the white mother could, due to her whiteness, choose her husband and the father of her children. Her whiteness allowed her to manage and protect her own family. Her embodied, intimate whiteness . . . amounted to the nation's most precious resource" (Ross and Solinger 2017, 23). Childless white women, especially those without spouses, enjoyed significant freedom.

The backlash was predictable. May (1995) describes this as the first period when experts began to warn of US "national decline" because of white women avoiding motherhood (72). The narrative of the decreasing white birth rate as a social problem white women must solve by following heteronormative scripts was born and reinforced by laws such as the Comstock Law from 1873 that blocked the postal service from being used to carry "obscene" materials such as contraceptives, putting "control of pregnancy and matters constituting gynecological and obstetric medicine legally in the hands of physicians alone" (Ross and Solinger 2017, 24). In reinforcing such laws, it was common to label single women as pitiable "spinsters," a burden on families struggling to survive although they played a significant role by performing care work for both elderly people and children. Once again male doctors stepped forward with pathological explanations for (white) women's reproductive decisions, and hysteria became the pathological explanation relied upon to diagnose childlessness, in this iteration as a psychological problem. Other rhetorical scholars have examined how hysteria is part of a lineage of pseudoscientific and scientific diagnoses about women's bodies (Koerber 2018) and how the pathologization of women's bodies through hysteria has contributed to ongoing arguments about women's sexual function (Reilly 2020). Here, I draw on some scholars' historical work about hysteria and a brief analysis of accounts of hysteria by Charcot, Breuer, and Freud to demonstrate how hysteria was a response to challenges to hegemonic beliefs that still underscores rhetoric about childless women in the twenty-first century.[7]

Some scholars read hysteria as women's protests against social scripts. Sickness as evidenced through hysteria could allow women to resist what Dana L. Cloud (1998) labels "the cultural imperative to bear children and to fulfill the proper domestic role" (44). Although a mysterious diagnosis used to categorize and then treat primarily women for a variety of symptoms, hysteria can function, Elaine Showalter (1997) claims, "as a cultural symptom of anxiety and stress" (9) by serving as an outlet for things that cannot be spoken, such as a disinclination to become mothers. However, she also notes that "as a body language of women's rebellion against patriarchal oppression, [hysteria] is a desperate, and ultimately self-destructive, form of protest" (10). Indeed, physicians who advanced the narrative had platforms in their lectures and published work that reached many, and in these spaces women's voices are largely ignored and written over.

For example, French physician Jean-Martin Charcot, who experienced fame from the 1870s until his death in 1893, popularized hysteria and, despite his belief that men and women were both susceptible, solidified the view that hysteria is primarily women's illness. Harkening back to the witch trials, Showalter (1997) describes how Charcot "used techniques that suggested the diabolism of the witch-hunt, such as searching for the hysterical 'stigmata' and pricking or writing on the sensitive skin of patients" (32). He, like Plato, Galen, and others who proposed the wandering womb, also focused on women's reproductive systems, especially the ovaries, as the source of hysteria.[8] Charcot's descriptions of hysteria relied on female stereotypes and commonplaces about women, such as that they were "vain and preoccupied with their appearance, deceitful and self-dramatizing" (34). Many of his patients were young, working-class French women who had migrated to the cities for work and, therefore, faced many obstacles and dangers, including sexual dangers to which Charcot typically attributed their hysteria. Often, Charcot recommended solitary confinement and lifelong treatment, which silenced women's experiences and kept them out of society. In other words, their treatment essentially removed their challenges to heteronormative scripts from the public sphere, diminishing their challenge to the hegemony.

One of Charcot's colleagues, Sigmund Freud, became the spokesperson for women's hysteria, particularly in the 1890s. Taking Charcot's attention to sexual experiences further, Freud (1962) claimed in his 1896 Seduction Thesis, which he later abandoned, that "*one or more occurrences of premature sexual experience*" caused every case of hysteria (203), which the practitioner must then help the patient remember. Historian Jeffrey M. N. Boss claims hysterical women were cast as " 'commonly a maiden, widow or spinster . . . or a woman who is failing to menstruate' " (quoted in Koerber 2018, 29), reinforcing the connection between heteronormative scripts and the pathologization of childlessness. As James B. McOmber (1996) and others point out, even though Freud's "talking cure" gave the patient a literal voice, it was not intended to give space for challenges to heteronormative scripts. Instead, it primarily functioned to give the physician the power to convince the patient (and other audiences) that their symptoms reflected a sexual trauma and to appropriate the patient's voice in lectures and published work. Such work reinscribed the normality of the hegemony and the deviancy of women who challenged it, most notably those women who were not or refused to be mothers.

Rhetorical tactics to silence women's challenges to hegemonic beliefs are most evident in Josef Breuer and Freud's case Anna O.[9] and Freud's most well-known case, Dora.[10] Freud and Breuer pathologize both these patients because of their (in Dora's case temporary) resistance to wifehood and motherhood, turning them into what Showalter (1997) calls "great hysterical stars" (93) whose cases serve as a warning to other women who want to challenge heteronormative scripts and an exhortation to doctors to intervene. Because hysterics were frequently young, they were particularly vulnerable to explorations of their sexual activity—a way to judge how well they took up gendered happiness scripts—and to physicians' desires to force them to align with these scripts. Anna O.'s case appears in Breuer and Freud's 1891 text *Studies on Hysteria*. After her father's death, Anna O. manifests a number of symptoms Breuer and Freud diagnose as hysterical, including loss of facility with language. The cure Breuer and Freud devise is one in which "the patient [describes] that [traumatic] event [her father's death] in the greatest possible detail and [puts] the affect into words" (6). In this way, "language serves as a substitute for action; by its help, an affect can be 'abreacted' almost as effectively" (8) as taking action. In the case of women with hysteria, the action could be socioculturally disruptive because it could involve acting against the scripts set out for them. Therefore, the cure must involve male physicians effectively squashing women's challenges and reinforcing the need for women to follow heteronormative scripts. In the case of Anna O., she experiences hysteria unless she can talk to Breuer, what she herself calls "a 'talking cure'" or "chimney-sweeping" (30). In this process, Anna O. challenges such scripts and then depends on Breuer to persuade her of the value or need to align with them because she does not recognize this desire in herself, despite the sociocultural expectation that she must.

Freud (1993) published his account of Dora's case in 1905 as *Fragments of an Analysis of a Case of Hysteria*. Dora ultimately marries, but during her treatment she demonstrates greater resistance to gendered happiness scripts than Anna O. did. Freud precedes the case with a general discussion of the difficulty hysterics have in voicing their own experiences: "As a matter of fact the patients are incapable of giving such reports about themselves. They can, indeed, give the physician plenty of coherent information about this or that period of their lives; but it is sure to be followed by another period as to which their communications run dry, leaving gaps unfilled, and riddles unanswered; and then again will come yet another period which will remain totally obscure and un-illuminated by even a single piece of coherent information. The connections—even the ostensible ones—are for the most part incoherent, and the sequence of different events is uncertain" (10). In the silences and gaps Freud perceives in Dora's narrative, he finds ample room to assert heteronormative scripts as a normal and desirable cure for her deviant sexuality. He claims she takes "no interest in anything but sexual matters" (19) and that she has "a feeling of jealousy [for Fraulein K.] which had that lady as its *object*—a feeling, that is, which could only be based upon an affection on Dora's part for one of her own sex" (52) because adolescent affection for those of the same sex was seen as natural. Freud also describes Dora as having no interest in sexual intercourse and being overinvolved in intellectual activities (16, 112). An excessive interest in sex, a complete lack of interest in sex, and possible lesbianism or bisexuality are all viewed as in need of a cure, ideally through "marriage and normal sexual intercourse" (71). Thus Freud circulates hegemonic beliefs about reproduction in a new psychological framework (Koerber 2018) with the same conclusion: women must conform to heteronormative scripts in order to be mentally and physically well.

The pathologization of hysterics at the turn of the twentieth century thus reified the already-existing heteronormative scripts women were expected to follow and recirculated hegemonic beliefs about reproduction at a time when they were being challenged. In this instance, reproductive doxae even more closely follow heteronormative sexual experiences and motherhood, severely limiting the types of women's sexuality viewed as normative and the roles women were expected to assume. There is no doubt one of the reasons Anna O. and Dora became the "great hysterical stars" Showalter identifies is because their cases demonstrated the sometimes-forcible means men could use in order to silence and realign women, particularly young childless women who were identified as deviant or outside sociocultural norms, with heteronormative scripts. But their cases also reveal the ways some women tried to challenge these scripts, even as those attempts did not ultimately change the scripts and, through the groundswell of support for psychological techniques curing hysteria, may have further reinforced them.

Racializing Reproduction and the Twentieth-Century Eugenics Movement

While pathologization was one way some childless white women were cast as deviant and punished for weaving new happiness scripts, BIPOC women's reproduction in the United States has historically been forcibly controlled through state-sanctioned violence. Even before the formation of the United States as a nation-state, links between reproductive ideologies and white European citizenship reinforced the control of BIPOC women's reproduction by white oppressors who manipulated reproduction for their own ends. This control and manipulation racialized reproduction and embedded racism into the reproductive hegemony, as Ross and Solinger (2017) claim: "Racializing the nation depended on the development of a culture and a politics—and a body of law—that declared that white babies had a different, dearer, and non-negotiable value compared to nonwhite babies and that enforced those different values" (15). Racializing reproduction in this way, Solinger (2005) argues, was an integral part of building racist, nationalist ideologies that continue to inform hegemonic beliefs about reproduction in the twenty-first century: "The reproductive capacity of enslaved and native women was the resource whites relied on to produce an enslaved labor force, to produce and transmit property and wealth across generations, to consolidate white control over land in North America, and to produce a class of human beings who, in their ineligibility for citizenship, underwrote the exclusivity and value of white citizenship" (29). Hong (2012) also notes the links between reproductive control and citizenship in her examination of the ways people of color have been used and seen as surplus labor in the US nation-state's economy. From before the United States was founded, Dorothy Roberts (2017) claims, "control of reproduction [was] a central aspect of whites' subjugation of African people in America" that "marked Black women from the beginning as objects whose decisions about reproduction should be subject to social regulation rather than to their own will" (23). However, European settlers exerted population control differently over enslaved Africans, whom they needed to reproduce in order to work the land, and Indigenous populations, whom they needed to keep from reproducing as the settlers brutally stole their lands. During the seventeenth through nineteenth centuries, whiteness allowed some women to experience some reproductive control, even if not having children was viewed as a pathological problem. Stripping reproductive control from women of color was one central way white oppressors defined what scripts women of color could take up and controlled not just women of color but their entire communities.

Legally establishing different reproductive ideologies for Black women began early in the United States with the Virginia Colony's 1662 law An Act Defining the Status of Mulatto Bastards, which linked a child's enslaved status solely to their mother's enslaved status (Solinger

2005), limiting the status of enslaved women's children while not necessarily limiting the freedom children born of white women might
experience even if those women had children with Black men. This
law ratified that enslaved women's reproductive lives were available for
manipulation to white, wealthy owners who could try to increase their
property by forcing enslaved women to have children. During slavery,
Black enslaved women's reproduction was encouraged and valued as
an essential part of owners' estates; as Maria del Guadaloupe Davidson
(2017) argues, they were "the valued machine creating generation after
generation of bonded labor" (57). Systemically, then, enslaved Black
women encountered very different reproductive ideologies underwritten by white supremacist beliefs about their and their children's value
as property rather than as human beings. The Virginia law, Solinger
(2005) claims, also set up a pattern for "using sexual regulations—who
had the right to have sex and reproduce with whom—to reinforce and
police racial boundaries. . . . These laws sexualized race and racialized
sex" (32). The lack of paternity tests at the time would make it difficult
to definitively prove the paternity of a child born to a white woman. In
1692, however, Virginia passed the first antimiscegenation law (followed
shortly by Maryland) to address this problem by "clamp[ing] down on
the births of racially 'mixed' children, outlawing intermarriage, marking
all racially indeterminate children as 'illegitimate,' and forcing them to
work for many years as bonded labor" (Ross and Solinger 2017, 19). This
was the first such law in the colonies to restrict marriage based solely on
race, and many other colonies and, later, states enacted such laws. This
change was enacted precisely to police white women who might violate
the racial "purity" of the nation-state by having children with Black men
and, as a result, calling into question the racialized differences on which
the colonies were founded.

Indigenous women in the US also had reproductive control stripped
from them by white European colonizers. Solinger (2005) explains that
the power Native American women had as childbearers and leaders in
their cultures was often targeted as white colonizers forced their beliefs
on Native American tribes. She describes "restricting female authority"
as a first priority in "civilizing Indians" (43). Although some Cherokee
women specifically tried to "argu[e] from a position of power derived
from their reproductive and maternal capacity" against land agreements
with the US (44), ultimately these efforts failed and Native Americans
were assimilated and/or displaced into reservations. Ross and Solinger
(2017) recount the devastation to the reproductive capacities of Native
American communities caused by the forced movement of Indigenous

peoples: "During coerced marches westward, pregnant, parturient, and mothering women were under terrible physical stress and also unable to observe cultural rituals and traditional practices associated with health and well-being. Consequently, many women and their infants did not survive" (22). Even for those Indigenous women who did survive these atrocities, white colonists stripped them of their reproductive autonomy: "In the new settings, women's health and their lives were threatened by sexual assaults by white men, deadly diseases, insufficient food, and poverty. Consequently, the reproductive potential of Native communities was devastated" (22), which has had ongoing effects on the Indigenous communities that exist into the twenty-first century.

The pathologization of white women's childlessness through hysteria supported arguments made by eugenicists at the turn of the twentieth century that reproductive control through contraception and sterilization should be used to limit some women's reproduction and enhance other women's reproduction to create "a better (white) 'race'" (Ross and Solinger 2017, 32). Throughout the twentieth century, eugenicists, lawmakers, and even members of the women's movement made arguments that created race-based divisions between the ways white women and women of color experienced reproductive control. This brief examination of these arguments demonstrates how reproduction continues to be racialized into the twenty-first century, circulating differently for different groups of women and constructing an intricate web of constraints that differently operates on individual women depending on their identities.

Prior to the eugenics movement but in keeping with the reproductive control previously exerted on people of color, the United States Page Act of 1875 and the Chinese Exclusion Act of 1882 sought specifically to limit Asian women's immigration to the United States and, as a result, to limit the Asian immigrants who could reproduce in the country. As Asian immigration, particularly from China, rose due to the California Gold Rush, white citizens cast Asian immigrants as job stealers and wage competitors. The Page Act prohibited the immigration of women who "entered into a contract or agreement for a term of service within the United States, for lewd and immoral purposes" (US Congress 1875), while the Chinese Exclusion Act was the first act in the United States that prohibited a specific group of people from immigrating to the country. These laws meant few Chinese women immigrated to the United States, even if their husbands were in the country, and it "ensured that Chinese men could not legally have sex in the United States and that few ethnic Chinese babies would be born here" (Ross and Solinger 2017, 29). Later, the Immigration Act of 1924, including the Asian Exclusion Act and National Origins Act, set the precedent for the United States to further limit immigration that continues today. This act prevented immigration from Asia, set quotas on immigrants from particular locations, and set up funding and enforcement for carrying out this xenophobic work. The racialized reproductive ideologies already circulating in the United States at this time became further tied explicitly to immigration through the passing of these laws, contributing to beliefs about immigration and reproduction that remain in circulation in the twenty-first century.

The eugenics movement at the turn of the twentieth century demonstrates how reproductive ideologies about women of color underwrote arguments white women made to challenge the hegemonic beliefs about reproduction that circulated in scripts about their own reproductive lives. In a 1903 speech to Congress, President Theodore Roosevelt expressed concern about race suicide, or the declining rates of white, middle-class births in contrast to the higher rates of immigrant births.

> Surely it should need no demonstration to show that wilful [*sic*] sterility is, from the standpoint of the nation, from the standpoint of the human race, the one sin for which the penalty is national death, race death; a sin for which there is no atonement; a sin which is the more dreadful exactly in proportion as the men and women guilty thereof are in other respects, in character, and bodily and mental powers, those whom for the sake of the state it would be well to see the fathers and mothers of many healthy children, well brought up in homes made happy for their presence. No man, no woman, can shirk the primary duties of life, whether for love of ease and pleasure, or for any other cause, and retain his or her self-respect. (May 1995, 61).

His speech echoes the belief of eugenicists that some undesirable people's birth rates should be lowered (negative eugenics), whereas desirable people's birth rates should be encouraged (positive eugenics).

Diverting attention away from white women's falling birth rates, Margaret Sanger and other white birth-control activists at the time argued birth control was needed to encourage specific populations not to have children.[11] Those "unfit," as Solinger (2005) outlines, included all people of color, immigrants (particularly poor ones), low-income people seen as excessively fertile, and all disabled people (including those identified as disabled without evidence that they were) (90). Fears about reproduction led to laws intended to shape the population, including laws addressing immigration, naturalization, interracial marriage, and racial segregation (91). As Roberts (2017) and other scholars claim, these fears meant that racism marked the movement for reproductive rights "from its very inception," indeed that "the spread of contraceptives to American women hinged partly on its appeal to eugenicists bent on curtailing the birth rates of the 'unfit'" (56). Beyond using eugenics to push for access to birth control, the "science" of eugenics led to state-sanctioned sterilization programs that targeted immigrants, people of color, poor white people, disabled people, and people who transgressed sexual norms. One of the first such laws in the United States that tied negative eugenics with sterilization was a 1907 law in Indiana that allowed for the involuntary sterilization of "confirmed criminals, idiots, imbeciles and rapists." Although later found to be unconstitutional, this law set the stage for thirty-one other states to pass eugenics-based sterilization laws. In total, more than sixty thousand people were sterilized through state-sanctioned sterilizations, often without their full knowledge or consent (Stern 2020).

Ross (2017) highlights how sterilization reinforced negative eugenics: in North Carolina, one of the states that most aggressively used state-sanctioned sterilization, 65 percent of procedures were performed on Black women, and "by the 1970s, nearly one-quarter of Native American women in the United States had been sterilized" (65). Although state-sanctioned sterilization programs were largely abandoned by the 1960s, particular groups of women have continued to face pressure and coercion to undergo sterilization based in part on reproductive doxae that continue to circulate about which women are "fit" to have children for the nation. As recently as 2013, the Center for Investigative Reporting found that almost 150 women in California prisons had been coerced into undergoing sterilization from 2006 to 2010. Taken altogether, antimiscegenation laws, immigration and segregation laws, and state-sanctioned sterilization programs were used to, as Ross and Solinger (2017) argue, "regulate who could live in the United States, who could become a citizen, who could live where, who could be 'white,' who could love and have sex with whom, who could marry, who could be born. These laws structured the reproductive lives—and even the physical appearance and the 'race'—of people living in America. And they attempted in various ways to associate citizenship with whiteness" (37).

The racialization of reproductive ideologies embedded in North American and particularly US contexts has had ongoing, lasting racist effects on BIPOC communities and reproductive experiences. Understanding these ideologies is an integral part of understanding how reproductive doxae circulate in different ways through different communities and women's lives and in examining the ways childfree rhetorics intersect, at least in part, with racist systems of oppression.

Women's experiences with sterilization are one such example of the ways reproductive doxae circulate differently in different communities and women's lives. The racist and nationalist threads interwoven with sterilization complicate how sterilization is viewed today and the reproductive ideologies at work in different women's experiences of sterilization. For example, one of the most cited examples of negative eugenics and sterilization is Puerto Rico, where sterilization, alongside emigration, was viewed as a solution to widespread economic problems. Because of sterilization campaigns and lack of access to other birth-control options, by 1974, two hundred thousand, or 35 percent, of Puerto Rican women had been sterilized (Lopez 2008, 8) through what the government called *la operación*. However, Iris Lopez (2008) contests the binary representation of Puerto Rican women who have been sterilized as either agents or victims (xxi); her ethnographic research focusing on the reproductive experiences of women in five Puerto Rican families in New York City asks what reproductive rights mean to women who make the choice to be sterilized themselves but whose choices are constrained by socioeconomic, political, and cultural factors. Although sterilization is one of the most commonly used birth-control methods in the world in the twenty-first century (xiii), the ties among racism, xenophobia, and sterilization mean individual women—particularly white women and women of color—have "profoundly different" experiences of sterilization, with white women often denied sterilization procedures while some women of color are forced or coerced into being sterilized (Ross and Solinger 2017, 51–52). Historical and cultural beliefs about race, immigration status, class, disability, and so on continue to shape individual women's reproductive experiences and the reproductive ideologies circulating through childfree rhetorics.

CHILDFREE WOMEN'S INTERVENTIONS
IN REPRODUCTIVE HEGEMONY

Childfree women who reject hegemonic mothering scripts challenge reproductive ideologies in offering new ways women can experience their bodies and reproductive lives, a challenge that threatens to unravel the threads on which these ideologies are built. If we return to Anglin's comments about Heyer, his hatred centers around the fear that white, middle-class women choose not to have children by white men, and, for him, perhaps her involvement in antiracist protests suggests she might engage in miscegenation, leading to a loss of white dominance. As can be seen in this chapter, such fears about control—or lack of control—over women's lives have circulated in similar forms for millennia, and they have often been tied to race/ethnicity and nationalism. Women such as Heyer who choose not to have children circulate a new idea of womanhood that rejects the reproductive control they have historically experienced, albeit in different ways, and that operates outside the hegemonic norms that have suppressed women for millennia, norms previous childless women have resisted to their peril and for which childfree women today can still face social consequences.

Even though childfree women contend with different forms of reproductive ideologies depending on their intersectional identities, as is seen in the following chapters, they by and large must contend in some way with the expectation that they will follow social norms and have at least one child so they can become mothers (as seen in part through their self-identification as childfree women). Judith Lorber's (1994) *Paradoxes of Gender* speaks about some of these norms, asking in part, "Why are all women expected to have children and care for them in modern society? How does this responsibility co-opt women into a system of inequality? Why is domestic work the wife's responsibility in modern societies even when she earns more than half the family income?" (8). Lorber's identification of these particular inequalities illustrates how hegemonic mothering ideologies built on articulations of happiness, selflessness, and care are being challenged even as this web has an overwhelming chokehold on sociopolitical arenas.

Another historical example of the ways childless women have been punished for resisting reproductive ideologies is the accusations and punishments for witchcraft many women endured in the fourteenth through seventeenth centuries across Europe and New England. Like hysteria, witchcraft constructed a social category linking childlessness on a larger scale with danger to social order. This movement partly countered the trends of women's childlessness and reproductive control achieved in the second half of the fourteenth century through infanticide, the use of contraception, and "the widespread use of coitus interruptus by married and single persons" (Ben-Yehuda 1980, 20) by targeting women as the reason for social and religious upheaval. As Nachman Ben-Yehuda (1980) describes, at least 20 percent of women aged fifteen to forty-four were unmarried (21). Fears built up during this time about this relatively large group of single women who typically worked outside the home and their sexual power and depravity, inspiring the witch hunt. May (1995) explains that childlessness, having fewer children than the average married woman, and being over forty and thus unlikely to be caring for small children were clear risk factors for being accused of witchcraft (28–29). Witchcraft thus reinforced reproductive doxae. Although women accused of being witches did not choose to be labeled as such, they were what feminist writer Shulamith Firestone (1971) calls "women rebels" and "women in independent political revolt" (15) against the reproductive control of women. The witch hunt ended, Ben-Yehuda (1980) describes, in the later seventeenth century when a "new European pattern of marriage and spinsterhood" that brought such women under familial control "was institutionalized" (23).

In a contemporary social context in which more people are speaking out about the ways gendered happiness scripts produce happiness in vastly different ways for men and women, childfree women are finding a collective voice that publicly intervenes in the arguments being made about childfreedom and circulates a new perspective on women's identities and reproductive lives. The next chapter explains how I interviewed thirty-four childfree women to explore the ways reproductive doxae circulated through affectual and discursive exchanges in their lives, including through commonplaces about women's reproduction, which I develop further throughout the rest of this book. Ultimately, I analyze to what extent the ideologies formed in these historical contexts have shifted and changed in contemporary contexts and how childfree women have tried to intervene to create new gendered happiness scripts for themselves and others.

2

REPRODUCTIVE COMMONPLACES AND RHETORICAL ROADBLOCKS

Nicole: *"I want other women to understand when they make that choice [to have children or not], it's theirs to make and not to feel pressured because of what society or your family dictates because after the baby showers, everybody else goes home."*

Dianna: *"I think society still has a real problem with women being viewed purely for being baby producing machines, and I don't think we're gonna get past that any time immediately."*

As seen in these words from interviews I conducted with thirty-four childfree women, hegemonic beliefs about reproduction that have evolved across time and sociocultural milieus, as the previous chapter demonstrates, continue to impact many women in contemporary Western cultures. Although more widespread acceptance of birth-control methods such as the pill and IUDs have opened avenues for some women to choose not to have children, the gendered happiness scripts woven through with articulations about gender and motherhood continue to inform the rhetorics used to talk about women who choose not to have children. While reproductive beliefs have evolved over time, many of the same ideologies about women's reproductive lives and what these should look like continue to affect how women think about their reproductive experiences and their identities as women. In this book, I focus on interviews with childfree women to explore what reproductive doxae about motherhood and childfreedom circulate around them and how these affect rhetorics about childfreedom and their agency over reproductive decisions about their bodies.

In this chapter, I analyze how the hegemonic reproductive beliefs, values, and ideologies discussed in the previous chapter circulate through media outlets in the twenty-first century and through commonplaces

https://doi.org/10.7330/9781646424399.c002

childfree interviewees often hear that seek to align their bodies and lives with happiness scripts. I then turn to childfree interviewees' experiences to explore how changes to articulations of reproduction are gaining ground as women in the United States, Canada, and the United Kingdom increasingly choose not to have children. I analyze commonplaces about childfreedom and motherhood that circulate around childfree women and how reproductive doxae underscore these commonplaces. I also examine the effects of such doxae on the decisions even women who have reproductive options are able to make and how these beliefs constrain their control over their bodies.

METHODOLOGY

Table 2.1 provides some key characteristics of the thirty-four women I interviewed, largely via Skype or phone, between Summer 2019 and Spring 2021. I recruited women via social media platforms and snowball sampling, through which interviewees sometimes recruited other childfree women to contact me for an interview. All data is according to participants' own reports; some data was not provided, and I purposely anonymized some data to ensure participant anonymity, which I have abbreviated as U (unavailable) in the table.

As qualitative data gathered through nonprobability and random-sampling techniques, the quantitative data reported here are not generalizable, although they do highlight some of the results found in other studies. The high proportion of white women (62%) and women with advanced degrees (76%) amongst my interviewees reflects some of the associations among childfree status, race, and educational backgrounds other scholars have also found (Basten 2009). However, the "class growing up" category illustrates how this group may have more varied experiences than those demographics, which are more commonly reported in sociological studies, indicate; for example, 35 percent reported they were working class or poor when growing up and another 12 percent reported they were lower middle class when growing up. Throughout this project, I focus on the intersectional identities the interviewees brought up themselves, trying to remain sensitive to those issues they found meaningful rather than imposing my own framework on them. Further research about the positionalities of childfree women and of the arguments particular populations of childfree women make is needed, however, to more fully capture the ways reproductive ideologies are woven differently and taken up in different communities' childfree rhetorics.[1]

Table 2.1. Childfree interview participants

Name[a]	Race/ethnicity	Nationality	Education level	Socioeconomic class growing up	Age at time of interview
Cassie	White	US	Some college	U	24
Jeanette	White	US	BA	Middle class	55
Sandra	U	US	MA	Middle class	33
Christina	African American	US	Clinical doctorate	U	40
Tasha	African American	US	MA	Lower class/poor	28
Silvia	White	U	PhD	lower middle class	36
Nicole	Black	US	BA	U	45
Mary	U	Canada	MA	Working class	63
Claudia	Latina	Panama/US	MA	U	38
Suzanne	White	US	PhD	Working class	42
Meghan	White	US	MA	Lower middle class	45
Cynthia	U	US	PhD	U	54
Traci	White	US	BA	Upper middle class	49
Grace	Black	Caribbean/ England/US	MA	Working class	54
Leigh	White	US	PhD	Working class	36
Shanna	U	US	PhD	Working class	39
Bonnie	White	Canada	PhD	Working class	34
Kari	White	US	MFA	Working class	44
Christie	White	US	PhD	Lower class/poor	46
Rachel	White	US	PhD	U	38
Tara	U	US	MA	Middle class	39
Alison	White	US	MA	Upper middle class	34
Dianna	White	England	PhD	Working class	31
Katherine	Black	US	Some college	Working/middle class	45
Jessica	White	US	MA	Lower middle class	41
Devori	White	US	PhD	Lower middle class	38
Allison	U	US	BA	Upper middle class	55
Elizabeth	White	US	PhD	Working class	36
Celia	White	US	PhD	Middle class	35

continued on next page

Table 2.1—*continued*

Name[a]	Race/ethnicity	Nationality	Education level	Socioeconomic class growing up	Age at time of interview
Sarah	White	Canada	AA	U	39
Brittany	White	US	PhD	Upper middle class	35
Irene	Asian American	US	PhD	Working/middle class	39
Gail	White	Scotland/ Canada	MA	Working class	59
Alicia	White	US	MA	Upper middle class	31

a. *As mentioned in the introduction, I asked interviewees if they wanted to be identified by their real names or not. In the text when I talk about interviewees, I do not distinguish between pseudonyms and actual names.*

In semistructured interviews, I asked fourteen questions (see appendix A) while also allowing for follow-up questions, interviewees' own topics, and so on. These interviews ranged in time from twenty-three minutes to ninety, and the average time was thirty-nine minutes. Interviewees had been provided the interview questions before the interviews; while some admitted to not having really looked at these ahead of time, others clearly had used them to think through answers to the questions before our interviews. I did not explicitly ask interviewees about the reasons they did not want children or the life patterns that led them not to have them; that work has been done in the past several decades by scholars, primarily sociological scholars, such as Sharon K. Houseknecht (1987), Park (2005), Julia McQuillan, Arthur L. Greil, Karina M. Shreffler, Patricia A. Wonch-Hill, Kari C. Gentzler, and John D. Hathcoat (2012), Braelin Settle and Krista Brumley (2014), and Amy Blackstone (2019). Instead, I focused in large part on the background of my interviewees and the interactions they have had with others (family, friends, colleagues, strangers) about their decision not to have children, which allowed for more attention to the affectual and rhetorical nature of interactions around childfreedom. While interviewees did often mention reasons they had chosen to be childfree, my questions allowed us to focus on the ways they have talked with others about their decisions not to have children and about reactions, both positive and negative, to this decision from a variety of people. This approach provided me with information about reproductive doxae circulating through childfree rhetorics and how interviewees negotiated articulations and disarticulations of these doxae with others.

I developed my coding process while continuing to conduct interviews, which let me ask more focused follow-up questions in later interviews about themes previous interviewees had discussed that connected to themes later interviewees mentioned. After the interviews were professionally transcribed, I used Dedoose software to identify thirty-five parent codes arising from these, following Johnny Saldaña's (2016) methods of attribute coding, as well as structural coding to identify common themes across interviews. In this coding process, I used extant literature about childfreedom, including many of the texts mentioned throughout this project, to guide my development of categories and codes (a process Thomas R. Lindlof and Bryan C. Taylor [2017] discuss). There are many overlapping themes throughout this work, and these informed how I approached reading and analyzing interview material. However, I was also attuned to the ways the focus of my interview questions on interactions with others opened up new avenues to consider the circulation of social scripts through these interactions. Coding for standard demographic categories such as race/ethnicity, class, educational attainment, age, and so forth also spoke to some diversity among my interviewees, which provided new lenses through which I could reconsider some of the themes in previous work on childfreedom that does not address such diversity.

The thirty-five codes provided a window into how interviewees interpreted childfreedom in their own lives and what events, people, things, and so on were notable to them in reflecting on their identities as childfree women. After my interviews were complete, I further examined and recoded these codes, ultimately combining them into ten interrelated categories (see table 2.2), focusing on common threads that related to reproductive doxae as they wove happiness scripts, whether in the identities of childfree women, interactions between interviewees and others, experiences that related to their childfreedom, their own explanations for their own childfreedom and its rising prevalence, or some other area.

In coding, I did not try to develop completely exclusive codes that did not overlap in any way; as can be seen in table 2.2, quite a few codes did overlap across categories. This overlap maintains the messiness inherent in the ways interviewees spoke about childfreedom and the ways many intersecting understandings of their childfreedom developed out of their interactions and experiences with others. While this approach to coding is not in keeping with the completely grounded approach explained by Lindlof and Taylor (2017), it rejects the premise that coding must lead to completely separate and neat categories despite the

Table 2.2. Primary interview categories and codes

Category (percentage of interviewees who mention)	Parent code(s) and child code(s) included in category[a]	Example interview text
Social scripts (76%)	Social expectations, choice, other people's reactions, media	Irene: In "a lot of working class families, especially immigrant families . . . your plan in life that's sort of handed down to you is you get a job, you have a . . . you get married, you have kids . . . so I kind of grew up expecting that's what would happen to me."
Reasons for not having children (94%)	Reasons for not having children, other people's reactions	Meghan: "And I think people are just often . . . they just, I mean, not my friends but strangers, it's like, they just don't really actually believe, like 'Oh no, you're wrong. You really want kids, you just don't know it yet. You have to want kids!'"
Medical interventions (44%)	Medical interventions, other people's reactions, strangers, choice	Traci: "And even when I was into my 30s and on to my serious relationship, and what was going to be my second marriage, nobody would tie my tubes. And I know that like it's most complicated for women if you want it undone blah blah blah, but I would say to doctors, even women doctors, I would say, 'I will sign papers until my arm falls off, and I will not sue you.' And still college educated, professional, with a job, same job for years and years and years, nobody took me seriously. . . . Yeah, it's infuriating."
Women's identities and cultures (97%)	Gender/sexuality, race, religion, class, geographical location, family, friends, colleagues, strangers, dolls, babysitting, mother-*role*	Grace: "There's also the racial component to that, right? Where people expect Black women to have children, like there's got to be a child somewhere. . . . And it was just sort of like this expectation of it."
Grandparenting (71%)	Grandparenting, parents, fathers, mothers, in-laws	Leigh: "I think my mother tries to pretend that she's not devastated that she's not having grandchildren. And so for a while she would guilt trip me and subtly drop hints."
Care and self-care (94%)	Social expectations, roles, childless role models, workplace environment, selfishness, other people's reactions-*selfish*, reasons for not having children, pets	Elizabeth: "I think that we get called selfish and I'm okay with that. If it means that I'm a happy person, sure, that's fine because I don't want to be guilted into taking care of another human."

continued on next page

Table 2.2—*continued*

Category (percentage of interviewees who mention)	Parent code(s) and child code(s) included in category[a]	Example interview text
Unsupportive interactions (94%)	Family-*unsupportive*, father-*unsupportive*, mother-*unsupportive*, siblings-*unsupportive*, friends-*unsupportive*, colleagues-*unsupportive*, dating, partners' feelings about children	Christina: The most "hostile responses" she had received from anyone about being childfree were from men she had dated, including men who had told her, "You're denying your purpose on earth."
Rhetorical strategies about childfreedom (59%)	Rhetoric, family, friends, colleagues, strangers	Tara: "I'm very straightforward. I'm like, 'I don't have kids. I don't want them.' If that person has an issue with it, then, I mean, that's their issue at that point is kind of how I look at it."
Supportive interactions (97%)	Family-*supportive*, father-*supportive*, mother-*supportive*, siblings-*supportive*, friends-*supportive*, friends-*friends without children*, friends-*friends with children*, colleagues-*supportive*, workplace environment, partners' feelings about children	Bonnie: "My biological mother also has been incredibly supportive of my decision, and even though she says that her children were the best thing she's ever done in this world, she's never thought that I wasn't doing, you know, I'm not kind or nurturing or a woman if I don't have kids."
Aunt identity (44%)	Roles-*aunt*, childless role models, reasons for not having children	Sarah: "And I'm, I, although I never want to be a mom, I'm very, very, very much proud of being an auntie. That's a pretty big thing in my life, and my family is my little niblings."[b]

a. *I can't help but remark on the fact that even qualitative coding is characterized in terms of parent-child relationships.*

b. *"Nibling" is a gender-neutral term used to refer to the child(ren) of a person's siblings.*

complexities of the subject being studied. Instead, I sought to embrace these complexities by identifying common categories across the interview set that different codes fit into and across. This approach maintains the systematic nature of coding while also being more transparent about the how the interview material often linked to different categories and codes, revealing the many layers of information each interview contained and communicated. As I identified categories and codes, my approach was to focus on those that most directly related to the ways reproductive doxae circulated through interviewees' experiences and interactions while also taking into account as much as possible what kinds of differences existed between individual interviewees and how these differences shaped their experiences.[2]

In this chapter, I turn attention to reproductive doxae interviewees identified circulating through media about motherhood and childfreedom and to some of the commonplaces interviewees heard from others, particularly medical professionals, about childfreedom. This analysis demonstrates how contemporary reproductive ideologies have been rearticulated from reproductive ideologies seen in previous time periods, illustrating how tightly woven ideologies tied to reproductive doxae are and how difficult they therefore can be to challenge. It also illustrates how I use interview material to build my analysis of reproductive doxae as they circulate through and contribute to gendered happiness scripts affectually and rhetorically.

A METHODOLOGICAL NOTE ON POSITIONALITY

Because of the historical centering of white women, the reproductive ideologies operating on them are most often brought to the surface and challenged through political action, demonstrations, and so forth, whereas the reproductive ideologies working on other women often remain invisible except to them. This invisibility means a project such as mine focusing on childfreedom is tricky to research and write. While I draw attention to reproductive doxae circulating through childfree rhetorics, my analysis is only part of the picture. Because many of my interviewees are white women, they necessarily speak from a white perspective about their experiences with reproductive ideologies. Further, because I am a white woman myself, my positionality as an interviewer necessarily shapes the types of interactions that occur with interviewees, particularly women of color who, correctly, may not feel that I can fully understand their experiences.

For instance, at one point in an interview with Christina, an African American woman, the different communities we belong to came to the forefront; in describing her family, she said, "And we have what we call . . . I have another aunt who's more like an adopted mom." (Perhaps she was going to say "othermother," a term I discuss in chapter 5, although I'm not certain.) This was an obvious point at which it felt to me that my whiteness interrupted our communication. It demonstrates how my positionality as a white woman interviewer affected how some interviewees interacted with me, even as we shared identification as childfree women and even as I tried to refrain from interjecting my own perspectives into the interviews.

In addition to my own positionality as a white woman researcher, a lack of diverse lenses through which childfreedom is interpreted indicates the need for more diverse perspectives about childfreedom. Scholarship about childfree women has often been conducted by white women, although there are exceptions (Kendrick 2019; Martinez and Andreatta 2015; White 2017). This gap in understanding how reproductive doxae uniquely circulate through the lives of childfree women of color may also demonstrate how whiteness works in reproductive ideologies to call all women to relate to particular happiness scripts in order to align themselves with ideas about what is good, regardless of race, class, sexual orientation, (dis)ability, and so on. So while my interviewees do represent different races, ethnicities, social classes, national backgrounds, sexualities, and so forth, their experiences cannot fully unravel and reweave the hegemonic beliefs about reproduction at work in all women's lives. Instead, they provide insights into their own experiences unravelling and (re)weaving these threads in relation to those around them, and my analysis demonstrates how attention to the affective circulation of reproductive doxae can be used to understand how different groups of women experience reproduction as doxae circulate in rhetorics around, by, and about them.

AFFECTUAL WEAVINGS OF REPRODUCTIVE IDEOLOGIES

More than three-quarters of my interviewees mentioned the scripts they saw around them that reinforced hegemonic mothering ideologies and the articulations of selflessness, care, and happiness tied to motherhood that circulated through their lives, although I did not ask about this specifically. These experiences suggest how buried and unexamined doxae often are until someone resists them. My interviewees often described themselves as living outside the common representations of women in their communities and, more broadly, in media. As several pointed out, reproductive ideologies often circulate through affectual rather than explicitly rhetorical threads, in spite of their impact on childfree rhetorics. I argue that the growing attention to childfree women in the twenty-first century signals another historical moment when reproductive ideologies are being brought to social attention and made available for argumentation and critique.

Several interviewees themselves were aware of the some of the interwoven threads in sociocultural contexts that affect childfreedom and whether women, especially on a large scale, feel comfortable and are able to make a childfree choice. Mary, who was sixty-three at the time of the interview, attributed her decision not to have children to having grown up "through some of the feminism in the sixties and seventies and eighties." By implication she referenced the role of the twentieth-century feminist movement in advocating for reproductive choice through birth control and abortion—a change that does not address the facts that choice is very contested for many women and that the rhetorics of choice can mask constraints on the reproductive options available to different women.[3]

A central part of the social control exerted on women is the circulation of reproductive ideologies through affectual, or unspoken, threads. Several interviewees talked about having made assumptions earlier in their lives they would one day be mothers because motherhood did not seem to be an articulated choice. Brittany said, "It's not that I never really thought about it, I just always automatically assumed that I would have children, that it would happen someday it's just . . . it wasn't ever going to be today. And then it kept just getting pushed off and pushed off and pushed off." A number of interviewees said they had expected to become mothers and gradually realized they did not have to. Suzanne mentioned women feeling as if they must have children is "social conditioning" that presents "very limited models of adulthood." In other words, she recognized the weaving of reproductive doxae through affectual social networks that contribute to happiness scripts that, for women, revolve around motherhood. For both Brittany and Suzanne, going to graduate school outside their own communities and meeting people without children were turning points in their thinking about motherhood as a choice rather than as compulsory. Tara also said her thinking about motherhood was complicated because of the messages around her. She mentioned thinking when she met her husband that she "wanted to have a kid" but felt she had this thought only because "so many people were talking about it" and asked her about it. She felt "a tremendous amount of pressure" from family and friends about her becoming a mother. Eventually, she decided she was "entitled to make it [her life] [her] own creation," which she did by embracing childfreedom. However, it was not an easy process for her to shift from a path of assuming she would have children and having this script reinforced by those around her. Although now Tara felt confident telling others she was childfree, assuming an identity as a childfree woman had taken time: "But it took me a long time. I'm acting like I'm all cool and stuff, but I'm not. It's taken me a long time to get there, to get to that point." Beliefs, values, and commonplaces supporting these ideologies often circulate through the communities childfree women grow up in and, to some extent, in the media around them, operating at such an unconscious level that many women grow up thinking they will necessarily one day have children.

Quite a few interviewees attributed the gendered happiness scripts about motherhood that surrounded them when younger to the articulations of adult life in communities in which they had grown up. Cassie felt that neither of her parents "ever felt like they had the option not to have kids." She attributed this to their growing up in a rural Southern area and the expectations that "the nuclear family was the priority." Sandra also attributed the pressure to have children to being raised in a Southern community, where she said many women get married early and have children. Elizabeth, who grew up in the Midwest, said that in her very small town "everyone has children" and that growing up she didn't "know anyone who didn't have kids." Rachel grew up in a rural farming town in the Midwest. She said women in her community were raised to be "farm wives." The scripts she identified included staying in the community, marrying a man, having children, and running a family farm, scripts in which "women don't have a voice. You don't really have any agency over your life."

Other interviewees referenced factors such as race, class, and immigrant status that articulated the gendered happiness scripts they were expected to follow. Irene, whose parents were Asian American immigrants and who grew up working class, said, "[In] a lot of working-class families, especially immigrant families, your plan in life that's sort of handed down to you is you get a job, you get married, you have kids . . . so I kind of grew up expecting that's what would happen to me." For Gail, who emigrated from Scotland to Canada as a child, class status and a working-class environment were associated with pressure to have children. She said, "I often wonder what it would have been like if I had stayed in Scotland. If I'd stayed in a working-class community or environment, I would have had a lot of family pressure to have children." Instead, the opportunities she experienced in Canada and the friends she made "became really strong influencers in [her] going to school and [her] life choices" that ultimately meant she did not choose to have children. Although Gail and her mother were close, Gail still felt like "the black sheep" in the family because she was educated and did not have children, which was in stark contrast to her mother and sister, who had both had a child when they themselves were very young. Essentially Gail moved out of the community that exerted pressure to have children, much as other interviewees did, but she moved out when still a child.

It is difficult to extrapolate from a small sample, but it is possible that moving to Canada was crucial to Gail's experience. Two other participants who did not sense the pressure of reproductive ideologies as strongly grew up in Canada, although the Canadian rates of those who are childfree are approximately the same as those in the United States (around 7%), and Maura Kelly (2009) has found that experiences of childfreedom are similar across the United States, Canada, and the United Kingdom (161). The first, Mary, had grown up working class in the 1960s and 70s, but she said she "never really felt pressured by society" to have children. On the other hand, she attributed this freedom mostly to her own attitude, which she said was one of "I do what I wanna do" rather than her geographical context. Bonnie grew up in Canada three decades more recently than Mary, but she said, "I don't feel a lot of social pressure to have children. . . . The only time I felt pressure is kind of by proxy through my stepmom and her sons, and she's been much harder on them than she has been on me." Bonnie recognized her stepmother believed people need to have children, but she did not directly feel pressure. However, the pressure interviewees felt about having children may have been more about the individual communities they grew up in rather than specific national contexts. Jeanette, who grew up in the United States, also said, "[I] never felt particularly targeted [to have children] but I have heard about women who have." She gave an example of a woman she knew who had been "shamed in her [Baptist] church for not wanting children" such that the pressure ultimately "drove her out of the church. And [Jeanette] thought, that's really sad."[4] Generally, interviewees acknowledged a more general association of happiness scripts with motherhood in their broader sociocultural contexts, even if they themselves had different experiences with negotiating such scripts in their own communities.

Dianna spoke specifically about the larger context that weaves together gender ideologies and motherhood. She explained, "I think too much of society defines women according to being a mother." She said motherhood is a huge part of many mothers' identities. Being childfree can also be a big part of identity, but Dianna felt it is not a big part for her. She also said few people believe she "actually" made a decision not to have children instead of being forced into childlessness through infertility and trying to act happy about it. Her example points to how pervasive reproductive ideologies are and how they often circulate affectually through scripts around people without many openings in which they can speak about childfreedom, making it difficult to articulate their happiness and contentment.

While most interviewees focused on the ways reproductive ideologies affectually circulated in the communities and social fabric around them, a few discussed how it circulated through media. Leigh had been studying romantic comedies, and she said one thing she had noticed was how "strikingly pro kid" and "pro parenting" these are. She also explained that so much media "show[s] sad women without kids, the cat-lady stereotype" and that this depiction contributes to "a lot of fear mongering" about childlessness, which "make[s] women feel like they're supposed to feel like horrible people if they're not excited by a [positive] pregnancy test." Alicia also mentioned specific scripts embedded in media. She talked about the television show *Bones* and how she "absolutely loved it" for the first few seasons because the main character, Bones, did not have children and did not express a desire to have them. Alicia stopped watching the show when Bones became a mother through an accidental pregnancy. She said television shows use pregnancy and having children as "a really unfortunate cultural narrative" and "lazy plot device" that can "put women in their place." She recognized these narratives as circulating the belief that even women who claim they do not want children actually do and eventually will. Christie was sensitive to this as well, and she mentioned an exception: a scene in *House of Cards* in which a childfree woman, who in the show is the First Lady of the United States at the time, responds to the question as to whether she regrets not having children with her own question: "Do you regret having them [children]?" Christie said, "That was my favorite scene."

Other interviewees had slightly differently perspectives on the evolving sociocultural milieus that support or constrain women's reproductive choices. Jessica delved into how much sociocultural ideologies rather than individual women's choices influence whether or not a woman has children.

> I think it's also interesting to know that we [childfree women] see ourselves and our decisions as being so much influenced by current events, and cultures, and political, that sometimes I think we put, women put this child or not child question, it seems like an individual personal decision that is so personal and so important. But actually, it's not so incredibly important, really personal. It's not so personal. It is this . . . that decision in 2019 is different than it was in 1996, it's different in the United States than it is in Peru. . . . I think about what if I ever lived in a different time, or a different political landscape, something like that. My conception for my own body might be different.

She points out that the ways people think about reproduction, especially in relation to whether or not they have reproductive choices, shifts depending on the sociocultural contexts in which they live and the ideologic webs that exist in these contexts. While women's childlessness has been stigmatized for thousands of years, the forms of this stigma and how reproductive ideologies have been articulated have evolved across times, places, and women's identities. In the twentieth and twenty-first centuries, larger groups of women have had reproductive options, and yet sociopolitical constraints are put on these options. As Elizabeth explained, this tension raises the question, "If you're not a mother, then how are you being controlled?" The answer historically has been pathologization, threats of death, and absorption into other family structures that put women under male control, among others. While powerful political forces are seeking—with some success—to limit reproductive options, when women can work in their own jobs and create their own households without male control and oversight, there are fewer legal mechanisms in place to align them with gendered scripts. Instead, the affectual circulation of reproductive doxae through social interactions and ideologies is even more crucial because it is one of the central ways women with reproductive options can be aligned with articulations of motherhood.

DISCURSIVE CIRCULATIONS OF REPRODUCTIVE IDEOLOGIES

While the childfree women in my study often recognized the affectual circulations of reproductive ideologies working somewhat invisibly on women's lives, their own decision not to have children made such ideologies visible not just to themselves but also to those around them. This visibility led to explicit discursive interactions about hegemonic reproductive beliefs that demonstrate the relationship between the affectual and rhetorical. Future chapters delve more deeply into some of these interactions. Here, I end this chapter with an examination of common questions interviewees were asked about not wanting children to demonstrate how reproductive doxae bind these questions and how these women's responses demonstrate a recognition of the constraints of happiness scripts on their lives and their attempts to make these threads visible to others. I also examine examples of discourse between interviewees and medical professionals to illustrate how childfree women's bodies are suspect because they do not align with happiness scripts about the reproductive capacities women's bodies are supposed to fulfill.

As a feminist rhetorical scholar, I was interested in the types of interactions interviewees had with others about their decision not to have children. I also wanted to know about their backgrounds because research into childfree women does not always account for past experiences that could shape their childfree decision, instead often focusing on current demographic data about women (their race, class, educational achievement, etc.). Nonetheless, all but one of my thirty-four interviewees talked about reasons they decided not to have children. I took this as a sign of the pressure they face to explain why they were not following happiness scripts and to explicitly rearticulate womanhood apart from motherhood. I did provide space at the end of interviews for childfree women to talk about any topics we did not cover, and sometimes reasons came up during this part of the interview. Reasons also often came up in other questions, including a question about formative events or people that influenced their decision not to have children. Having well-formed reasons about childfreedom is one way for childfree women to circulate counterhegemonic beliefs about womanhood as they dialogue with others.

It was clear that not having children was often, although not always, a deliberate choice the interviewees had thought carefully about. They had also considered how to present this choice to others in rhetorically strategic ways (as also seen in chapter 5). The two most cited reasons for not having children, each mentioned by fourteen women, were travel/lifestyle and not wanting to care for children, with no desire to have children closely behind and economics or money a close fourth. Only four women mentioned caretaking of siblings or parents as a reason they do not want children, despite this being an often-assumed reason they don't want children (see chapter 4). Nine women did mention babysitting had reinforced their decision not to have children. A common theme was that concerns about having children revolve around the choices interviewees are able to make about their daily lives, including choosing how to spend time and money. They also represent new articulations of womanhood these women weave through childfree rhetorics.

My interviewees' reasons for not wanting children align fairly well with reasons cited in sociological research about childfree people. In Houseknecht's (1987) review of sociological studies about the childfree, she found the most cited reasons for not having children were "freedom from child-care responsibility/greater opportunity for self-fulfillment and spontaneous mobility" (79%), "more satisfactory marital relationship" (62%), "female career considerations" (55%), and "monetary advantages" (55%) (377). Park's (2005) more recent interviews with twenty-one childfree men and women found childfree women were more likely than childfree men to "be affected by parenting models—displayed by their own parents and by friends and colleagues—when making their decision." Their assessment of the things they saw around them "produced fear or anxiety about or distaste for the parenting experience" (395). Childfree women in her study also viewed "motherhood . . . as compromising career and leisured identities that were currently experienced as satisfying and intending to be further developed" (396). In alignment with some of my interviewees, Park found about half the childfree women she interviewed mentioned not being comfortable with or being interested in children as an additional reason. While not statistically generalizable, her finding that childfree men were more likely than women to cite financial reasons as motives for not having children is suggestive. Like other researchers, I found childfree women developed new threads and revalued things such as time to oneself, making one's own choices, and so forth that are not reflected in happiness scripts about motherhood tied to articulations of selflessness and care for others. These threads reveal the tensions between the weaving of this happiness script and the alternative weavings childfree women make for their own lives.

While quite a few interviewees readily identified as aunts who have some role in children's lives (see chapter 5), others had no such ambitions. A few said they did not even like children, a reason for not having children they often kept quiet about because it is perhaps the most subversive statement that unsettles the supposedly natural, biological connection between women and children. Given the assumption many make that all childfree women do not like children, and the hostility directed at them as a result, this unravelling of articulations is a particularly tricky one for childfree women to voice without being attacked as unnatural or deviant. In the space of our interviews, however, some interviewees did explain how they did not want to use their bodies to reproduce and/or did not like children. Affectually and rhetorically, this position is difficult to openly express, as seen in other chapters in this book as well, and it shows some of the tensions that circulate around childfree women's reproductive experiences that are underscored by reproductive ideologies.

Aside from not wanting to provide the actual care children require, several interviewees mentioned not wanting to go through the bodily experience of being pregnant and giving birth. Celia talked about wondering what it would be like to be pregnant and not wanting that experience: "What would I do if I had people touching my belly, you know, one example of many . . . I think I'd be anxious about the physicality of all of it, too." Katherine similarly mentioned thinking of pregnancy as "a very not pleasant experience, being sick and stuff like that a lot." Sarah and Brittany also mentioned not wanting their bodies to be changed by having children. Sarah said she and a childfree friend had agreed: "We didn't want our bodies to be destroyed by babies. That's an important thing." This seemed to involve both the physical nature of change but also mental changes through things like lack of sleep. Brittany also talked about the pride she took in her body and not wanting it to change: "I also take a lot of pride in working on my body physically, and it's not necessarily because I'm trying to achieve some aesthetic goal, but I know that if I had a child it would completely ruin all of that . . . it's happened to all of the women in my family and I don't want that." Although there are of course many women who have gone through childbirth and maintained their physical bodies, Brittany assumed her own family's "genetics" would work against her personal goals, which she said are more about pride in accomplishment than an aesthetic goal.[5] Elizabeth was particularly concerned about "the pain of childbirth"; she said that if she were pregnant, she "would spend the whole nine months terrified of what was coming." While these women's concerns did not necessarily rise to the point of tokophobia (or fear of being pregnant), they did influence their decision not to be biological mothers. Although pregnancy and childbirth are often presented in somewhat idealized terms (e.g., Douglas and Michaels 2004), these interviewees recognized women's bodies and the relationships between women's bodies and others necessarily change through pregnancy and childbirth, and they did not want these changes to happen to them. This resistance was a part of counterhegemonic challenges to reproductive doxae and their valuing of how women's bodies carry and birth children that also affects how adoption, surrogacy, and other nonbiological means of becoming a mother are viewed.[6]

Apart from the bodily experiences required of biological mothers, other interviewees did not view themselves as baby people and/or did not like children. This view was a more direct challenge to articulations of hegemonic motherhood and the caring feelings women are assumed to naturally have towards children. Several interviewees mentioned they are not drawn to babies as some of their friends and family members are, a feeling they saw as indicative of their not wanting children. In recounting some of the formative events that shaped her childfreedom, Traci mentioned, "If I was around a neighbor's little baby or a cousin's little baby or something, I'd be like 'okay,' and it just never really seemed to be in me," in contrast to her desire to be around pets. Devori experienced anxiety around her lack of desire for babies: "I've never been a baby person either and that caused me a lot of grief, I would say in my late twenties and early . . . and I think I spent a lot of time, some years, that I'm kind of embarrassed about now, but I think it's sort of natural, I don't know . . . I spent a lot of years worrying there was something psychologically or emotionally wrong with me like I had a hormone deficiency, and . . . I'm not getting the baby craze." Eventually Devori started listening to podcasts that interviewed childfree celebrity women, which empowered her to become "comfortable with the decision." The stress she felt, though, speaks to the powerful nature of reproductive doxae and how they impress upon childfree women who do not like babies or children that they are abnormal and out of line with gendered happiness scripts. In these instances, they must figure out their own identities they can be comfortable with and situate these identities in new weavings of womanhood.

Elizabeth was the most open about not liking children. She said, "I don't like being around kids. I don't know how to talk to them. I don't know how to deal with them. Babies are fine 'cause they sleep, that's okay, but kids, I don't understand and I just don't feel comfortable around them." She tended "to avoid spaces where there are a lot of people with children" and had turned down invitations to events such as children's birthday parties to avoid children. These feelings are perhaps the most difficult for other people to understand because they completely challenge the articulation of womanhood with motherhood and the happiness women are supposed to experience when they selflessly care for children.

Sarah described "a divide" between childfree women who don't like children at all and childfree women who like children but do not want to be mothers. This division is visible in childfree groups on social media, some of which seem to embody an openness about any person's decision to have or not have children and some of which take a more openly hostile stance towards parents (sometimes referring to them as "breeders"). Childfree women who do not like children reject the reproductive ideologies that connect womanhood with selfless care, which makes it more difficult for them to weave happiness scripts not connected to selfishness.

Tensions around how childfree women are positioned outside the social center are also seen in some of the common negative reactions the childfree women in my study often received from others when they revealed they were childfree, reactions that often reinforced the deviancy of their identities (see Kelly [2009] for further discussion of these types of responses). Brittany said that when she "first kind of flew the idea" of remaining childfree by her mother, her mother suggested she was following the lead of her two close childfree friends. Brittany didn't entirely deny it, and her mother responded by saying, "No, no. You'll change your mind." Such claims demonstrate an unwillingness on the part of others to challenge happiness scripts and what appears to be a combination of ageism and sexism. As Brittany summarized, "And so I was treated as though I was still a child. And I was in my early thirties at this point."

Participants had often experienced the assumption that childfree women were not yet mature enough to make reproductive decisions and that they would eventually want to become mothers, echoing forward ideas about the naïveté of young women associated with hysteria in the early twentieth century. Sandra's mother's reaction was similar to Brittany's mother's. Sandra was thirty-three at the time of the interview; she recalled, "When I was younger, my mom kind of did the 'Oh, you'll change your mind when you're older.' " The persistence with which people react to childfree women in this manner speaks to the expectation that women of childbearing age who haven't yet had children will simply alter course and conform to happiness scripts eventually. Sandra's mother gradually came to accept her decision, but she still faces such reactions. Sandra explained, "But as I eventually got older, [my mother] finally kind of recognized that was the real deal. And she's been okay with it. She . . . there was never any conversation about why or something's wrong with you." But Sandra said many strangers express the "assumption that [her disinclination to have children is] a phase."

Meghan's experience reflected the idea that there is a biological imperative to have children, the absence of which is pathologized. She said, "And I think people [strangers] are just often . . . they just don't really actually believe, like, 'Oh no, you're wrong. You really want kids, you just don't know it yet. You have to want kids!'" Her perception of strangers' reactions emphasizes how having children is seen as an inevitable outcome of being a woman, a part of happiness scripts that cannot be avoided. The disbelief around childfree women's choices speaks to an unwillingness to examine and/or challenge hegemonic reproductive beliefs and the difficulty others have in (re)weaving happiness scripts for women that don't revolve around motherhood.

Medical professionals also refused to confront their own reproductive beliefs and deconstruct happiness scripts, according to interviewees. Almost half of interviewees mentioned these interactions, despite my not asking explicitly about interactions with medical professionals. Annily Campbell (1999) explores childfree women's choices to be sterilized in her book *Childfree and Sterilized*. In discussing the interactions child-free women can have with medical professionals, she explains, "When women who have chosen to remain without children find that powerful others refuse to countenance the decision to be sterilized then they say that they feel that their own freedom and determination is attacked and may experience a range of negative and undermining emotions: humiliation, frustration, anger and rage, and helplessness. Some speak of having been infantized [*sic*], not only by the refusal of their request but also through a denial even of their choice to make such a decision" (114). As other rhetorical scholars such as Owens (2015) and Harper (2020) show, interactions between women and medical professionals can be particularly fraught because the medical community often ignores and dismisses women's experiences of their bodies, especially if women are from historically minoritized communities.

Shanna described medical personnel's insistence that she take six separate pregnancy tests to establish that she was not pregnant when her abdomen was swollen, despite her insistence that it was "a waste of [her] money" because her husband had a vasectomy. The nurse told her, "But would it be so bad if you were pregnant?" and Shanna replied, "I am working on my PhD. I don't want children." She then said, "If I am pregnant, if by some immaculate conception I am pregnant, I am aborting this fetus as quickly as I can." She said the nurse was "appalled" at this reaction and kept saying, "But would it be so bad? I love my children," and went on and on about her own children. Shanna eventually asked for a different nurse. Experiences of having their decision not to have children questioned and even of others trying to intervene in this choice was not unusual in interviewees' accounts.

Elizabeth explained pushback to her decision not to have children usually came from "some sort of health professional" like doctors or nurses. She recalled an interaction she had with a nurse when she was in her midtwenties: "A nurse said something like I needed to start taking some kind of vitamin or something, and I was like, 'Why?,' And she was like, 'Well, you know, you know, 'cause you know, when you have kids, and blah, blah, blah,' and I was like, 'Whoa, whoa, whoa, I'm not having children.' And she gave me that look and was like, 'Oh, you'll change,' and I said, 'No, listen, I don't like children, I won't be having them.'" Such interactions speak to the embedded nature of reproductive ideologies and the medical community's ongoing and historical resistance to, if not pathologization of, childfree women.

Such interactions had happened to Elizabeth later in life, too. Just a week before I interviewed her, she had gone to the doctor to have her IUD replaced, and the male doctor and midwife were talking about the possibility of a hysterectomy. While the midwife said that would be possible, the male doctor hesitated, asked how old Elizabeth was, and tried to start a conversation about her age and reproduction. She stopped him by saying, " 'Oh, no, no, no, we're not having this conversation. I don't like children.' And that stopped, not just that I didn't want them, but that I don't like them, and he's like, 'Oh.' " Elizabeth suggested she had effectively ended the conversation largely because she had suggested she would be a bad mother; her preference was not sufficient. This rhetorical tactic reinforces happiness scripts by pointing to a woman's individual inability to assume the articulations of care and selflessness as a mother as the issue, not the scripts themselves.

An experience Devori, who is in her late thirties, had further emphasizes the ways medical professionals delegitimize childfree women's choices. After moving to a new town in the Bible belt, she went to see an OB/GYN for the first time. During this discussion, the doctor found out she had been on birth control for many years and asked if she wanted to renew her birth control. When she replied yes, he asked, "Do you want to have kids?" She said, "No, we're not planning on having children," and he said, "Well, I'll renew it now, but we should probably discuss this with your husband." In this instance, the doctor treated Devori as her husband's reproductive vessel without the ability to make her own reproductive decisions. The next year Devori went to another doctor in town—who she said was also an older man because that was the only kind in her town—but he was much more matter of fact about her right to choose to be on birth control.

Beyond unnecessary pregnancy tests and questions about vitamins or birth control, many childfree women struggle to find doctors who will provide surgical sterilization when they want it.[7] Often, this reluctance is because doctors assume women do not understand their own choices and are not capable of making these choices for themselves. Famously, as reported by Olivia Blair in the April 12, 2017, *Independent*, a British woman named Holly Brockwell fought for four years to get a doctor to perform a tubal ligation. Traci, who is white and grew up in an upper-middle-class household, had similar struggles. She said, "Nobody would tie my tubes. And I know that it's most complicated for women if you want it undone [that is, vasectomies are easier to reverse than tubal ligations or other female sterilization procedures] blah blah blah, but I would say to doctors, even women doctors, I would say, 'I will sign papers until my arm falls off, and I will not sue you.' And still [even though I'm] college educated, professional, with a job, same job for year and years and years, nobody took me seriously. . . . Yeah, it's infuriating." Traci said that of all the tactics she tried—emphasizing she was in a serious relationship and would not want to reverse the procedure, displaying her intelligence through her education, and reinforcing her stability as a professional—none worked. While it may be reasonable for a doctor to encourage women in committed relationships to consider whether their male partners could have the less invasive and consequently assumed-to-be-safer sterilization procedure available to men, ultimately women may have their own reasons for preferring to have what is in fact a very safe procedure,[8] including not being in an exclusive or permanent relationship or wanting to ensure their own bodies are unable to reproduce.

Cassie was unusual in that she found a doctor who would perform a tubal ligation when she was twenty-one years old, but first several doctors turned her down. All those who refused her were actually women. She said, "I had many women doctors tell me that I didn't have the right to choose. The last one that I went to, the last female gynecologist that I went to told me that it didn't matter if I wanted kids or not because I might need a man one day that did want kids and then it wasn't up to me." Much like Devori's doctor, this doctor was more concerned with Cassie's (potential) male mate than with her own reproductive choice, making the grounds for dialogue about this decision untenable. The doctor who granted her request was a man. She recalled that he said, "Hey, if you feel that strongly about it, I get it, but I wanna sit and talk to you for a little bit and see, you know, what you have to say, how long you thought about it, what your logical process was." Cassie said that ultimately the doctor acknowledged she'd be "a good candidate for" the procedure. While it's reasonable for a doctor not to want to provide surgery that is difficult to reverse without reassurance that the patient is making a rational decision, it is difficult to imagine a urologist insisting that a man who wants a vasectomy have such a conversation, or that a woman who declines to have her IUD replaced justify that decision. Indeed, Blackstone (2019) explains, "For men, their very resistance to the pressure to reproduce is understood as an act of manliness. For women, on the other hand, resisting the pressure to parent calls their womanhood into question" (106). Interviewees in my study noted their male partners or other men had different experiences than they did when interacting with doctors around reproductive choices.

To this point, Sarah mentioned that her boyfriend, who is in his twenties, went to the doctor and managed to get a vasectomy within a week. Hearing stories of resistance such as Traci and Cassie encountered can discourage some childfree women from even initiating conversations about sterilization with their doctors. Sarah hadn't tried to get a tubal ligation, but she assumed it would be difficult. She said, "I've heard a lot of stories from women who have been like, 'No, I'm very certain I don't want to have kids,' and just [have had] to jump through endless hoops to try. . . . I feel like even now at thirty-nine, if I wanted to get a tubal, they would be like, it would be hard, I would be questioned, whereas my twenty-seven-year-old boyfriend just went in and was just like, 'Yeah, I'm . . . I don't wanna have kids.' And they're like, 'Okay.' " She reflected, "I mean, don't trust us, right? They don't trust us as women. They . . . they're like, 'Oh, you'll change your mind. Of course, you'll wanna have kids someday.' " This is not to say men encounter no resistance. Dianna, who is from England, knew a male friend when she was in her late teens who "massively had to fight" to get a vasectomy. However, unlike Traci, he ultimately won that fight.

Stories like Traci's reflect the lack of rhetorical choices childfree women can face in interacting with medical personnel. They can argue, suggest they are unfit to parent, as Shanna did, or go from doctor to doctor as Cassie did and submit to the doctor's examination of the rationality of their choice. Women must depend on doctors for many types of birth control, yet those who choose to be childfree are often seen as people incapable of making rational, mature decisions about their reproductive lives. Rearticulating hegemonic beliefs about reproduction and, as a result, reweaving the happiness scripts that tie women's bodies to motherhood can be very challenging. Medical personnel are often gatekeepers of such beliefs and the types of decisions women are allowed to make about their reproductive lives.

In examining the ways discourses have circulated around women's reproductive decisions, a couple of commonplaces, which Crowley (2006) defines as beliefs or belief systems "taken as true or relevant on the basis of trust and confidence in an other, be that other an individual, a group, an institution, or a tradition" (70), show up in twenty-first-century arguments about childfree women and their choice not to have children. One of these is the emphasis on women's physical and mental imperative to function as mothers, a role that cannot be rejected without "unnatural" consequences. In contrast with the government's interference in the reproductive paths of "unfit" women who are cast as naturally bad mothers, those the government deems fit are especially demonized if they do not reproduce in accordance with the needs of the nation-state. Another is the reliance on men to explain women's experiences, a trope that often silences challenges to reproductive doxae. Finally, in response to these commonplaces, we see women's attempts to be heard about their own reproductive experiences, attempts that have often failed but have led to some changes in the reproductive options available to some women.

Those women who decide they do not want children recognize the need to articulate their identities to others and even themselves, both so their perspectives can be heard in their own voices and so they are not spoken for. In the process of doing so, childfree women try to make their lives legible within a culture that privileges hegemonic mothering ideologies and continues to make assumptions about women's lives based on this web stemming from thousands of years of beliefs about women's bodies, psyches, and social roles. Such ideological work is not easy, and a broader range of voices is needed in order to unravel the hegemonic ideologies of mothering, particularly the voices of those who may want to be mothers but are forcibly denied that option. As a starting point, the childfree women's experiences discussed in this book reveal how they have recognized the reproductive web that constrains them and have chosen to weave different beliefs and values about women's identities and encourage others to see these as valid and valuable. This path involves tricky work navigating their own and others' identities as tied to reproductive doxae, which the next chapter speaks to.

3

REPRODUCTIVE ARGUMENTS AND IDENTITY WORK

Christina: *"The women in my family are usually the ones in charge and doing stuff and taking on all the responsibility, and it's something I realized from an early age and it kind of pissed me off."*

Leigh: *"I don't have the same generational wealth that a lot of my friends with kids have."*

Suzanne: *"My mom loves being a grandmother and has pictures of her grandkids plastered all over. That is a huge part of her identity is being a grandmother and taking care of other people, which is a very Southern thing."*

Every childfree person has had a unique path to choosing not to have children. Although there are trends in who tends to decide to be child-free (as I discuss in the introduction), each person's story of being childfree takes a different road, involves different people, and is influenced by a variety of factors. In the introduction, I recount some of my own story of being childfree. In this chapter, I try to balance providing an overview of the types of factors that influence childfree women's choices not to have children and examining how interviewees identify the ways these factors affected their choice not to have children on an individual level. As can be seen in the interview snippets in the opening to this chapter, childfree women's choices can seem very personal, and at a micro level they certainly are: individual women do make conscious decisions about whether or not to have children. At a macro level, however, these choices are influenced by sociocultural factors beyond individual women's control (which one interviewee, Jessica, explicitly noticed, as discussed in chapter 2). Similarly, Probyn (1993) argues that "choice," while central to current conceptions of feminism, often centers around choices people appear to make but that have already been

https://doi.org/10.7330/9781646424399.c003

made for them by social systems (285), such as those feeding gendered happiness scripts. Thus, my own choice not to have children is simultaneously personal and also defined by forces outside me as a white, cisgender, bisexual (but seemingly heterosexual because I am married to a man), formerly working-class now middle-class, highly educated woman, and this choice does not fall in line with the hegemonic reproductive choices I am supposed to make and the subsequent prioritization of children over myself. These forces make the decision to be childfree more difficult for others to accept. As I have discussed, selfishness is viewed as one of the most destructive traits a woman can have.[1] The hegemonic belief that many women naturally are caring and nurturing and thus should be unselfish mothers reinforces an ambivalence or even hostility to those women who declare or demonstrate they are focused on their own lives. For women who choose not to have children, such reactions are often amplified because there is no obvious evidence childfree women care for or nurture others. They, like Lilith, are condemned for seeking out their own happiness in their own way.

Grappling with the judgments people make about childfree women is complicated by childfree women's individual identities and how these overlap with the happiness scripts they feel pulling on their lives, the kinds of judgments they face, and the kinds of choices that seem open to them. Aaronette White's (2017) book chapter "Tubes Tied, Truly Child-Free At Last!" reflects on her experiences as an African American woman who chose to be sterilized, a choice she recognizes "was shaped by race, gender, and class factors that intersect with my social and professional life" (409). As she writes, the reproductive ideologies women feel working on their lives and the reproductive options they have available are "often determined by a woman's race, class, education level, and other social factors" (411), although she recognizes that in most societies all women face some pressure to bear children. Different cultures also circulate reproductive doxae in different ways; the *Childfree African* (a now-defunct blog by Doreen Akiyo Yomoah, who runs a Childfree African Twitter account) described pressures African women face that differ in notable ways from those my study participants and I have faced.

Building on the previous two chapters' identification of the ways hegemonic beliefs about reproduction have been reinforced for millennia and continue to circulate, this chapter pulls apart the ways interviewees recognized the happiness scripts working on them and those around them and how they grappled with arguments about reproduction in relation to their own and others' identities. This chapter also analyzes how people's identities can intersect through happiness scripts in ways that can be difficult for them to negotiate with others, in this case through scripts about grandparenting. These struggles illustrate how difficult it can be for women to challenge reproductive doxae even when they are made visible as grounds for argumentation, providing rhetorical scholars with further considerations of the constraints wound around arguments about identity and the rhetorical positioning that occurs when groups try to articulate identities outside the "norm."

AFFECTIVE IDENTITY WORK IN (RE)ARTICULATIONS OF REPRODUCTIVE DOXAE

As childfree women negotiate hegemonic beliefs about reproduction circulating around them, make these beliefs visible so they can be articulated and argued against, and try to make interventions in them, this rhetorical work is complicated because their own identities as well as others' are implicated. Rhetorical scholars such as Johnathan Alexander and Jacqueline Rhodes (2015), Jean Bessette (2017), and Harper (2020) have explored the ways identities—particularly intersectional identities as tied to race, gender, and sexuality—interact with and impact the discursive interventions rhetors make in oppressive systems. Ahmed's (2015) argument in *The Cultural Politics of Emotion* that race, gender, and sexuality are particularly implicated in the ways bodies are bound by discourses around emotion and affect speaks to the deep connections between identity as borne out in individual bodies and the less visible but powerful effects of doxae as experienced through affect and emotion. For childfree women with reproductive options, the expectation that their bodies must experience childbirth in order to fulfill their roles as women affectively pulls not only on them but those around them. Even as they work to weave new identities for themselves that have the potential to create new affective and discursive connections with others (see chapter 5), their rejection of hegemonic reproductive beliefs has affective consequences on others that childfree women cannot account for themselves. The identity work childfree women do thus calls attention to a flexibility to pick up new threads and weave them in new ways, as well as the limits of these new articulations in reshaping the interconnected identities of others predicated on reproductive doxae.

The relationship between identity and doxae has been taken up by other rhetorical scholars. Anderson's (2007) book *Identity's Strategy: Rhetorical Selves in Conversion* perhaps most fully centers identity in rhetorical theory in its analysis of conversion narratives and how these persuasively appeal to others. He claims identity is "a person's ability to articulate a sense of self or self-understanding" (6) and that identity interacts with a culture's doxae: "For rhetoric to work from such a *doxastic* perspective on identity—an emphasis on how identity is experienced and articulated in culture—is to focus on how commonsense beliefs about identity and selfhood function in discourse, informing the actions of rhetors and audiences alike in specific discursive exchanges" (11). Although postmodern critiques of the concept of identity and selfhood have undermined identity as a stable category (Muckelbauer 2008), Anderson's definition of identity as someone's expression of their sense of self and the relationship of that expression to doxae about identity and selfhood opens space for considerations of the interactions between someone's conceptions of themself and sociocultural beliefs. The interconnectedness of individuals and communities with systems, objects, and so on—through affective, material, discursive webs—may undermine the idea of a stable self, but it does not in and of itself negate the ways many people conceptualize and express their places in these networks.

The connections between affective and discursive webs as they overlap with identity extends Anderson's theories to consider further what it means for individuals or groups to have their identities bound by the scripts at work around them and how they speak into or against these scripts. Ahmed (2015) argues sociocultural scripts can serve as bridges between individuals, communities, and global networks, scripts people then must negotiate not just affectively but with their bodily presences. Speaking to the script of compulsory heterosexuality, she claims, "It is important to consider how compulsory heterosexuality . . . shapes what it is possible for bodies to do, even if it does not contain what it is possible to be" (145). While such scripts do not necessarily determine identity, they do determine how bodies are oriented to other people and objects, which necessarily affects identity formation. Some bodies are able to do things other bodies cannot. Ahmed's explanation of the implications for working-class lesbian parents emphasizes how intersectionality affects someone's ability to disrupt scripts: "Maintaining an active positive of 'transgression' not only takes time, but may not be psychically, socially or materially possible for some individuals and groups given their ongoing and unfinished commitments and histories" (153). Although individuals may not always be able to disrupt scripts, Ahmed maintains that reflecting on transgressive work that has been done can help disrupt these scripts at a broader level. This chapter takes up this reflective work by focusing on the interactions among identity, doxae, and affect as childfree women negotiate identity formation and tensions in the scripts around them about reproduction.

The scripts operating on women and their responses to these scripts shift depending on their identities, including race/ethnicity, class, gender, sexuality, and (dis)ability. While it is impossible to sketch out all the permutations of reproductive doxae, some work in rhetorical studies provides insights into the ways women's identities relate to reproductive ideologies and their affectual experiences of reproduction, particularly in relation to race. For example, Maria Novotny and Juliette Givhan (2020) explore "how experiences of failing fertility shift depending upon one's socioeconomic status, sexuality, and race," creating a more intersectional understanding of infertility and "how infertility impacts each body differently" (193). Their article centers on the experiences of two women of color living with infertility and how representations of and access to fertility care differ along racial and socioeconomic lines in particular. Circulating through these reflections are reproductive commonplaces assuming Latina and Black women are very fertile and do not struggle with infertility, creating additional stigma for Latina and Black women who do. Harper's (2020) book is another notable contribution to understandings of how reproductive ideologies shift depending on a woman's identity. She traces how Black women's experiences with reproduction have often been cast in opposition to white women's experiences, creating what Collins (2000) calls "controlling images" that reflected "the dominant group's interest in maintaining Black women's subordination" and "functioned to mask social relations that affected all women" (72). These controlling images circulated reproductive ideologies that continue to shape Black women's reproductive experiences, affecting their reproductive rights and their health (Harper 2020). While these scholars and others, such as De Hertogh (2020), have explored ways such ideologies can be subverted or challenged, their work demonstrates how identities and reproductive doxae are interconnected and shape how individual women experience their reproductive lives.

In part because of the interweaving of doxae and identity, it isn't possible for anyone, including childfree women, to define their identities in isolation. Whether we explicitly or implicitly recognize it, doxae wind around the ways we speak about ourselves to others and think about our own identities. This process is tied to the affectual pulls people feel at work in their lives; in the case of childfree women, their articulations of their identities are often built either in contrast to or in relation to gendered happiness scripts, as these overlap with reproductive doxae, as described in chapters 4 and 5. However, like others, many of the affectual ties childfree women have are to those around them, and their choice not to have children affects not only their own identities but the identities of others. Childfree women in these instances can become Ahmed's (2010) feminist "killjoys"—or those who "spoil" the happiness of others by refusing "to convene, to assemble, or to meet up over happiness" (65)—who see unhappiness in the role of mother and fail to identify with portrayals of happy mothers, thereby making others around them unhappy. Their failure to have children of their own becomes a manifestation of their views and thus itself increases others' unhappiness.

A notable example of the ways childfree women operate as killjoys is found in the tension sometimes felt between childfree women and their parents who are denied the role of grandparents, another important script supporting hegemonic reproductive beliefs. Even some childfree women whose siblings have children face such censure. Bratta's (2018) argument that affect, ideology, and rhetoric are bound together in affective cultures speaks to the connections among reproductive ideologies, the happiness scripts at work on women's lives, and women's interactions with others. Similar to the operationalizing of the American Dream, motherhood and, as an outcome, grandparenting circulate as goods people should want. In this circulation, an "affective economy" as theorized by Ahmed (2015), or affective loop as theorized by Laura Gries and Bratta (2019), is created that begins with signs such as depictions of grandparenting in media and positive rhetoric around grandparenting in Western societies, which become affectively associated with happiness; this association further cements hegemonic reproductive beliefs and the happiness connected with having children that leads to the further circulation of these beliefs. This affective loop is so strong that creating a break in it necessitates making hegemonic reproductive ideologies visible (as discussed in the introduction) and then discursively speaking back to it by challenging the idea that motherhood and children are happy objects.

However, childfree women's parents do not always want to participate in this process of challenging motherhood, children, and, in their case, grandparenting as happy objects. Some experience what I call a commitment to doxae, which Ahmed (2015) describes as an investment "in social norms" (12). Like Judith Butler (1993), Ahmed views this investment process as occurring through the invisible repetition of norms, which speaks to the ways doxae invisibly circulate through symbols, signs, arguments, and so forth. The repetition for potential grandparents of the happiness in grandparenting as a social norm can occur through images of grandparents in media, friends who are grandparents, and rhetorics about the happiness of grandparenting. Some people's attachment to the identity of grandparent can be so strong the denial of this identity can create a lot of unhappiness, or, as

Ahmed (2015) puts it, they can "become *invested* in particular structures such that their demise is felt as a kind of living death" (12). While not all childfree women's parents react in this way, as I discuss later, many do struggle to reconcile their own identifications with (future) grandparenting and their daughters' decisions not to have children they can grandparent. This struggle reveals some of the limits of disarticulating hegemonic reproductive ideologies when other people's identities are also at stake in this work.

In extending work around affect, doxae, and identity formation in particular, this chapter draws attention to the interwoven nature of challenges to doxae and the ways identities are shaped through affective networks. Although other scholars have explored these connections, the identification of different scripts circulating around women and the tension around grandparenting bring to the surface more explicitly how reproductive doxae affectively construct identities. Chapters 4 and 5 of this project then examine ways childfree women attempt to challenge these doxae, even as these women experience varying degrees of identification and support from those around them.

NEGOTIATING GENDERED HAPPINESS SCRIPTS

In my interviews and in books, social media posts, websites, and so forth, childfree women frequently acknowledge the social scripts circulating around them that influenced whether or not they and others had children and how others responded to their not having children. Such awareness often came by recognizing what those around them expected or assumed as they were growing up, the role models they had, and the messages they received about parenthood or motherhood. In navigating these scripts, interviewees and other childfree women often recognized how particular aspects of their identities—gender and sexuality, race/ethnicity, class, religion, geographical areas, and cultures—influenced childfree discourses and how reproductive ideologies operated in relation to their individual identities. In speaking about other women's reproductive options, several of my interviewees also noted not all women have reproductive choice, identifying how assumptions made about women apply unevenly to different groups of women. Jessica spoke about the limitations on women's reproductive lives most broadly: "Women put this child or not child question, it seems like an individual personal decision. . . . It's not so personal . . . that decision in 2019 is different than it was in 1996; it's different in the United States than it is in Peru." Although Jessica doesn't dig into more particular differences between groups of women ostensibly living in the same time and place, she recognizes sociocultural factors work upon this seemingly individual decision and shape the decisions that are made.

Highlighting these types of sociocultural factors, Mary experienced a culture clash in Canada when she was helping support a Syrian refugee family. Upon hearing she didn't have children, they promised to pray for her, apparently assuming she and her partner were infertile. She recognized, though, that the "concept of choice" was "very foreign" to them, in part because of a lack of resources and in part because of their religious belief that God, not individuals, decides who has children. In thinking more closely about how socioeconomic class can affect a woman's reproductive decisions, Shanna talked about working with some high-school students who were living in extreme poverty in which housing and food were insecure and who had made a pregnancy pact. She noticed some of the pressures they faced and the ways their options could seem limited in this type of situation: "the choices women sometimes feel forced into by virtue of feeling isolated, by virtue of feeling like not a part of things." These women were "getting a lot of positive approval" from others and given more food to eat because they were pregnant, resulting in more security for themselves. In this type of situation, women may not feel as if they have many reproductive options available and may feel motherhood is their only clear path forward. These interviewees recognized making reproductive decisions isn't only a personal choice; indeed, power and privilege operate differently upon different women in ways that affect whether or not they become mothers. Here, I discuss childfree women's explorations of gendered happiness scripts and the intersections of their identities with the hegemonic beliefs supporting these scripts. This analysis demonstrates how childfree women make visible the affectual circulations of reproductive doxae for themselves and others, a necessary step in grappling with their own identities and their decision not to have children.

Reproductive Ideologies and the Perpetuation of Happiness Scripts

Interviewees and other childfree women are very aware of the reproductive ideologies circulating around their lives and the effects of these ideologies on them, perhaps because they make a choice not many others make and, in doing so, are out of alignment with hegemonic reproductive beliefs. As Ahmed (2006) notes in *Queer Phenomenology*, bodies themselves are inscribed by the repetition of orientations as seen through compulsory heterosexuality. Interviewees noticed they were expected to orient themselves toward motherhood and children in particular ways given the expectations of compulsory heterosexuality. Christie pointed out, "I was gonna say, the default is . . . being a mother. Then those who are not, have consciously decided not to have children, are the ones who are breaking the rules 'cause we're the ones who feel like we need to justify ourselves or explain ourselves. Why do we have to explain ourselves?" Ahmed's answer might be that childfree women are asked to explain themselves because they have oriented themselves away from motherhood and children, highlighting the reproductive options some women may have and potentially threatening happiness scripts built on hegemonic ideals.

Some interviewees noted they themselves had assumed they would be mothers, while those around them reinforced this assumption. Their attention to articulations of motherhood unraveled them and opened them up for questioning. As a few noted, this work can be difficult and exhausting. Almost all interviewees identified the reproductive ideologies that circulated through discourses from their upbringing into their adult lives, reinforcing motherhood as a good women naturally want to experience. Many felt pressure from themselves and others to conform to these happiness scripts and to literally inscribe these doxae onto their bodies through the embodiment of motherhood or just assumed they would have children because it's the way things work. Suzanne said she felt she "should have had kids because everybody else thinks you should" and calls this assumption part of "social conditioning" based in part on "limited models of adulthood" she had growing up. Similarly, Tasha said while she didn't necessarily feel *pressured* to have children, the assumption existed "because that's just how we're conditioned" to think "that's just how things work." This conditioning or felt sense that a woman must become a mother is predicated on hegemonic reproductive beliefs and the scripts built from these beliefs about women's roles. Even if women are not directly told they must have children, they affectively feel and take up this expectation themselves.

On the other hand, Tara did feel direct pressure from others: "So many people were talking about it. Like it would just be almost immediately. When they'd ask me, 'Hey, how are you?' You know? 'Hey, when are you going to have a kid with this guy, you know, that you love?' And you know, that was always the first or second question." By contrast, she never felt any inner desire for children. Because she was a heterosexual woman in a relationship, other people assumed Tara and her husband would have children and questioned why they did not. Such experiences demonstrate how reproductive ideologies circulate affectively through women's lives and overlap with compulsory heterosexuality, affecting their own inner dialogue about the reproductive choices they make.

Interviewees picked up on how reproductive ideologies affected what happened and the ways their own identities were positioned in relation to others. Their grappling with these ideologies shows how the affective can work in concert with discourse to create a felt and spoken sense that women are supposed to become mothers and that those who don't live outside the norm. Several women spoke to the sense of abnormality that accompanied their not having children. Celia mentioned a specific time when a friend's mother made an overt comment about her not having children, but she acknowledged that "there's just this constant felt, [that] it's inappropriate to not want to have kids, right? That's this social stigma around it; I feel that all the time." Her comment speaks to the affective circulation of reproductive doxae that occurs in tandem with any actual rhetorical exchanges; both of these together form pressures on childfree women and inform the ways they construct their identities as childfree women. Christie explored what it means to talk about childfreedom with others because "it feels like there should be some shame, right, because women are expected to be mothers. And so, how do we talk about it with different groups of people in ways that make them more comfortable?" Part of the difficulty she acknowledges is this tension between the affectual sense that there "should be some shame" around not wanting children because it doesn't fit with happiness scripts and the interactions childfree women have with others about this choice and how to make it easier for others to witness. Ultimately, though, Christie asked, "Who cares if I don't wanna have children and you do?" In other words, why are conversations about reproduction so vexed, especially when they occur between women? One answer is that childfreedom undercuts happiness scripts, threatening the reproductive ideologies on which these scripts are founded and potentially unraveling the entire web linking women with motherhood.

Part of the disturbance created by unsettling these doxae is predicated on the sense of control over women founded through compulsory heterosexuality as made visible through reproduction. Grace spoke about her family assuming she was a lesbian because she did not have children (see next section for further discussion) and how this choice was seen as a rejection of "the family structure" that is "quote unquote normal. And so you're just kind of completely out of control and [they] don't know what to do with you." Part of the trajectory of this family structure was that, as a girl, "you do girl things [air quotes]. So you're very domestic, etc. etc. You go to school and you're probably gonna work in a helping profession of some sort and then you have children or get married and have children . . . regardless, children are a factor in your life. Period." She recognized the gendered nature of happiness scripts underscored by reproductive doxae, scripts tied to care work—working "in a helping profession"—and motherhood as the ultimate care work. This pressure and set of expectations can result in what Tasha called a "moral obligation on women . . . to have kids." If a woman doesn't want children, she is automatically called "selfish," and that word is used as a weapon to level a moral accusation at women (Kelly 2009; Rich et al. 2011). Dianna echoed Tasha, saying that "too much of society defines women according to being a mother" and that identifying as childfree, even if an individual woman does not think this choice is a huge part of her identity, is seen by society as "a massive part of what defines who [she is]," and that means "clearly there's something wrong with [her]." Their understandings of how childfree women are caught up in social pressures echo the messages conveyed about childless women historically that continue to prop up happiness scripts and construct childfreedom as deviant or abnormal.

Katherine's discussion of social expectations pulled together many of these threads about how reproductive ideologies are woven through affectual and discursive means and push childfree women to the sociocultural margins. First, she described the correlation people make between women and mothers: "People think of women, they think of mothers." Second, she identified the commonplaces that govern how happiness scripts are posited to women: "I think women have been sold a bill of goods that being a mother or wife is what really makes you whole, makes you a real person and worth value." Third, she traced the happiness scripts that have been conveyed to women throughout their lives: "We all women, and we've all been taught the same stuff . . . little girls, you give them dolls . . . it's like we all get taught those same lessons. . . . But I think women just get taught from the time they were little girls that you're supposed to be a mother and you're supposed to want to be one . . . that's the thing. . . . We get the same, no matter where you are, you get the same messages that women are supposed to want to be mothers and that's what we're here for." Taken together, these threads create a web of happiness, care, selflessness, and motherhood that operates on women affectually and rhetorically in complicated ways. The affectual informs rhetoric, but rhetoric also informs the affectual.

Alongside these scripts, childfree interviewees noticed motherhood was held up as the ultimate role for women and the pinnacle of their lives as women. Katherine said she thought "motherhood is so glamorized," even as she noted the sanctification of motherhood was devolving to a degree. Nicole similarly noticed she felt as if "society as a whole tends to unfortunately value women more based upon not only their family situation, like whether or not they're married, but also whether or not they have children." This had happened to her in work situations, such as an interaction with someone from HR at her workplace who seemed to place "a higher value on the fact that [she] had been married before" and was now divorced rather than single. Nicole said, "I find that, just people I meet in general seem to have a more favorable perception of you if you are attached in some way, be it to a spouse or children or a dog, or what have you." Tasha also spoke to the affirmation mothers often receive through baby showers and accolades, like being told they are "hard-working mama[s]." In other words, motherhood is not only assumed but is also celebrated in ways that put pressure on women and that become part of happiness scripts.

A few interviewees spoke about how tiring it was to feel as if they had to respond to the expectations and questions of others about their child-freedom. Some noted that it was not anyone else's business whether or not women had children and that these questions could be inappropriate. As Katherine put it, "You don't have to tell anybody your decision. . . . You don't have to express it every time you talk to somebody." On the other hand, she did believe childfree women "should be open to saying, 'No, I don't want children,' " when it comes up and not "be shamed or feel any kind of way about it." She recognized the negotiation childfree women make between not feeling pressured to constantly talk about or justify being childfree and not trying to hide their being childfree when it came up. This tension is part of the affectual negotiation childfree women make in balancing their own needs with discursive openings to talk about being childfree.

Other interviewees felt the effects of these negotiations in different ways. Tara talked about having conversations in which she felt she had to justify being childfree as making her feel "kind of beaten down" because "conversation can only take you so far"; it won't make the other person "have some sort of revelatory moment where they're like, 'Oh, I guess everybody doesn't have to have kids.' " Her calculation with these conversations is whether there is an opportunity to persuade someone else to view reproductive choices differently and, if not, to try to preserve her sense of self instead of engaging in that conversation. Part of this preserving of self is recognizing the decision not to have children will make other people unhappy and having to come to terms with this reality, which can be particularly difficult for women who have been taught that making other people happy is paramount even to their own happiness. Cassie said, "[The] one thing that I struggled with my entire life and that was the hardest and best thing for me to overcome" was to figure out that "nobody should have to feel like their choices are up to other people's approval" and that "you can't feed off of other people to drive your decisions" because "that really let me grow into myself and become my own person." Like other interviewees, she understood being childfree meant going against social norms and having to affectually and discursively navigate what it means to be a childfree woman.

While many interviewees felt pressure on them as women to be mothers and felt as if being childfree went against sociocultural norms spanning their many different identities, several interviewees did not feel this kind of pressure, even though they still recognized it existed for other childfree women. Jeanette, who is fifty-five, said she herself never felt "particularly targeted" by pressure to have children, which she attributed to societal change over time. She did acknowledge having "heard about women" who had experienced such pressure. Allison, who was also fifty-five, said, "It was just never an issue. And [I] never had any negative, really, response to it." It is possible that as older women, these interviewees have forgotten pressure they felt when they were younger, especially if it was generally mild. Bonnie is two decades younger than either of them, however, and she said she'd never felt direct pressure either. Given that these women were from different age groups and locations—Jeanette and Allison from the US and Bonnie from Canada—it is difficult to attribute this exemption purely to cultural factors. In any case, their examples indicate childfree women can have more positive affectual and discursive experiences with childfreedom.

At the same time, women who experienced pressure through social scripts were not optimistic about societal change. Grace said, "I don't foresee society changing, you know, any time in my lifetime. Maybe one day we're gonna be able to say, 'Yeah, I don't want kids.' And not because I don't like kids, but, you know, I want to do other things first. Or, you know, if I have to choose between my career and children, my career wins or whatever your thing is. And just be, I think accepted is too much to hope for, but, you know, at least people can keep it civil. You know, you're not gonna get attacked if you don't wanna do it." Grace feels her best hope is someday not to be attacked for her choice. However, this change would mean challenges to hegemonic reproductive beliefs would have to be taken up and childfreedom articulated into gendered reproductive ideologies, which as chapters 4 and 5 demonstrate, is a slow and difficult process.

Navigating Personal Identities and Reproductive Hegemony

Childfree women frequently must navigate happiness scripts in processes that reflect the influence of their identities and/or how others view them as childfree women. Alejandra Martinez and Marie Marta Andreatta (2015) are both from Argentina, where, as they write, "representations [of traditional marriage] are strongly supported by a pronatalist culture heavily influenced by the Catholic church" (228). Part of this representation is that happiness scripts are comprised of heterosexual love leading to marriage and children. While this script of compulsory heterosexuality exists in many places (Ahmed 2006), individual women's experiences of it vary based on the cultures where they grow up, live, and experience life. As shown in chapter 1, historical time periods also govern discourses around childfreedom. Just as hegemonic reproductive beliefs have pulled on childfree women differently throughout history, as interviewee Jessica notes, they also circulate through individual women's lives in unique ways, based in part on women's intersectional identities. Here, I do not attempt to explain every possible way this circulation occurs, which would be impossible given the intersectional nature of people's identities. Instead, I offer some attention to ways specific interviewees' identities and cultures shaped their childfreedom and to the affectual and rhetorical effects of being childfree.

Gender was a formative part of my interviewees' experiences of being childfree, as can be seen throughout this book. They noted how gendered social scripts operated on their lives almost from birth, contributing to the assumptions they and others made about their lives. Strangely, to me, eleven interviewees explicitly talked about either playing or not playing with dolls growing up and how this choice signaled the reinforcement of social scripts in their lives, scripts they were taking up or already resisting as children. Over half these eleven interviewees mentioned playing with baby dolls, which often involved pretending to have children. Brittany remembered, "I grew up with all of the stereotypical girl toys. I had so many baby dolls, so many Cabbage Patch Kids. . . . When I played, I played cooking and I played cleaning and I played all of those things. And even my paper dolls and Barbies, I cared for them. So it's not that I never really thought about it [having kids]." Like other interviewees she recognizes the way dolls reinforce social scripts and affectively circulate gendered happiness scripts to young girls about their future lives.

Other interviewees had different experiences playing with dolls and what their mothers in particular read into this play. A couple explicitly mentioned not liking to play with baby dolls, identifying this dislike as a kind of foreshadowing of their not having children. A couple also told stories about their mothers interpreting how they played with dolls as signs they were not naturally developing mothering attitudes. Jessica talked about playing with Barbie dolls with her sister and the striking difference her mother noted in this play:

> My sister had a Barbie that had an office, and she had these shoes and went to office work and all this stuff, and my Barbie lived in my pom, and she hung out there and I called it the farm . . . and I remember her Barbie was, it was very carefully dressed, and mine was . . . had a hat, but no clothing, mine was just a sloppy mess. And anyway, my mother . . . was like, "What are you playing?" We're like, "We're playing Barbies." And she said . . . and my sister was doing all this Barbie work, and I was like, "Yeah, I think we're gonna be just hanging out over here by myself." And my mom was like, "Well, what are you gonna do during the day? Does your Barbie have a family?" and I was like, "No, my Barbie doesn't have kids." My mom said she was actually kind of freaked out.

Shanna also told a story about her mother interpreting how she played with dolls as a sign of her not wanting children: "I just put my baby doll in the sink and said, 'Well, I'm going to work now,' and just left. And she [my mother] was like, 'That's when I knew that, you know, you weren't really gonna be . . . you didn't wanna be a mom.'" These stories reveal the kind of affective work occurring when girls are given dolls to play with and how parents later interpret their interactions with dolls. Parents and others expect this play will reinforce gendered happiness scripts, and when girls interact differently or reject dolls, their parents may later read this rejection as a sign that their daughters at an early age rejected these scripts. Girls playing with dolls thus becomes interpreted as an affectual take-up or rejection of gendered happiness scripts and hegemonic mothering ideologies.

Babysitting formed another kind of test of whether girls were accepting or rejecting gendered happiness scripts. Twelve interviewees mentioned babysitting and how they and others interpreted their responses to babysitting as a sign they were or weren't taking up these scripts. Half mentioned not enjoying babysitting and seeing that dislike as a sign they did not like or want children. Leigh said, "[My] parents tried to get me babysitting . . . because it was basically easy money for the family. So I started babysitting when I was thirteen and I hated it. I hated being alone with children. I found it terrifying and boring." Similarly, Cynthia said she started babysitting when she was twelve or thirteen: "That was one of the few opportunities you had to make money . . . but I didn't enjoy being around kids. I didn't enjoy babysitting." Economic forces combined with gendered scripts to make babysitting a work option for these interviewees, but their experience shaped how they thought about having children and helped solidify their desire not to have children.

Several interviewees experienced babysitting as a positive experience even though they ultimately did not want to have children themselves. Bonnie said, "I really enjoyed taking care of my brother or babysitting or playing with younger children, so I definitely have a very kind of maternalistic drive, but it doesn't translate into desiring biological babies." Later, she noted, "So when I've babysat, I have loved the children I've cared for, and I would be incredibly protective of them if something was to try to hurt them." Here, Bonnie distinguishes liking or loving children from the need to have her own. While gendered happiness scripts are built around women caring for others and selflessly caring for their own children in particular, Bonnie points out such scripts limit our views of relationships between women and children and constrain our view of the affectual forces that bind people together.

One more aspect of how interviewees experienced the circulation of gendered happiness scripts was through their mothers' roles as they grew up. Thirteen interviewees talked about their mother's roles and/ or the patriarchal or matriarchal forces they saw working in their mothers' lives. While their relationships with their mothers were often complicated (as described in chapters 4 and 5), their perspective of their mothers' lives and how constrained these were by gendered happiness scripts informed their thinking about the options they did or didn't have as women. Ten interviewees mentioned their mothers had more traditional roles in the family. Shanna mentioned that most of the women in her family stayed at home and that "there was a prevailing attitude that women didn't work outside the home." Rachel, who came from a small town as Shanna did, similarly recounted,

> The assumption is that you're gonna stay, you're gonna marry some guy, you're gonna run a farm, and you're gonna be in these super traditional gender roles where women don't have a voice. You don't really have any agency over your life. I even remember my grandma worked for the church for a while as a pastoral associate and lived in a town one hundred miles away for a few years. My grandpa would be back and forth between the farm and [town] and it was fine, but I remember my dad thinking that she was like, and vocally say, "Well, her job is to be at home with her husband and how dare she take this job and do all this stuff."

Growing up in environments where gender roles are so tightly woven obviously affects how women think about their own lives and the kinds of options available to them. For many of these women, leaving their home communities was part of their recognizing they could resist these scripts.

A few interviewees mentioned that their mothers or other women around them worked against gendered happiness scripts and were more independent. Katherine, for example, explained, "I just always have [been] surrounded by women who were opinionated. . . . And nobody told me that I couldn't do this or say that because I was a woman." Suzanne had a similar experience, although her background and Katherine's were quite different: "I come out of this tradition of, you know, women take care of people. . . . Like my mom was a very . . . she's in charge wherever she goes, she's in charge. And so, even though she was a stay-at-home mom, she always had part-time jobs, too, and was always doing everything. So she was . . . she had a lot of influence and power in my family and still does." Although Suzanne did mention that part of the expected women's role was caring for others, she and a few other interviewees recognize the ways the women they grew up around asserted their own power and broke in some ways with gendered happiness scripts, even though they had children.

The reproductive ideologies associated with gender demonstrate the ways sexual orientation overlapped with gender in the scripts others expected interviewees to follow.[2] Only two interviewees explicitly said they were not heterosexual, one identifying as bisexual and polyamorous and one as nonheteronormative. The former interviewee and two heterosexual interviewees discussed the ways others associated queer identities—the lesbian identity specifically—with women who don't have children. They stated that as cisgender women without children, they are often presumed to be lesbians. This assumption directly relates to the ways compulsory heterosexuality demands people follow particular scripts. Interviewees' experiences partially demonstrate how reproductive ideologies function differently for queer women and heterosexual women.

Grace explained, "I've had people speculate that I'm a lesbian and I'm not, you know, which that rumor was in my family, that's the longest running rumor about me . . . it's almost like that's the only way we can make sense of this is that you just don't like men. And I was like, 'No, I like men plenty but I don't want to have children.' And it's kind of unknotting that thing in people's heads that is like, look, you can be both ways. You can like men and not want children." She also acknowledged many queer women do have children. She said that her having taken in a lesbian friend when the friend became homeless also increased this impression among her family, and that her mother was convinced she was a lesbian.

Grace's attempts to unknot the scripts associated with compulsory heterosexuality and the belief that heterosexual women must have partners
and children were ineffectual; in her family's mind, the association of
women not having children with lesbianism was fixed.

Meghan had a similar experience in one workplace where her
coworkers asked, " 'So are you a lesbian?' And I was like, 'That's none of
your business.' They were just like, 'How in the world can you not have
kids?' " Much like Grace's family, Meghan's colleagues refused to disarticulate sexual orientation from childfreedom, and they made assumptions based on compulsory heterosexuality. Bonnie had not had such
experiences, but she did talk about how gender identity and sexual orientation are problematically linked to hegemonic mothering ideologies.

> I think it's kind of a shame that the term *mother* has been so narrowly
> applied to biology and reproduction because I think those qualities can
> be exhibited in a variety of capacities. I also worry that to link an identity
> like womanhood to a biological function is a way of discounting different
> types of bodies, different types of abilities, and so I think we can refocus
> the discussion towards qualities or characteristics rather than biology or
> what, you know, your body can and can't do. . . . I do know a lesbian couple
> who have recently had a child and a gay couple who were hoping to have
> a child as well. . . . One of my gay friends is pretty clear that, you know, a
> child is nothing that he wants. So I wonder how it kind of impacts the ways
> in which we understand the parental capacity . . . in parental I mean just
> in a nurturing capacity . . . of people who don't identify as heterosexual.

As Bonnie points out, different folx may have the capacity to be biological mothers, and these folx may differ from those who take up mothering identities. She recognizes that by expecting childfree women to be
lesbians, we are also expecting lesbians will not be mothers (and queer
people will not be parents) and repeating scripts that erase different
folx from discussions about reproduction. Grace, Meghan, and Bonnie
all point to the ways reproductive ideologies are articulated differently
for heterosexual and queer women, as well as cis and trans women, and
how problematic it can be for motherhood to be linked to biological
capacity. Gender and sexual orientation formed the ways interviewees
experienced childfreedom in large part because of the gendered happiness scripts built around motherhood and the ways compulsory heterosexuality links to reproductive ideologies.

Race was called out specifically by several interviewees, mostly women
of color, who noticed how reproductive ideologies circulated around
them and affected their own thinking about childfreedom. Their thinking through the connections between race and childfreedom is echoed
in the written accounts of childfree women of color and research about

their experiences by Candice Vinson, Debra Mollen, and Nathan Grant Smith (2010), Martinez and Andreatta (2015), White (2017), Melda Sibel Uzun (2018), Keturah Kendrick (2019), and Kimya Dennis (unpublished), although this research remains very limited (Kelly 2009). This work speaks to the histories of race and reproduction that inform contemporary women's experiences of childfreedom and finds that women of color can face additional layers of sociocultural pressures to have children, particularly within their own communities. Almost all the white interviewees in my study made no mention of race, demonstrating the often-hidden nature of whiteness, but many did mention class, which to them seemed more salient to the topic of not having children. However, all interviewees who were women of color referenced race in some way, whether discussing how this aspect of their identities shaped their childfree decision or assumptions others made about their reproductive lives. In other words, they were aware of how their racial identities influenced their affectual and discursive experiences of childfreedom.

One of the factors that affected the ways two interviewees thought about reproduction was the violence people of color face in the US. Irene said one of two major reasons she did not have children and was okay with that decision was the racial injustice experienced by people of color in the US. She referenced the murder of Michael Brown by police in 2014, saying, "When the Grand Jury dismissed the case, I was just like, I don't want to bring up a kid in this environment, I just don't." Similarly, Nicole said the mistreatment of Black people in the US reinforces her decision not to have children: "And so as I've gotten older and I see the state of the world, and as a Black woman, how Black people are treated, I am so glad I did not bring another life into this world because it's sad. And the stresses that we go through, it's just incredible, you know, it's just incredible walking around in this skin, it's incredible." Their comments highlight how race and reproduction intersect to inform the decisions women make about having children. Nicole's comment also speaks to the lived and felt experiences of being a Black woman and how they shape her existence in the world. Clearly, the bodies individual women inhabit shape how reproductive ideologies are affectually and discursively woven through their lives and inform the decisions they make about whether or not to have children who will experience the world in different ways depending on their race.

The differences in the reproductive ideologies circulating about women based on their race are further made visible in the assumptions others make about individuals' reproductive lives. Four out of five Black women I interviewed explicitly mentioned other people assuming they must have children because they are Black women. In talking about interactions with colleagues, Grace said people just assume she must have children because she is Black. She said similar assumptions were made about other women of color: "I know my Latina friends have definitely been in the same boat as me. . . . I think it's partially economic and partially, you know, race." As she noted, the assumptions made about her are grounded in her identity as a whole, not just her race, but race is certainly a part of what leads others to make assumptions about her being a mother. Katherine felt people assume she must have children because she is Black: "I don't know if they just assume Black women always have children? I get that a lot. It's like I get, 'How many kids do you have?' Not 'Do you have kids?' 'How many kids do you have?' I get that question. And I'm like, 'I don't have' . . . and I'd be like, 'Zero.' And they like 'What?' 'I don't have any.'" White women did not describe this level of disbelief from others about their not having children, even though some of them experienced a good deal of pressure.

The belief that Black women must have children lines up with the stereotype or, in Collins's (2000) words, "controlling image" in the US that Black women are welfare cheats who try to grab government money by having children, according to the "welfare queen" myth. Tasha, an occupational therapist, felt her patients saw her identification as child-free through this lens, that there's an "aspect" of their surprise that is "kind of racial": "I think a lot of people assume that as a Black woman that I'm gonna have all these kids and all these baby daddies and stuff like that. . . . I do think though, generally, people, when people see a Black woman, they especially assume the most negative aspects and that you have a lot of kids out of wedlock and that you have several baby daddies and, you know, you're getting all this government help 'cause you're trying to, of course, take care of all your kids." Nicole also mentioned, "People have always assumed that because I am a Black woman, I'm a single parent." These experiences starkly demonstrate how the racist reproductive ideologies discussed in chapter 1 continue to circulate through assumptions made about Black women in the US and their reproductive lives. Their experiences also illustrate how closely individuals' identities are woven into the ways reproductive doxae affectively and discursively operate around and through them.

Other, less visible identity markers than gender and race also influenced how reproductive ideologies affected interviewees' decisions not to have children. Socioeconomic class was one such marker that certainly impacted how interviewees thought about motherhood. Among the interviewees who disclosed their childhood socioeconomic class, two identified as lower class or poor, twelve as working class, and four as lower middle class, with only five identifying as middle class and four as upper middle class. The impact of class was most apparent in interviews with those women whose families struggled with money in some way and who themselves did not want to give up economic stability and even flexibility by having children.

Gail's experiences perhaps most clearly highlight the weaving of socioeconomic class with cultural expectations and reproductive ideologies. She talked about being from a working-class white Scottish family and forcibly moving with her mother and sister out of their house when she was thirteen because her father "was physically and mentally abusive," which led to their moving to Canada. As noted in chapter 2, Gail feels she would have faced a lot more pressure to have children if she hadn't left Scotland, not least because she would have remained in a working-class community: "And I say by now I'd be divorced, working in, you know, a Booth's Drug Store with children and some deadbeat [ex- or second] husband." She said people she knew when she was a child in Scotland stopped going to school at fifteen so they could work to support their families of origin, and that they get married so they can keep their earnings. In other words, compulsory heterosexuality was articulated to economic independence, forcing women to make decisions about marriage and, as a part of heterosexual marriage, reproduction based in part on their desire to be financially separate from their families. This intersection of compulsory heterosexuality and economic class creates additional pressure for women to follow these scripts.

Alternatively, some interviewees found themselves resisting reproductive doxae in part because they identified the economic constraints parenthood put on their parents and themselves growing up and wanted financial stability they had not experienced. Mary, who had been born in Canada to Catholic parents and had four siblings, talked about how her parents' issues were "always about money." Her mother felt forced to go to work and "always felt very guilty about going back to work and kinda couldn't let that go" because her family had issues that led to "somewhat strained relations with [her] older brother." Mary identified finances as a key reason she didn't have children herself: "My parents always arguing about money was huge and that was a big part of my decision not to have kids, 'cause they're so expensive and I just wanted to do other things. It might be . . . I don't know. It's just weird, but my mom telling me, 'Don't ever have kids.' " While other interviewees' parents didn't necessarily tell them not to have children, Mary was not unusual among participants with lower-income backgrounds in that several remembered their parents struggling with or fighting about money and this tension having a role in their decision not to have children themselves. Socioeconomic class thus shaped the social scripts interviewees encountered and how they struggled with reproductive doxae themselves. It often demonstrated to them the constraints of motherhood and reinforced their resistance to these scripts.

Religion was another factor mentioned by twenty-three interviewees. Among these, in childhood, twelve were Protestants, five Catholics, and one a Jehovah's Witness, and five were not religious; fourteen referenced their current religious beliefs, and among them only five actually identified as religious, of which all considered themselves Protestant or Christian. Childhood religious communities influenced how interviewees identified gendered happiness scripts as woven with reproductive ideologies, and those who were immersed in religion as adults had to navigate how others saw their religious beliefs as articulating or not with their decision not to have children.

Celia talked about her family's connections to Protestant religion and its relationship with her identity formation overall. She said when she was in middle school, her parents put her in a "super Christian Baptist school" because they thought she was "making friends and hanging out with people who [we]ren't good for [her]." They also took her to a church, where she became really involved with the youth group, including going on a couple of mission trips. However, she gradually separated from the church; the factors she mentioned were being made to feel ashamed of her body because she developed a curvy figure, an incident wherein the senior pastor mishandled money and lost his job, and disagreement in the church when Celia's youth pastor became the interim pastor but was not voted to become the senior pastor. Yet she said she had been "terrified of marrying somebody like [her husband]"—that is, an atheist—and that even though she was not "religious any more but kind of believ[ed] in God," she would face the expectation, perhaps from herself and certainly from others, that she would bring children to church if she had them. The expectation that she should take her children to church if she had religious beliefs formed part of the reproductive doxae that circulated through the religion she grew up in. While avoiding this expectation was certainly not Celia's only reason for not having children, she seemed to consider avoiding it to be an advantage.

Reproductive ideologies shifted depending on how religion overlapped with other aspects of women's identities, such as race. Kendrick (2019) writes about how the Black church circulates pervasive sexist rhetoric that "there [are] only two roles in which [women] could find their ultimate worth: wife and mother" (85–86). Tasha, an African American woman, had strong religious beliefs that affected how she thought about her childfreedom, although she had found ways to resist the reproductive doxae Kendrick references. She became a Christian when she was nineteen, and she was aware of how reproductive doxae circulated in different ways in her church. She mentioned that Christianity is often associated with a "focus on the family" and "expanding the nuclear family with children" that leads those in the church to think "Oh, yeah, you're gonna have to have . . . you have to get married, you have to have kids." Tasha identified as single by choice, as well as childfree, and she pointed out that Christianity actually includes space for such choices: "Actually, there's a practice, some practices that are in the Bible that actually talk about singleness. And I thought that was so interesting because in the church, there's a little cult, we're gonna call it, a lot of people are still hyperfocused on creating a family. And I thought it was a contradiction because I was like, 'Well, there's this whole question in the Bible where they actually say that single is actually better.' "[3] She pointed out that the fact that Christian beliefs call for sex between only married people implies that as a single woman, she should not have children.

Tasha also had many single and childfree role models in her church who demonstrated what it means to be a Christian who does not have a traditional family. She explained, "And then also in my church that I was at, I met a lot of older women who were also single and also didn't have children and they were living their best life. They were hanging out, they were going fishing and kayaking, they were traveling, and they were doing all this kind of stuff and they did not have children. But, you know, they interacted with the kids at that church and they enjoyed their time with the kids, but then they also lived their own lives. So I'm like, 'This sounds amazing.' And that really appealed to me." She was friends with and talked with some of these women and felt as if they affirmed her desire not to have children. Meeting them, she said, was "kind of the pivotal moment": "I realized that that's actually what I wanted out of life." She realized she could resist reproductive doxae in the church and rearticulate different beliefs supported by the Bible as well. She relied on other scripts laid out in this text to challenge the happiness scripts typically circulated that linked Christianity with having a traditional family. Celia's and Tasha's experiences illustrate how religious beliefs can overlap with happiness scripts and circulate reproductive doxae in different ways that counter or confirm women's childfree experiences.

Finally, geographical areas and cultures that circulated reproductive ideologies and shaped their childfree lives formed part of the interviewees' identities. Interviewees came from a wide variety of places, and the places they grew up and resided in reflected reproductive doxae somewhat differently, with some differences showing up most clearly for those who were part of Southern US cultures, those who were part of Midwest US cultures, and those who identified a difference between rural and urban cultures.

Six interviewees specifically spoke about how Southern communities circulated gendered happiness scripts. Cassie in particular noted differences between the community in Texas where she grew up and the community she now was part of outside the South in Colorado. She mentioned her parents' upbringing in small Texas towns and the social scripts that circulated there: "Both of them just come from a very stereotypical Southern lifestyle. My mom was raised way out in the country; all of her people were taught to, you know, you get married, you settle down, you have babies, you go to church on Sundays, you do things that you may not like but you do them anyway 'cause that's what you do. But they were taught that the nuclear family was the priority." These scripts were passed down to Cassie, who resisted them. Other interviewees also noted that Southern cultures reinforced similar scripts. Sandra explained, "I was raised in a very Southern community where girls get married in their early twenties, and I'm thirty-three and still not married. So I feel like, I mean, I've always had a lot of pressure about that, and my mom's friends, just community members, it's kind of like something is wrong or not right because [I don't] want to have children." These scripts became even more visible when interviewees interacted outside white Southern culture. When Cassie talked about her roles, she broke them down into her role in Texas and her role in her new community: "So in Texas I felt really out of place. I did not feel like my ideals and my views in politics and my religious beliefs and everything, what I wanted out of life, I didn't feel like I felt part of the Southern ideal." Later on, she noted about her new community, "Everything has been, I feel so much more accepted for who I am up here than I ever did in Texas." These interviewees emphasized how compulsory heterosexuality and hegemonic motherhood were tightly woven into their communities' reproductive ideologies.

Similar scripts circulated in the US Midwest. Five interviewees spoke about the reproductive doxae that circulated through their Midwest communities. Rachel talked about growing up in a German Catholic family in a very small farming town with fewer than two hundred people.

The approach to reproduction in the community was "everybody had ten to fifteen kids because the philosophy at that time in these farming communities in the rural Midwest was you needed a lot of sons to work the farm; you were literally birthing your free labor, and then you needed the girls to do the house stuff and the cooking and the cleaning because it was legitimately full-time jobs for everybody." While that stance "generally . . . stopped with [her] grandparents' era," Rachel was the oldest of eight children her parents had within ten years and, as I've already discussed, the gendered happiness scripts that circulated around her were very conservative and traditional. Elizabeth similarly spoke about growing up as the next-to-youngest child out of seven children in a very small town of about two thousand people in northern Wisconsin. She talked about how her family "was very traditional growing up" and telling her mother "she inadvertently made [Elizabeth] a feminist" because of the strict gender roles reinforced in her household. Like Rachel, gender roles were clearly defined in her family, and she resisted the expectations of those scripts.

Gendered happiness scripts circulated through rural and urban communities differently as well. Gail, Mary, Cassie, Rachel, and Elizabeth were all from small rural towns through which reproductive doxae circulated in traditional ways that conformed to compulsory heterosexuality. Jessica explained how rural and urban communities could affect someone's identity by pulling apart her own experiences in a small town: "I grew up in a lower-middle-class family in a rural area outside of Pittsburgh, Pennsylvania. . . . I have parents that were both teachers. And, let's see, we had a very, I would say that the background was kind of interesting, in terms of formative, in terms of . . . being in that rural area. We spent a lot of time, weekly or biweekly, doing things like going to Pittsburgh to see symphonies or baseball games. So we had kind of a wide range of different cultural activities and more exposure . . . relatively a lot more exposure to diverse lifestyles, cultures, etc. to . . . relative to the area that we lived in." Jessica's experiences add another layer to understanding how geographical locations and particular communities can influence a person's attitude toward reproduction; these factors can be more or less important depending on how insular a community is. Shanna's discussion of her family's community, described in this book's introduction, also highlights how reproductive doxae can circulate differently in different geographical areas and communities.

Reproductive doxae were woven through each individual woman's life in unique ways depending on the cultures she was situated in and her identities and how these influenced her decision to reject gendered happiness scripts. Childfree women's negotiations of culture and identity and the discursive threads these women notice at work around them make hegemonic reproductive beliefs, and some of their permutations, visible even as they complicate the ways we think about reproductive doxae and how they circulate through women's lives. As should be clear, childfreedom is an individual choice women come at differently through the affectual threads at work on them and through contesting what those are and mean in their lives. Their work in doing so positions them as killjoys who question hegemonic reproductive beliefs and pinpoint motherhood as not entirely happy. As the next section describes, this positioning affects not only their own negotiations of the childfree identity but others' negotiations of different identities, namely grandparenting.

HAPPINESS SCRIPTS ALL MIXED UP: THE CULTURE OF GRANDPARENTING AND CHILDFREEDOM

A couple of years ago I was visiting my grandparents at Christmas, and my family was watching an old home video. In the video, my parents and grandparents are sitting around talking with relatives while my siblings and I—I think there were five of us at the time (eventually there were six)—were playing in the middle of the screen. In the midst of our play, a ten-year-old me was carrying around my sister, who was around one year old, on my hip. Watching, my dad commented, "What are we doing? Why is Courtney holding the baby? No wonder she doesn't want kids!"

My parents lamented not having grandchildren after I, as the oldest child, reached adulthood until a few years ago when one of my younger sisters finally had a child. I can see that in addition to a genuine desire for grandchildren, they feel some pressure to be grandparents and that not having many grandchildren is seen as a kind of failure on their part. Just as childfree women face pressures to take up social scripts around motherhood, older adults are expected to take up social scripts around grandparenting. When childfree women's parents are unable to do so, this inability creates conflict because childfree women are viewed as those whose refusal of reproductive ideologies prevents their own parents from being part of the affective economy around grandparenting. Such tension demonstrates the complexities binding affect, doxae, rhetoric, and identities; when identities do not complement each other, discursive interventions are not always possible.

Just as mothering or parenting is often seen as a particular stage of life, one integral part of happiness scripts, grandparenting—and particularly grandmothering—is seen as another distinct, important stage of life. Reinforced through grandparenting blogs and websites and often featured in media, an affective economy has built up around grandparenting, one that intersects with and comments on mother and childfree identities. The proliferation of social media posts by and about grandparents speaks to the strong identity many people associate not just with having their own children but also with their children having children. Ahmed's (2010) arguments about happiness speak to grandparenting as part of happiness scripts; returning to the framework explicated in this book's introduction, she argues that "going along with happiness scripts is how we get along: to get along is to be willing and able to express happiness in proximity to the right things" (59) and that "parents can live with the failure of happiness to deliver its promise by placing their hope for happiness in their children" (33). Both these claims point to ways grandparenting is associated with happiness. The latter offers additional security because if their own children haven't fulfilled happiness scripts, then perhaps grandchildren will. Thus, a perpetual cycle of the hope for happiness is created through children, grandchildren, and future generations. As with parenting, women (grandmothers) are often linked more strongly to grandchildren, particularly given the number of grandmothers who often become primary or secondary caretakers for their grandchildren.[4] For women in particular, then, becoming grandmothers can assume particular sociocultural importance that forms part of gendered happiness scripts.

Almost three-quarters of my interviewees mentioned grandparenting in some way; of these, fourteen interviewees were in their thirties and thus likely facing additional pressure about this topic at the time of the interview, five were in their forties, three were in their fifties, and one was in her sixties. Their mentioning grandparenting illustrates the pervasiveness of the affective economy of grandparenting when childfree women think about their choices, even if they are beyond the point of having direct interactions with their parents about being grandparents. Several interviewees talked about the grandparenting identity and the external pressure people face to become grandparents. Alicia mentioned talking with others about how "someone wants grandkids and you're supposed to have kids," an expectation difficult to refuse when it is so closely tied to parents' identities. Jeanette talked about how her parents, despite being supportive, still felt pressure to have grandchildren: "I mean, I think my parents, even though I think they were way ahead of their generation, they're used to hearing about everybody else's grandkids. And it's . . . it was an expectation. And even though they were way ahead of the curve, it was still an expectation. So not having grandkids sort of equated for them with that kind of, something's wrong. Yes. There's that something wrong . . . in the picture." Her comments point out that despite parents not being in control of whether or not they have grandchildren, the pressure is still put on them, as well as their children, for them to become grandparents. Irene explained how her parents' friends directly put this pressure on her, as well as on her parents: "And I feel like when I do go back to see my parents, they, her friends will be like, 'Oh' to my mom, '[mom's name] do you have grandkids yet?' in front of me. . . . And I think, you know, our friends [meaning her and her partner's] wouldn't do that to us. Yeah. So that's where the conversation has shifted, I think, is that her friends are assholes . . . I'm just like, 'Mom, you should ask them, how many degrees do your kids have?' or something. 'How many books are they writing?'" Irene wants the conversation to shift to other ways she can be happy, such as through her professional life, but this shift is difficult when happiness scripts are so tied to reproduction. Similarly, Devori said, "And I remember [my parents] saying something about you know, it would be nice to have grandkids, and I think I said something to the effect of, 'Well, when I get my PhD, I'll roll it up in a blanket and hand that to you.'"

Other interviewees noticed how the affective economy of grandparenting was built up, especially on social media. Leigh commented on how strongly her mother's friends reinforced her mother's desire to be a grandmother: "And so all her friends are posting pictures of their grandkids, and so, at one point when my mom and I were discussing this, she was mentioning that these kids that I used to babysit for, well each have three kids of their own. And, I said to her, I was like, 'Mom, neither [this person] nor [that person] finished college. They hate their spouses. You know, they're twice divorced,' you know, like all of this stuff, your daughter is like, 'Maybe I don't have grandkids but I'm hugely successful. Can't you just be proud of me?' . . . There isn't a lot of social focus on being proud of your kids after the age of thirty." Leigh's frustration with the received logic tying success to reproduction and her discussion of the expectations placed on grandparents, which echo Alicia, Jeanette, and Irene, speak to Ahmed's ideas about happiness. If a woman doesn't find happiness in her own children, there is the hope she will find it in grandchildren. And, if happiness scripts, particularly for women, are built around mothering, grandchildren are what women's parents feel they can brag about to others in legible, valid ways (rather than their children's professional or personal accomplishments). The inability to brag about grandchildren thus can cut parents off from affectual and discursive interactions with their friends that validate them, just as childfree women can be cut off from validating interactions with others. Childfree women's interactions with their parents about having children are not just about their own identities; instead, their parents' identities as grandparents are also wrapped up in the decision to be childfree.

Pressures about having children typically come from parents and in-laws, but they can also form internally in childfree women themselves as they grapple with what it means to deny their own parents the identities of grandparents (or, in Ahmed's terms, to function as killjoys). This pressure can be eased somewhat if they have a sibling(s) with children. However, the arguments childfree women make about their own happiness and identities without children are more complicated when they run up against arguments made about the identities of others depending upon grandchildren. Leigh's mother was one of my interviewees' more persistent parents. Leigh said, "I think my mother tries to pretend that she's not devastated that she's not having grandchildren. And so for a while she would like guilt trip me and like subtly drop hints." While other interviewees experienced this type of guilt tripping, and many felt they had disappointed their parents, they did not express anger at their parents. Meghan spoke about this type of pressure: "And, you know, my mom has been pretty accepting, although certainly she's been like, 'Oh, I just wish I could have some more grandkids.' And I finally was like, 'I'm just going to have to be the big disappointment in your life, and you're going to have to deal with it.'" Similarly, Jessica said she inferred that her mother "felt like she was getting ripped off . . . She tried to play it cool, but like now, I think I can totally see she's looking at me like, 'Well, you know, you didn't [give me grandchildren].'" Cynthia's parents also waited a while to verbalize their disappointment when she told them she didn't plan on having children. But she still felt they supported her choices. At the same time, it was uncomfortable for these childfree women to feel they were disappointing their parents.

At the same time, in-laws, specifically their mothers-in-law, could be a far greater source of pressure than interviewees' parents. Leigh mentioned her mother-in-law "hardcore guilted [her husband and her] for a long time," saving items for potential grandchildren until finally giving up. Alicia, who had dated her husband from her early twenties, also noted getting "a lot of pressure very early on" from her mother-in-law about having children. Tara explained that every Christmas her mother-in-law asks about her having children "in front of a group of people," and it was "the first thing" out of her father-in-law's mouth any time she and her husband talked with him on the phone. Her mother-in-law had also called her husband a few years after they had been married to ask how long they had been married and said, "Where are the grandkids?" Tara's in-laws actually have a grandchild and some step-grandchildren from her husband's brothers, but she explained, "No, it's just like it, she just can't get enough. Yeah, it's just like she's got to collect them all. Like here's a Pokémon situation or something. . . . She had three kids, and I guess she kind of thought, 'Oh you know I had three kids. I'm going to have all these grandkids.' But, you know, [it] hasn't really exactly worked out that way." Although some childfree women feel the pressure is off once a sibling has children, Tara's mother-in-law had constructed an idea about her identity as a grandmother that has not materialized, which she is unhappy about. This disappointment has led to her being particularly pushy in her interactions with Tara and her husband.

Rachel's in-laws do not have any grandchildren. When Rachel's mother-in-law told her about things she had saved from her husband's childhood for grandchildren, Rachel had to tell her, "We don't plan to have kids," to which her mother-in-law responded, "When did he decide that?" As Rachel reflected, "The idea that we would choose together not to have kids or that I would have anything to say about that was totally foreign to her." Her husband finally told his parents directly that they should stop pressuring them. They stopped bothering Rachel about it, but, she said, "They just come after him and not me" because "they're clearly not okay with it." It can be difficult for childfree women to speak with their in-laws about this choice because they do not typically have the long-term, familial relationships with their in-laws that they have with their own families, which means their reproductive decisions very much affect their in-laws' lives. But there is a level of understanding that can be missing from these relationships to help in-laws understand childfree women's perspectives.

These types of familial pressures, as well as the sociocultural expectation that women will have children and that older people will become grandparents, can lead some childfree women to question their childfree decision. Tara said, "[I] very much felt like, 'Shit, maybe I should give my parents grandkids.'" Although eventually she realized she could make her own life decisions and that her parents were "not going to be crushed by it. Their lives are going to continue. They're going to be fine," this internal conversation recognizes the power the grandparenting script holds. Jeanette noted feeling regretful that neither she nor her sister had a grandchild for her mother, who is "very, very maternal." Silvia also talked about grappling with not having grandchildren for her parents: "So I think for me the only actual serious challenge [with] not having kids, the only thing that ever seriously really gives me pause, is feeling guilty for my parents because I owe them a grandkid or something." Her guilt has been assuaged somewhat because her brother had a child, but she said that if he hadn't, "maybe that would have changed [her] decision, made that feel more important to [her]." The denial of someone's identity as a grandparent is very real to many childfree women, and it creates internal struggles when these women may not otherwise have questioned their decision.

Almost half the interviewees pointed out their siblings have children, illustrating the relief these women found in their parents not having to depend solely on them for grandchildren. Some interviewees mentioned their parents having so many grandchildren there wasn't much pressure at all; Sarah said her cousins and siblings "have had plenty of babies for everyone." Mary said there were "lots of grandkids around and no need to produce a grandchild for anybody," and Elizabeth said her mother "has twelve grandchildren." Rachel said in her own family there are thirty-three grandchildren "distracting them [her parents]." In these situations, the number of grandchildren seemed particularly comforting to childfree women because it made their choice seem less significant. Even childfree women whose siblings had fewer children still felt relieved they were not solely responsible for fulfilling their parents' grandparenting script. Sandra mentioned she told her mother outright, "I'm glad he's having kids [meaning her brother] so you're still a grandma," even though she had known from an early age she didn't want to have children herself. Shanna didn't feel a lot of pressure from her family to have children, and she mentioned her sister has two children and she thought "they [her parents] got their fill with that." Similarly, Allison felt her brother's children "totally deflected any of that ever from really probably coming up" and kept her from having to hear from her parents that they wished they could be grandparents. Having siblings with children, regardless of how many, kept many of my interviewees from feeling too guilty about denying their parents' grandparenting scripts since their siblings had technically fulfilled them.

The interviewees' external and internal dialogues about their choice affecting their parents or their partner's parents becoming grandparents illustrate additional complexities at work when one person's identity constrains another person's identity. This contingency can make even more visible the social scripts childfree women are refusing and create tension in conversations about their not having children. As interviewees noted, these interactions can be difficult because they are asking their parents to refuse these scripts as they have, and their parents do not always want to participate in this work. The affective economy around motherhood thus extends to grandparenting and shapes the identities of childfree women's parents. Childfree women whose parents are unhappy they are being denied the identity of grandparent must grapple with what this denial means for their relationships with their own and/or their partner's parents. Reproductive doxae, then, affect these relationships in particular as identities are aligned with or opposed to these doxae.

RHETORICS OF REPRODUCTIVE NORMALITY

This chapter demonstrates the complexities statistics can obscure when accounting for various facets of childfree women's identities and how these facets relate to their not having children. Each individual must negotiate their childfree identity differently depending on how hegemonic reproductive beliefs affectively and rhetorically move through their own and others' lives. In 2013, Lauren Sandler's piece about childfreedom, "Having It All Without Having Children," was featured on the cover of *Time* magazine and drew attention to the growing numbers of Americans, and particularly American women, deciding not to have children. The research she discusses and the women interviewed for her article mention many ways their identities overlap with childfreedom, including socioeconomic status, gender and sexuality, race/ethnicity, and cultural expectations. Throughout this article, echoing threads found twenty years earlier underscoring Ann Landers's May 26, 1993, satirical piece in the *Chicago Tribune*, "Pity the Lonely Lives of Childless Couples," is an emphasis on how hegemonic beliefs continue to reinforce the imperative for women to become mothers even as individual women's identities mean this imperative operates differently upon them.

Sandler (2013) argues this imperative has become even stronger with advances in fertility treatments, in addition to the possibility of adoption, that hypothetically allows all women, even those who in the past would have been biologically incapable, to become mothers. Landers's (1993) piece ends with a reinforcement of the normality of parenthood: "See what the years have done. He looks boyish, unlined and rested. She is slim, well-groomed and youthful. It isn't natural. If they had kids, they'd look like the rest of us—tired, gray, wrinkled and haggard. In other words, normal." Given the reinforcement of reproductive doxae, twenty years later Sandler still finds childfree women are asked to justify why they don't have children because this decision is seen as abnormal. While some of these views may be changing, as Jeanette suggested, they still reflect the normalization of parent identities and the deviancy of childfree identities. While this chapter demonstrates how different forms of reproductive doxae can circulate through childfree women's lives because of the identities and cultures they inhabit, childfree women still collectively understand motherhood is set up as normal and childfreedom as abnormal. Our identities as childfree women are constantly negotiated through this lens, even as those negotiations occur in myriad ways.

As this chapter demonstrates, childfree women's intersectional identities and their relationships with others form a large part of their grappling with gendered happiness scripts and how to take up or resist them. The affective networks that form not just around these women but around others they are connected to, such as their parents, shape their own and others' identities and the rhetorical approaches they take when interacting with others. In the case of grandparenting, childfree women function as killjoys who are asking their own parents (or their partners' parents) to also reject the happy objects of children and grandchildren. While a few interviewees' parents were able to do this work and shift their own thinking about sociocultural scripts, many had parents who were somehow embedded in affective networks around grandparenting and wanted to fully participate in these networks. The inability to participate felt like a denial of a crucial role and the erasure of identity work they wanted to perform. Aside from the interactions with medical professionals discussed in chapter 2 and the complicated negotiations of childfreedom around grandparenting discussed here, interviewees generally struggled in many instances to articulate their childfree identities and make them legible to those around them. While they identified some flexibility in how reproductive doxae can be contested, others did not always support them in this work, which meant childfree women were often in negotiation with others about childfreedom, and some of these interactions could reinforce their marginal status in relation to reproduction. The next chapter examines how interviewees tried to negotiate reproductive doxae with others, particularly by taking up an idea of care typically linked to gendered happiness scripts and transforming this concept. It demonstrates how even this attempt to rearticulate how care is woven into women's lives—a less risky move than those discussed in chapter 5—can lead to negative interactions with others about childfreedom.

4

THE LIMITS OF REARTICULATING
HEGEMONIC REPRODUCTIVE BELIEFS

Nicole: *"I felt like I was parentified when I was a child. I had so many additional responsibilities being the oldest girl, being the oldest granddaughter on my paternal side of the family. And then also when my parents split, my mom was single for a while, so I had a lot . . . I felt like I had a lot of responsibilities as far as cooking and cleaning and so forth, looking after my sister. So I felt like I was kind of put into that type of role."*

Bonnie: *"I tend to take on more of a motherly, nurturing role, especially with my own mother. So I've taken on the primary financial caretaker for her, and I've been playing that role off and on since I was sixteen to varying degrees of, I guess, assistance."*

Meghan: *"I think that I . . . most of my life I've worked with children, so I think I tend to be, you know, have a nurturer side of me for sure, especially in the workplace."*

Devori: *"I think the characterization of us [childfree women] is that we're selfish or too fixated on our own goals or something like that . . . but you can find women who are amazingly kind, loving women, and most of us are."*

Although care is tied to many women's roles, it is perhaps most commonly articulated to motherhood which, as I argue throughout this book, makes it difficult for childfree women to assert they are caring or selfless since they are not mothers, despite the care many childfree women perform for those around them, as seen in the epigraphs. Hegemonic beliefs that women who do not care for others are actually dangerous have circulated for thousands of years. Part of the warning for other women in Lilith's myth is that she never provides care for others: she prioritizes herself above Adam by trying to assert her own agency, and she agrees to murder one hundred of her own children a

https://doi.org/10.7330/9781646424399.c004

day rather than return to him. Lilith represents the antimother who thus will kill children in the quest for her own agency. The commonplace that childfree women choose their independence over care for others follows them. Hayden (2010) identifies the struggles childfree women face as they try to assert their identities in a society in which reproductive doxae interweave with many aspects of childfree women's lives: "Women who are childless by choice thus face a bind. Through their reproductive choices they open up the potential to craft identities rooted in their individual talents and actions. In doing so, however, they simultaneously abdicate a key attribute of femininity, making it difficult to claim the mantle 'good woman'" (270). The childfree women Hayden studied either play into the idea they are selfish because they have chosen to live their lives without children or counter this idea by talking about ways they still care for others. This latter tactic reflects the affectual and discursive moves I sketch in this chapter.

Both this chapter and the next show how childfree women resist cultural representations of themselves as selfish or deviant. I found that, as Park (2005) argues and like me, study participants found ways to "cope with social expectations, censure and stigma" (376). She writes that some of the rhetorical strategies the childfree use include "passing, identity substitution, condemning the condemnors . . . , claiming biological deficiency, and redefining the situation" (376); I found instances of my interviewees using all these strategies alongside other rhetorical tactics I discuss in this chapter. One of my own strategies, echoing Nicole's experiences in the epigraph, is to invoke the caretaking I perform as an oldest daughter with five siblings as a way of asserting my value by working with the threads already assigned to women. I find I am not alone: other childfree women sometimes struggle to rearticulate or disarticulate the gendered happiness scripts already in existence that tie women to motherhood, and as a result some of us try instead to articulate childfreedom within discourses familiar to us and those around us. As a result, we sometimes utilize rhetorics that echo motherhood rhetorics so our lives are legible in spite of a reproductive decision that undermines gendered happiness scripts. My analysis of interviewees' rhetorical strategies helps explain why this group uses these rhetorics, given the sociohistorical and personal contexts outlined in chapters 1, 2, and 3, and how childfree women attempt to construct communities as a way to work around and against gendered happiness scripts.

As a way of moving into such analysis, this chapter analyzes the ways childfree women construct portraits of themselves as nurturers and caretakers, still working within gendered happiness scripts articulated through the rhetorical threads of happiness, selflessness, and care. Doing so allows them to work with the happiness scripts already established for women while expanding those scripts to include care for people besides children. Such rhetorical moves do not greatly unsettle happiness scripts tied to the act of caring through mothering; instead, they are moderate rhetorical tactics childfree women use to articulate their similarities with mothers through the function of care in a bid for validation. This chapter also demonstrates the types of conflicted interactions childfree women can face that call into question how successfully they can rearticulate care, selflessness, and happiness with childfreedom rather than with motherhood. Collectively, this chapter demonstrates how care affectually and rhetorically circulates through childfree women's lives and what is possible and not possible when they try to remake gendered happiness scripts.

REDEFINING CARE IN GENDERED HAPPINESS SCRIPTS

Articulations such as those among motherhood, happiness, care, and selflessness can both constrain and open up the ways women rhetorically position arguments and their positions. As work by other feminist rhetorical scholars such as Campbell (1989), Royster (2000), Buchanan (2005), and Rebecca Richards (2017) demonstrates, many women rhetors recognize the constraints hegemonic reproductive beliefs place upon them and have tried to work with and counter these so others will hear, listen to, and respond to their arguments. Childfree women similarly recognize how reproductive ideologies shape their identities, and they try to work both with and against these ideologies. Building on the previous chapter's discussion of this work, this chapter analyzes how reproductive doxae affect childfree women's rhetorics and the ways they respond to these doxae by realigning and redefining part of this articulation—care—without completely challenging these threads or the web they weave about women's reproductive lives.

One of the central aspects of doxae I mention in the introduction is that they are social in nature. Doxae have been described as invention's social dimension (LeFevre 1986); as the heart of rhetoric because persuasion rests on shared beliefs and values that are part of a social milieu (Ritivoi 2006); and as common beliefs that spur people to "become activated, charged, and mobilized" around cultural narratives built on ideology and affect (Bratta 2018, 95). The social nature of doxae and their ties to identity as seen in chapter 3 directly affect the arguments individuals and groups make in particular sociocultural contexts, despite the historical knowledge that often accumulates and accretes from past generations that feed into doxae and, as a result, new ideas (LeFevre 1986). Thus, according to LeFevre (1986), the circulation of doxae creates "a foundation of knowledge" people "may dismiss, confirm, or build on" (34). Often, doxae can limit invention in that social collectives can open or close down certain lines of thinking and social groups can discipline rhetors and audiences to avoid social margins (Hariman 1986). However, people can challenge and change the assumptions of their communities by bringing to the fore new arguments, which extends the limits of social circulations of doxae and creates space for new ideas to take hold (Ritivoi 2006). Rhetorical strategies for accomplishing this work, as Bratta (2018) argues, offer a unique opportunity to study affect and ideology, as they coalesce in "affective cultures" I discuss in the previous chapter, because affect and ideology are often most clearly articulated in various arguments at work in a particular culture.

A social understanding of doxae explains the tensions childfree women can feel as they try to reweave the articulation of care with motherhood, happiness, and selflessness so they can build arguments about childfreedom on the cultural connection already established between care and women. As this chapter demonstrates, however, the persuasive power of this realignment has limited impact on childfree women's interactions with others. Childfree women try to shift from the social margins to the social center through strategies such as their alignment with care, yet they can be shut out of the social center by those around them who reject this rearticulation of reproductive ideologies.

Some childfree women try to rhetorically weave care with womanhood, not motherhood, in two distinct ways. The first is by connecting care with relationships apart from motherhood such as those in their workplaces, families of origin (as in my case), and social circles. The second is by privileging care for themselves as something that should be as important as caring for others. Such rhetorical approaches to childfreedom alongside rearticulations of care demonstrate childfree women's attempts to weave new patterns for those around them that challenge hegemonic ideologies about their reproductive lives. Taking this approach in analysis demonstrates a rhetorical approach Raymie McKerrow (1989) views as shifting focus from what symbols are to what they do (104). Care here is part of the articulation of hegemonic mothering ideologies childfree women are trying to undermine, even as some of them are compelled to speak to it given its rhetorical power in their sociocultural milieus. Muckelbauer (2008) argues an approach that can change tradition must be built around interactions between newly invented ideas and tradition to make them legible to an audience: "Both innovation and tradition must somehow be at work for actual change to occur" (146). Similarly, Crowley (2006) claims doxa are useful platforms for launching arguments that can elicit disapproval (71). By integrating care as a part of childfree women's identities, some childfree women try to build on the connections between care and women typically identified with motherhood and to reweave this connection as one that can exist for any woman, regardless of whether or not she has children.

Understanding how childfree women rearticulate care matters in understanding the rhetorical work they do to delineate their identities in relation to motherhood, but care itself is a complicated concept. Tronto (2013) acknowledges the difficulties in defining care and parses some meanings that are both "dispositions and specific kinds of work" (19). She and Berenice Fisher (1990) define caring "as *a species activity that includes everything that we do to maintain, continue, and repair our 'world' so that we can live in it as well as possible.* That world includes our bodies, our selves, our environment, all of which we seek to interweave in a complex, life-sustaining web" (40). While most humans demonstrate care, society places higher expectations on women than on men to care for others, not the least for children. Furthermore, psychological and biological theories such as Gilligan's (1993) reinforce the belief that care for others is an innate aspect of women's psyches and biological makeup, thus justifying these unequal expectations. Mary O'Brien (1978), in her article "The Dialectics of Reproduction," identifies the biological and psychological role of fathers as fundamentally different from mothers because paternity is, in some ways, chosen through a man's willing declaration. As she explains, "Fatherhood is a *right*, in other words a political phenomenon" (237) because, up until recent widespread availability and use of paternity testing in the late twentieth century, fatherhood was a claimed, not bodily, identity.[1] Conversely, women, O'Brien claims, have been tied to motherhood through embodied labor that links them with their children through childbirth. Maaret Wager (2000) echoes O'Brien's attention to the ties that bind women, children, and care, stating: "At the heart of mothering there is an ethic of caring—women are supposed to think and feel and act in the interests of others, in both their public and private lives" (391). Given these historical links between women and children, feminist theorists themselves can struggle to separate care for children from women's identities; Rosemary Balsam's (2000) work points to this difficulty: "I do want to speak of childbearing as the anatomical and physiological potential of the female body, though in the context of the woman's developing psyche. I think this can be done without imposing value judgments, masked as science, about how a mature woman ought to be" (1341). Balsam recognizes her focus on the connections between women's bodies and their psychological development risks reinscribing the links between women's identities and childbearing. Even calling childbearing the "potential" for women means those women who do not have children have not fulfilled their bodily potential.[2]

The pressure to care for others carries risk. Helen O'Grady (2005) argues that the constant turning outward of women toward care for others results in "a need to please and accommodate others" that elides care for the self and results in women's constant self-surveillance and judgment (2). Using Michel Foucault's idea of the panopticon, O'Grady (2005) outlines how women have historically been denied self-care and others' care because nurturing takes place in domestic spaces, primarily through mothering (30). As a result, women self-police their ability to care for others and, in turn, ignore the need to care for themselves or to demand others care for them. This self-denial has wide-ranging effects that, according to O'Grady, include a "patchy" or nonexistent "knowledge about one's own desires, needs, values, tastes, beliefs, and so forth" (84). While men's lives have been oriented around the self, women's lives have been oriented around caring for others, work that enables men to focus on themselves to the detriment of women's lived experiences. Childfree women thus face a difficult task in rearticulating care because they are drawing attention to different aspects of their identities that do not involve childbearing or childrearing. Even when they demonstrate the care for others women are assumed to need or desire, childfree women who try to weave new articulations between care and other humans who aren't their children may be disparaged. Childfree women who try to rearticulate care are attempting to undermine hegemonic reproductive beliefs that have been at work for millennia (see chapter 1) and that continue to constrain the ways they can make arguments about their reproductive lives.

Beyond tracing how care circulates around childfree women's identities in these ways, this chapter also examines what it means when childfree women have unsupportive interactions with those around them. Often, these interactions result in someone (or a group) in a childfree woman's community failing to understand the woman's decision and resisting realignment of their conceptions of womanhood apart from motherhood. As one of my interviewees observed, these interactions involve not only words but also the unfelt or unseen circulation of affective cultures. Crowley (2006) speaks to the connections between rhetoric and affect in claiming that although proofs must be provided to support persuasive arguments, affect establishes "ethical, evaluative, and emotional climates" that make it possible for beliefs and behavior to change

(58). While chapter 5 speaks primarily to the successes of shifting affectual climates around childfree rhetorics, this chapter speaks mainly to its failures, when childfree women and their interlocutors prove unable to come to terms about reproductive doxae, such that childfree women are shut out of the social center and kept on the margins.

While affect is difficult to analyze, the ways interactions speak to gendered happiness scripts reveal some of the affectual moments circulating through reproductive doxae, moments that are often hidden but, in these cases, have become more visible. Anderson (2007) argues that "for rhetoric to work from such a *doxastic* perspective on identity—an emphasis on how identity is experienced and articulated in culture—is to focus on how commonsense beliefs about identity and selfhood function in discourse, informing the actions of rhetors and audiences alike in specific discursive exchanges" (11). My interviewees' experiences demonstrate what commonsense beliefs about women's reproductive lives are circulated through gendered happiness scripts predicated on the articulations of motherhood, happiness, selflessness, and care. They show the limits of reweaving these articulations, at least in their interactions with some people, and they discuss the effects of these exchanges on their conceptions of themselves as childfree women. However, it isn't clear whether these exchanges affected their audiences, but, in some cases, it seems clear they did not. Farrell (1993) claims rhetoric can "perform an act of *critical interruption*" in inventional moments when the rhetor's own interpretive framework and the audience's sociocultural mores, including doxae, intersect (257–58). While rhetoric is at work in the interactions described throughout this book, interviewees' experiences in this chapter speak to their attempts to shift others' reproductive doxae. This chapter therefore demonstrates how childfree women work to represent childfreedom in terms others may understand and accept, particularly through a rearticulation of care, and the difficulties they face in unraveling hegemonic reproductive beliefs and socially centering childfreedom.

REARTICULATING CARE IN CHILDFREE WOMEN'S LIVES

Although doxae function in silent and unspoken ways, they are not always invisible. Resistance to doxae, such as resistance by childfree women, can indeed make doxae more visible, more obviously constructed around sociocultural beliefs rather than natural, as some of their defenders might suggest.[3] By questioning the supposedly natural connection between womanhood and motherhood, childfree women surface hegemonic reproductive beliefs for both themselves and others to contest. This process also helps make visible the gendered happiness scripts constructed for women around reproductive ideologies and the interwoven connections of motherhood, selflessness, happiness, and care that inform these scripts. Childfree women have different ways of attaching to, challenging, and intervening in these scripts, dependent in part on their own identities (see previous chapter) and in part on the interactions they have with those around them.

The ways the interviewees talked about care in efforts to help others understand their identities as women without children varied depending on who they were and whom they were talking to. This chapter focuses on their care relationships with colleagues, family, friends, and even themselves to explore how reproductive doxae affectually and rhetorically circulated through interviewees' lives. Care was brought up by 94 percent of interviewees, demonstrating their awareness of the ways care is linked to gendered happiness scripts, as seen in the last chapter's discussion of gender in particular. In talking about her love for her dog, Brittany said, "And so the caregiver part coming out, right? Because it's socially expected that a woman would be a caregiver." The same proportion of interviewees mentioned having interacted with some unsupportive people around their decision not to have children. Dianna said her grandmother believes "a woman's role in life is to produce children, and to take on care and responsibilities for the older generation," including the woman's parents. Dianna's attainment of a PhD and her childfreedom created tension with her grandmother such that they stopped speaking to each other for a period. Such contentiousness demonstrates how engrained reproductive doxae can be for people who see childfreedom as an affront to normalized life patterns that have revolved around women caring for others, especially children.

Some of my interviewees emphasized that their experiences with others had been overwhelmingly positive and did not fit the stereotypes of childfree women being denigrated for their decision, but most who had unsupportive interactions seemed to feel these interactions deeply. They described difficulties navigating these interactions rhetorically, demonstrating some of the complexities of challenging hegemonic reproductive beliefs when this work largely occurs through individual interactions rather than more collective interventions from childfree women as a group.

Talking about Caring Careers as a Strategy

In the same way I articulate I am a caring person through reference to my younger siblings, some childfree women talk about the caretaking of others through their careers as a way of addressing negative interactions about their childfree status. Reflecting overall gendered patterns in the workforce, many childfree women are involved in careers that capitalize on their relationships with others and involve nurturing of some kind. Women's involvement in these types of careers is not limited to childfree women; Rocheleau's (2017) chart that appeared in the *Boston Globe* reflecting national career patterns showed that preschool and kindergarten teachers, speech-language pathologists, dental hygienists, childcare workers, dental and medical assistants, nurses, and administrative assistants are all predominantly women. Undermining assumptions that childfree women are cutthroat career women, Amara Bachu (1999) found on the one hand that childlessness is most common among managerial and professional women with high education achievement and high family incomes, but on the other hand that childless women were participating at high rates in service industries. I found that highly accomplished participants in white-collar jobs emphasize the caring work they do in their jobs as well.

Perhaps in part due to my snowball sampling methods, eighteen of my interviewees worked in higher education in some capacity; fourteen of these worked as faculty in English studies.[4] Five women worked in a health or medical profession, two in nonprofits, two in media, two in offices, and the remaining five in various other industries. A few interviewees who work in education emphasized that care for their students is an integral part of their professions, which satisfied their desire to interact with children and young adults and to have an impact on the future. Rachel, for example, commented that as a college professor she has "thousands of students." She added, "They're all my kids and I do not need to have them running around at home and [have to] deal with the toddler stage." Similarly, Bonnie said her job in higher education was part of what fulfilled her need to "nurtur[e] others or car[e] for others." Silvia, who also teaches in higher education, said, "Just because you aren't a parent doesn't mean that you can't influence and influence for the better and be there in many ways. And I've had all these, you know, individual experiences with certain students where I really do think that I was . . . I had the space to answer phone calls at night and listen to hysterical crying for an hour." The implication was that she would not have that "space" if she had children of her own.

Other interviewees mentioned the types of support and mentoring they provided to others in their careers, which was another way for them to rearticulate care as part of their lives. This type of care work formed an integral part of Claudia's career in the Christian church;[5] she was a leader in "belonging and mission." She described this work: "[It involves] helping people who are connecting to our church initially to feel in a sense that [they have gotten] to the point where they feel like they belong, and so I work very hard to connect people, both socially and spiritually, and to help our congregation understand what it means to have a posture towards other people that is welcoming." Her work also concerned "making sure that people are cared for in every sphere of their life" through the church's health and educational initiatives. These types of work involve caring for others by paying attention to their needs and helping them find a sense of belonging. Claudia also mentioned she has observed most women in ministry ultimately leave this work when they have children so they can stay home and raise their children. She did not feel the desire to have children and saw being childfree, in part, as a way for her to fulfill her ministry work, which she felt she "was meant to be doing."

Childfree women in other fields had similar experiences in caring for others and serving as childfree role models. Gail, an architect, said she often plays "a mentoring role" at work to younger women. She also explained that "architecture is a really tough business for women. It's really very, very male dominated." Because of this she takes on a mentoring role with young women in her field, which, she said, made her "feel like [she's] almost playing that mothering or mentorship role now." She also viewed herself as a childfree role model who shows other women in her field they don't have to have children unless they want to. Thus, she made it clear she sees supporting other women as an important part of her work and a way she could positively impact others' lives.[6] At the same time Gail expressed frustration that after a recent position change at her job she is expected to be "partly babysitter" to younger colleagues who need constant follow-up from her in order to do their work. In these instances, she distinguishes between the types of care work she wants to do—mentoring other young women in the field—and does not want to do—cajoling adults into doing their jobs. Making such workplace interactions visible was part of how childfree women reframe narratives about their relationship to care. Centering care work that is not mothering but that does offer valuable support to others, much like my care work as an oldest sister, leaves particular articulations about women intact. This rhetorical move is one way childfree women take up threads commonly associated with motherhood while weaving new happiness scripts that potentially disrupt hegemonic reproductive beliefs.

Childfree women who work in high-paying, time-consuming, prestigious careers are likely to be labeled through commonplaces as "selfish" or "antisocial" (Lisle 1996, 196). Research suggesting childless women earn higher wages than mothers (see Anderson, Binder, and Krause 2003; Correll, Benard, and Paik 2007; Wilde, Batchelder, and Ellwood 2010) that has only been mounted in the context of the COVID-19 pandemic (Ruppanner et al. 2021) may contribute to this narrative (in spite of some countervailing evidence; see Joan R. Kahn, Javier Garcia-Manglano, and Suzanne M. Bianchi [2014]), although it represents a misplacement of anger towards a system that unjustly marginalizes people with caring responsibilities and a sexist system that demands women behave in certain ways and then punishes them for doing so. Participants referenced this system as part of the reason they were child-free. Over a third of interviewees explicitly said they had not had children in part because of their careers, and others indicated they saw having children and maintaining their careers as incompatible, in line with other scholars' research showing careers are a primary concern among women as they make reproductive decisions (Dykstra and Wagner 2007; Hayden 2010; Kemkes-Grottenthaler 2003). Participants were aware of the systemic constraints mothers face in balancing a career and motherhood and how careers affected mothering practices. Their statements echoed Jeanne Safer's (1996) claim that "women who have worked hard to establish their autonomy . . . see motherhood as a threat to their liberty. Because of their potential overinvolvement and difficulty setting limits, they're afraid that a child's requirements would compel them to give so much that they would give themselves away" (80).

Several women emphasized the lack of adequate childcare options as one reason they did not think being a mother and having a career were compatible. Kari, who works as an administrator and professor in higher education, described her career as "an influence" in her childfreedom. She said she would feel uncomfortable using daycare or a nanny, mentioning she considered the latter option "really exploitative." She also said watching colleagues at her university struggle to balance dual careers and parenthood "made it [having children] not as appealing." Similarly, Mary, who worked first as a nurse and later taught nursing in higher education, said she would want to stay home if she had children: "I have very, very particular views about politics and society, and those would be the things I would've wanted to kind of develop in a child. Whereas if you send them off to, you know . . . and I have nothing [bad to say] about daycare, it's great . . . but I just don't want . . . I want to make sure that my child would grow up at least exposed to my perspectives, so then, there goes the career, there goes the money, there goes the pension." While these particular women had reservations about particular aspects of the childcare they believed would be available to them, their comments also suggest concern about the expectation that they prioritize their children above everything else, including their careers. These expectations fuel the lack of political momentum to improve the US childcare system, but they also fuel participants' lack of interest in having children. They also align with Hayden's (2010) finding that some voluntarily childless women expressed a reluctance to have divided identities as mothers and career women.

In my study, participants' ability to define what would make them happy and what would not was an integral part of their negotiation of their childfree identities and careers. Alicia, who worked in health policy, talked about the centrality of her own education and career in her life: "I've always needed and loved having something to do, whether it's being in school or having a job that I can dive into, and the times that I've been between jobs or in unfulfilling jobs or things like that it's just, I don't like . . . I feel very lost." Focusing on her own education and career was of primary importance to Alicia's well-being. Grace also mentioned the flexibility she was able to embrace in her work as a freelance journalist because she didn't have children to care for: "I freelance, and it's a different ballgame when you have children I imagine, you know, because I'm like, if I don't get paid, if someone doesn't, you know . . . pay off the invoice by a certain time, there's nothing catastrophic that's gonna happen. I'll just have to tighten my belt for a little while and chase them. But when you have obligations for children, you can't tell kids that . . . the invoice wasn't paid so, oh well. . . . another thing for me that I was like . . . my entire life will be impacted by that one decision [if I have kids]." Similarly, Alison's work in wine sales meant she travelled a lot, which she recognized she likely would not be able to do if she had children, particularly because women who had previously held this type of position in her company had switched to other positions once they had children. Centering their own careers was one way Alicia, Grace, and Alison, as well as other childfree women, were able to prioritize themselves, even as a focus on careers counters reproductive doxae and can lead to others' disregard for them as "selfish career women."

Given the tensions around women in the workplace and how their roles do or don't align with gendered happiness scripts, it is not surprising some childfree women said some of their most difficult negotiations of childfreedom involved colleagues. Relationships with colleagues exist in a liminal space—they can be friends or they can simply be workplace acquaintances. However, for working childfree women, colleagues often form an important part of their social environment, and interactions with them can contribute to the levels of support or lack of support they feel about being childfree. Perhaps because under the current system in which workers with caring responsibilities rarely measure up in terms of time commitment in the workplace—or are stigmatized as failing in this way—and thus workers without such responsibilities may feel they benefit from the childfree state of their colleagues, most interviewees felt at least some of their colleagues were supportive.

Although interviewees did not seem to care as much about whether their colleagues supported their childfreedom as whether their family and friends were supportive, they still found working alongside unsupportive colleagues a challenge. They also noted this burden falls on them because they are women. For example, Shanna noted male colleagues do not have to answer the question about whether or not they have children. As she noted, "[Parenthood is] an identity feature for the women" but not for men.

Leigh, a college instructor, lamented that "almost no one" at her job understood her decision to remain childfree, and the most difficult was a staff person who frequently asked her when she and her husband were going to have children. Like Claudia who worked at a church, Mary said that when she was teaching at a Catholic university, she felt there was prejudice against childfreedom, as she was barred from teaching future nurses about birth control in a maternity nursing class. She noted that she only stayed two years and that her time with that employer was "very challenging," suggesting she not only felt she was barred from preparing her students in the manner she wanted but also that she took the assumption that all women should "be fruitful and multiply" and directives against birth control as opposition to her own choice. Nicole, who is divorced as well as childfree, described an interaction with a male hiring manager who said he considered the fact that a female job candidate had a family was a reason to hire her.

> He said, "Yeah, I'm really pleased about her. Not only is she sharp, but she also has a family."[7] So of course I key in on that. I'm like, "So what do you mean?" He said . . . , "I'm glad she has a family because she's less likely to leave." I said, "Well, why would you say that?" He said, "Well, because she has a family. She's not so quick to pick up and go as a single person." I said, "Well, . . . you do see me sitting here, right? . . . I've been at this company almost ten years." . . . [Another male colleague who was part of the conversation pointed out that this was] "discriminatory." He said, "Just because someone is married does not mean that they're any better . . . that they will be a better employee than someone who's single."

Nicole and her colleague pointed to the way assumptions were based in this job candidate's family status and factored into a myriad of assumptions about those who have partners and children, as well as about those who do not, in this workplace.

Nicole also said she felt discriminated against because her colleagues who are parents could take a day to stay home with sick children but she couldn't take a day for her own health. This created a somewhat hostile workplace environment: "I feel like I've had to stand up for myself and I feel like people, society as a whole, tends to unfortunately value women more based upon not only their family situation, like whether or not they're married, but also whether or not they have children." She similarly mentioned a married coworker of hers being "singled . . . out" as a "target" for criticism because she was open about being childfree. Vinson, Mollen, and Smith's (2010) study of female university students' attitudes about childfree Black women suggests that Nicole's identity as a Black woman may also have increased her negative experiences of colleagues who disapprove of her choices.

On the other hand, Shanna, who worked as an administrator in higher education, recounted a story about being applauded for being childfree on the job. She described a time when an older male professor—whom she described as "tweed jacket with the patches"—poked his head into her office soon after she joined her current institution and asked if she had children. When she said she didn't, she recounted, "He said, 'Good. You'll go far.'" She considered this interaction problematic, reflecting an attitude women can't "ever get away from," but she chose to "speak back to it." Thus, she aligned with the notion that being a mother does not automatically hinder women in the workplace and that being a childfree worker is not always positive, even though her own career and childfreedom were compatible.

Other childfree women had encounters in the workplace that were extremely negative. Perhaps the most negative was recounted by Cassie, who had previously worked at a large hardware store. She admitted to a colleague who was at the time seeking a surrogate in order to have her own child that she had chosen tubal ligation because she was childfree, not for health reasons. As Cassie described it, the woman responded that Cassie was "an idiot and that everybody in the world should have at least one kid because nobody can determine that they can't be a parent without already having a child." Similarly, Traci had a colleague who objected so strenuously to her childfreedom "that [she] had to threaten to go to HR. . . . [she] had to say, 'This is not appropriate. This is harassment.'"

The ways childfree women navigate their careers—including what careers they have, how they negotiate their identities as childfree women in their careers, and how they interact with colleagues as childfree women—demonstrate how hegemonic reproductive beliefs inform professional aspects of their lives. Their identities in workplaces can be contested, drawing attention to stereotypes of mothers and career women and how these stereotypes interfere with the work all women do. Some childfree women attempt to negotiate care as part of their careers to reweave how they take up care as women. However, these attempts cannot completely unsettle some of the systemic and personal constraints that still inform how childfreedom is viewed in workplaces and how childfree women negotiate their identities at work.

Talking about Care and Families of Origin as a Strategy

This section focuses on interactions with family of origin, including parents and other caretakers, siblings, and extended families, while the next section focuses on social relationships, including friends who might be seen as family. Interviewees grew up in a variety of family backgrounds: twenty-two interviewees' parents were still married, ten interviewees' parents were divorced, and one interviewee's parent had been widowed. Number of siblings varied substantially, too, although only one interviewee had no siblings; of the other interviewees, eighteen had one sibling, six had two siblings, four had three siblings, three had four siblings, and two had five or more siblings.

As discussed in chapter 3, talking with families—especially parents—about the decision not to have children can be complicated, and often some of the most serious pressure about this choice comes from family members. Families also govern much about how a childfree woman grows up and constructs her identity when young, including her own assumptions about whether or not she will eventually become a mother. Most interviewees felt their families' attitude toward their childlessness was mixed. This section discusses some of the unsupportive interactions childfree women had in their familial communities; they experienced these interactions as difficult points in negotiating their childfree identities and their disarticulation and rearticulation of hegemonic reproductive ideologies.

Mothers, in particular, were central figures in many of my interviewees' interpretations of why they decided to be childfree and whether/how much they felt judged because of that decision. All interviewees mentioned their mothers at some point, although they experienced varying degrees of support from them. Some said their mothers had come around to the idea of their daughters being childfree, while a few felt their mothers had been supportive from the beginning (see next chapter). Many interviewees thought their mothers had trouble accepting, at least for a period, that their daughter was not going to become a mother—a role that shaped most of their mothers' lives in meaningful and deep ways. Part of what the interviewees thought occurred, although this idea circulated affectually perhaps more than discursively between interviewees and their mothers, is that their decision to be childfree felt like a rejection of an identity that cements relationships between mothers and daughters. As Allison explained, "[My mother] probably took it personally as a rejection of her mothering that I didn't want to have kids." Here I begin by briefly discussing some of the complications in these relationships before analyzing how childfree women portrayed the unsupportive interactions between themselves and their mothers and the effects of these interactions on their identities as childfree. This section concludes with a discussion of the caring support participants provided to their families. Like articulations of their caring roles at work, the discussion of such roles represented a rhetorical strategy for articulating women's roles as caregivers without becoming mothers.

Some childfree women recognized that their mothers' attitudes about motherhood or sometimes-inadequate modeling of motherhood affected the ways they thought about becoming a mother. Kari said she knew she did not want to be the sort of mother who prioritizes parenting over everything else in her life: "But I also felt like I knew what not-priority parenting looked like. I knew what that looked like when you knew someone didn't really want to have a kid and had kids." Christie said that growing up in an abusive home and the lack of a positive model affected her own views of motherhood: "[My mother] was not a very good mother. I never felt mothered, and so I always felt like I wouldn't know how to be a mother 'cause I didn't have a model." Even more bluntly, Gail said that her mother "was immature and a battered wife who never should've had children" and that this model played a role in her decision to be childfree. Interviewees recognized that following gendered happiness scripts does not always have positive outcomes, even though hegemonic mothering ideologies present those scripts in a positive manner.

Other interviewees recognized the web of mothering ideologies may have made their mothers feel they did not have any options but to become mothers, regardless of whether they wanted to or not. Allison said, "I probably think that my mom didn't feel like she had the choice to not have kids. I don't know that if in a different day and time that she might not have had children. You know? I'm glad she did obviously.

But I don't know if it was her life's mission to have kids." Christie was more definite: "I never got the sense that my mother wanted to be a mother; I got the sense that she did that because she was supposed to." Mary said her mother had advised her outright not to "ever" have kids. Mary recalled, "She was not particularly, from my sense of it, wasn't a particularly happy woman. . . . I think she wanted to be perhaps more of a career person. And it just . . . then she just . . . and being Catholic, you know, you gotta have kids. And so then here she . . . and then dad's like, you know, all of a sudden here they are, you know, with five kids. And that's pretty life changing." Interviewees' recognition of the ways the power of reproductive doxae had shifted between their mothers' generation and their own demonstrates an evolution of ideas about mothering ideologies, even if being childfree is still largely positioned as deviant.

Celia's feelings about her relationship with her mother were complex. She said that she had a good relationship with her mother in adulthood and that her mother had always been supportive of her, not pressuring her to have children. She noted that when younger, she had not considered her mother "very motherly," stating, "I don't think she knew how to create a relationship with me very well, growing up, and I don't think she . . . I think she wanted one, if you would've asked her, but I don't think she knew how." Celia felt her mother was often busy with crafts, something she said her mother did very well, and that she felt distanced when her mother preferred to be left alone. She said my questions had made her think differently about her mother's behavior.

> I think that when I was younger, I always saw this as antimotherly or whatever, but your questions and thinking about this also made me reflect on kind of like, where did I get that idea? Maybe she's just showing me a different version of being a mother. As a feminist, I'm kind of like, "Why didn't I read it that way?" . . . Now I see . . . I can think of her more as this amazing kind of feminist alternative to motherhood that you don't have to be all consumed with your children, and you don't have to be motherly in a traditional way. Now, I can see that, but I never thought that growing up.

Self-reflexively, Celia realized as an adult that when she was a child she had expectations that conformed to hegemonic mothering ideologies, both about what it means to be a mother but also about what it meant to have a particular type of mother-daughter relationship. She explained, "I wanted a closer relationship with my mom that I never had, but at the same time, she's never been comfortable pressing me about things like children. . . . Like I said, my mom's always kind of let me be. And there's again, good parts to that and bad parts to that." Celia's ambivalence about her relationship with her mother was more pronounced than other participants', but it illustrates the sometimes-conflicted feelings childfree women can feel about these relationships and how their reflections on their decision not to have children can help them think differently about how reproductive ideologies are woven through women's lives.

A couple of interviewees faced judgments from their mothers about how their decision not to have children would factor into heterosexual relationships with men. Traci first talked with her mother about being childfree when she was in her late teens, and her mother told her, "No man will ever want to marry you if you don't want kids." Alison had a similar experience; her mother believed if she met the right man she would want to have children. Alison explained,

> My mother is very romantic . . . her story with my dad was, "I met your dad and I knew that he would be a great father." And that's what she wants . . . and she's like, "So you're going to meet a man and you're going to know that he's the one who you want to be a father." And, so she still very much has this in mind for me, that it's just a matter of the right man showing up and me knowing that it's him. . . . And then as I've gotten older, it's been more of a, I think almost a fear from her of like, "Well, you don't know. You don't know. He still might be out there." But it's hard to get her to take me seriously, despite the fact that I've been saying this forever.

These comments illustrate heteronormative values around marriage and motherhood that reinforce happiness scripts, scripts that childfree women contest in these interactions but that their mothers often ignore.

Mothers expressed their disapproval of their daughters' choices in various ways. Leigh's mother tried to make her feel guilty about being childless and suggested she needed to spend time holding babies so she would change her mind. Her mother actually has a framed picture of Leigh and her husband with their friends' two children in her house, a visual representation of an idealized image of Leigh as a mother. Dianna's mother deliberately tried to spring conversations about having children on her when she couldn't easily escape those conversations, and she talked about the ways Dianna could have a child as a single person. When rebuffed, her mother asked her, "Do you not love children? Do you just hate them all?" Dianna viewed these conversations as evidence that her mother "is convinced that I'm kidding myself." Interviewees said their mothers try to force existing scripts on them because they cannot see what new happiness scripts their daughters can weave for themselves.

Several interviewees reported their parents had promised to help with childcare if their daughters got pregnant, especially if they were unmarried at the time.[8] For instance, Silvia's father told her when she was single, "Just have a baby with anyone, we'll look after the baby." Such promises seemed to be supportive in that they recognized there are concerns about childcare and labor linked to mothering parents could potentially help alleviate. However, the sense of humor with which interviewees related such stories indicated they felt such promises also overlooked other factors beyond childcare that shape women's lives in deciding to be childfree. Many interviewees viewed these offers as demonstrating interviewees' parents recognized some of the constraints around mothering and how reproductive doxae worked in mothers' lives and were trying to find ways to address their daughters' objections to having children without seeing childfreedom as an integral part of their daughters' identities.

Interviewees' interactions with their fathers around childfreedom were generally less complex than those with their mothers, although they were also mixed in terms of whether fathers were supportive or unsupportive. In general, fathers of childfree women seemed less invested in whether their daughters became mothers and, sometimes, more invested in their daughters being self-sufficient, as discussed in the next chapter. However, some still struggled to see how their daughters could live as childfree women.

Silvia's father pushed her to have a child more than her mother did, and in their case it was he who offered to help take care of the baby. She said, "Sometimes I get annoyed and sometimes I'm also . . . I think that being a dad was my dad's favorite thing. And I think he wishes . . . I think he wants to do it again a little bit and then I think he doesn't want me to miss out on this thing that he experienced so happily." Similarly, Allison's father told her "that he felt bad for [her] because having his children . . . was the greatest joy in his life." These comments demonstrate some interviewees' fathers recognize how much labor mothers often must do[9] and seek to remedy this burden, even as they fail to recognize how women's decisions to be childfree are often about more than simply the labor of childrearing, although that can certainly be a factor. In perhaps an extreme example of heteronormative happiness scripts influencing other people's reactions, both Sandra's father and Grace's took their desire not to have children as an indication they are lesbians (see the previous chapter). Sandra no longer speaks to her father, and his error suggests how deeply happiness scripts are tied to heteronormative ideals of adulthood and how challenging hegemonic beliefs can break down communication.

Siblings also formed an important part of interviewee's interactions with family around childfreedom. Perhaps reflecting siblings' common experience in coming from the same nuclear family background and their lower investment in one another's choices, most interviewees felt their siblings were at least partially supportive. However, sisters who had made different reproductive decisions were often the most persistent siblings in questioning a childfree woman's decision. Elizabeth actually reported one of her sisters is more resistant to her decision than her mother is.

Others reported a mix of understanding and resistance. Kari's sister asked her why she doesn't want children and whether their mother's approach to mothering had influenced that decision, reflecting an intimate understanding of Kari's calculus. She also to some extent dismissed Kari's concerns, telling her she could make different and better choices as a mother, something Kari agrees her sister is demonstrating as a mother herself. Kari sensed, though, that her sister had felt judged in some way because she had chosen to have children, and Kari felt she had to reassure her sister that she was a good mother despite their shared history in their own family. One of Rachel's sisters denigrated Rachel's decision by saying she is not "really fulfilling [her] purpose in life." She has also joked Rachel might not have the patience to be a good mother. Rachel seemed annoyed by this presumption that she wasn't patient, which tagged her as not having the personal characteristics that fit with articulations of motherhood, although she said in general her family left her alone about being childfree.

Some interviewees mentioned reactions from extended family members such as grandparents, aunts, uncles, and cousins. In general, such interactions raised less intense feelings than interactions with closer ties. Sarah simply stopped talking to an aunt and a cousin who were offended by a Facebook conversation that followed her publication of an article about reasons not to have children. While she said their taking offense "was the worst, I think, the worst reaction I had" to her choice not to have children, she eventually began talking to them again, and they avoid the topic now because it isn't "productive." In this instance, multiple layers of interactions occurred—personal and public—that created a rift. These overlapping layers of complication demonstrate how complex the affectual uptake of reproductive doxae can be, spilling into people's relationships with others.

Dianna's rift with her grandmother over her childfreedom was layered with her being a first-generation college student. She said her grandmother "would just force [the topic of childfreedom] in" whenever she was around.

[She believed m]y role in life as a woman is to provide children that will then care for me in my old age, and when I said that I was going to university, I was the first one to go to university in my family, and she was absolutely horrified. And, just disgusted, that I would dare to go get a degree. Why on earth would a woman want to get an education? And then when I announced I was getting a master's degree, she like hit the roof, and by the time I finished my PhD, we just weren't even talking anymore. It had just become such a contentious issue.

The additional layer of a woman obtaining an education is added onto the issue of childfreedom here (something echoed in Gail's experiences with her family as well), emphasizing that Dianna had rejected gendered happiness scripts and chosen a completely different path than her grandmother. This example demonstrates the ways articulations of womanhood with motherhood, selflessness, care, and happiness play out in childfree women's lives, potentially distancing them from others.

One interviewee had a difficult situation with her sister-in-law that forced her to divulge information about her reproductive experiences she had not wanted to. This interviewee identified as childfree, but she became pregnant and experienced a miscarriage. Only her partner knew about the pregnancy or its conclusion. She said that in this "still very raw, still very new" state, her sister-in-law asked her repeatedly when she was going to have children. She felt very wounded by her sister-in-law's pushing her, and she ultimately told her sister-in-law about the miscarriage. She described this interaction as "a bizarre, really traumatizing situation" in which she felt forced to tell her sister-in-law about this experience because she needed a way out of the constant line of questioning and did not see any other way to end it.

In some cases, relatives who are themselves without children put pressure on respondents. Alicia mentioned feeling judged by a cousin who had not had children even though she wanted them because she had not found a partner with whom to have a child: "[She acts] like, why aren't you using your fertility if you're, if you have it?" Meghan's childless aunt mentioned to her that not having children "was the biggest regret of [her] life." Although Meghan wasn't certain whether her aunt was childless by chance or circumstance, she understood her aunt thought she should try to become a mother. In these more negative interactions, interviewees often found themselves feeling as if they had to explain or answer to their family members about their childfree decision, defending the choice not to have children and articulating new identities for themselves.

For some interviewees the pressure from relatives exists in a surprising context, which is that they are giving support to members of their families of origin, some of which might be difficult to supply if the interviewees also had children. This care work, despite being codified into the role of daughter, however, was often even more invisible than the care work mothers perform because children, especially younger (not adult) children, are not often recognized as caregivers in their own households (Evans 2013; Miller 2005). As with the care they provide in professional contexts, childfree women used this care to weave articulations among care, selflessness, happiness, and family apart from motherhood, but even those who benefit from this care do not necessarily acknowledge these connections.

For example, Tasha said that now she is an adult, her mother and grandmother call her for advice regularly, even though she generally must research the answers. Tasha and her older brother were at times homeless and at other times lived with both these family members; her mother has schizophrenia and bipolar disorder. This history meant Tasha was used to caring for herself and others even as a child. Others mentioned caring for older relatives when they were still children, such as Leigh, who said she had "done enough care taking for a lifetime" growing up in a household with an alcoholic father. She said in her family she has "always been kind of the fixer, the peacekeeper . . . the adult." Broadcaster and comedian Maureen Langan (2013), who served as a substitute mother for her sister who was fifteen years younger than herself in an abusive household, and who embraced childfreedom later in life after several miscarriages, reflects on similar caretaking she performed as a child: "I may not be anyone's official mother, but I have done a lot of mothering in my life. I was more of a mother when I should have been more of a child. I don't resent it. Life isn't always linear or chronological. In fact, I'm glad I got to experience that mothering energy. It's a part of me. It always will be. It's why I can be okay with not having children because I have nurtured" (118).

My findings align with Safer's (1996) statement that girls who "felt forced to act in their mother's place and raise their siblings" frequently decide "once was enough; now that they are adults with choices, they want to live for themselves" (104). As the epigraph to this chapter demonstrates, Nicole said she felt parentified as a child because she was expected to care for her sister. She also cared for her nieces and nephews at times, and while she enjoyed the work, it gave her a sense of what she did not want to do. Rachel similarly talked about taking on a lot of responsibilities as the oldest daughter in her family with eight children: "As a kid, I had to take on a lot of responsibility really fast as the oldest. And it was a small farming community, which is way different. You know, here I see my twelve-year-old neighbors, and they're not allowed to stay home for more than an hour by themselves. . . . I was mowing the whole town and babysitting the whole town . . . by ten, right, so this is a different world." She was preparing eggs and toast by the time she was in kindergarten and helping change her siblings' diapers shortly after. Similarly, my own experiences growing up the oldest of six children meant I had increased responsibilities in the household, including baby-sitting that extended into my college years, preparing food, cleaning the house, and generally being responsible in part for the well-being of my siblings (responsibilities my siblings still, somewhat disparagingly, note I performed).

Claudia's two siblings are both parents, and she provides her mother as well as her siblings a fair amount of care work she would find difficult to provide if she had children of her own. She took time to care for her mother when she had surgeries and spent a month with her helping her pack up her house to move and house shopping with her. She also cared for her siblings' children when their parents went on vacation. As she said, she and her husband are "able to do those things" because they do not have children. Similarly, Cynthia performed extensive care work in her family as an adult. She cared for her disabled older sister before her sister was moved to a group home, and she has served as her sister's legal guardian for thirty years. Cynthia and her husband were also living with her parents because they felt "it was time to come home and help our families, so we have a helping role right now in our families." She said their families "look to [them] for help." Such care doesn't fit neatly with gendered happiness scripts, but it is clearly an important part of the care work some childfree women perform.

Families of origin are an important part of childfree women's naviga-tion of hegemonic reproductive beliefs and gendered happiness scripts. The types of care work performed by childfree women in their families of origin influence the ways they rhetorically position this care work in rela-tion to their childfreedom, often positioning such work as a reason they are childfree. Thus they do not question the assumption that all women must perform a certain amount of care in our lives. Tactically, when we reference this care we have provided or are providing, we articulate our lives to reproductive doxae while maintaining our childfree identities.

Talking about Care and Social Relationships as a Strategy

Childfree women also expand definitions of family as part of negoti-ating their identities. While compulsory heterosexuality reifies " 'the structurally normal' family . . . as tied to the conjugal unit and a family of procreation" (Dykstra and Hagestad 2007, 1281), childfree women reject this definition and envision family in more capacious ways as they explain their own care work in families.[10] Because of childfree women's decision not to have children, society often criticizes them for "being associated with 'excessive' individualism and loss of family bonds" (Park 2005, 376) as a way to reinforce the heteronormative ideologies surrounding family, and motherhood in particular, telling childfree women they will be lonely and sad if they do not marry and have children. By refusing to give in to these tactics and constructing their own ideas about family, childfree women disarticulate hegemonic reproductive beliefs and family. Childfree women may rearticulate as family anyone for whom they perform ongoing care work, including partners, close friends, and pets, and these relationships are often important to their identities. As blogger and television writer Danielle Henderson (2015) writes, "Choosing not to become a parent means that I've had to redefine my concept of family. I consider my family to be a cobbled-together group of friends and people I'm related to, all defined by the fact that I can count on them" (160).

Almost all my interviewees mentioned finding supportive social relationships in contrast to the mixed level of support in families of origin. However, while they were selective about who they connected with socially, they did not necessarily experience complete support from those they had social relationships with, and without family bonds, negotiating childfreedom in social relationships could endanger a connection. Unsupportive interactions with friends could also be some of the trickiest for childfree women to navigate because these interactions, like other relationships, were to an extent affectually driven, leaving childfree women unsure about the tensions that they felt but that were not always openly expressed.

Interviewees often discussed the care they were able to show to friends, children of friends, and others in their social circles because they had time to spare since they did not have to care for their own children. Although this type of care is not part of typical happiness scripts, it is an important part of childfree women's weaving of care apart from motherhood. For example, Sarah said, "I do tend to take on kind of a mama-bear role in some of my groups." She said she had grown to be "very, very protective of" a local social group she had joined whose mission is offering support to people who practice polyamory. She said, "So when people criticize my group or criticize someone in my group or something or, you know, have complaints or things, I get pretty upset and I get pretty maternal about it, I guess. So yeah, I do tend to . . . that's how my maternal instincts come out in my social groups and my niblings." Sarah's view demonstrates, however, how women's caring for others is interpreted readily even by themselves through the lens of motherhood rather than through any other lens, reflecting the strength of the articulation of care with motherhood when women practice it.

Several other interviewees reflected on the centrality of friends in their lives and how important caring for those friends was to them. Dianna said that while she is "not always necessarily the best at supporting the emotional crises," she is "quite good at practically being there when people need me to be": "I think all my friends know that they could ask for anything and I'll do it if it was within my power." She said she has "a good number of friends" who "are very, very important to [her]," and because she has no children, she has "a reasonable amount of time to invest in [her] friends and [her] family when they need [her]." This investment included activities such as traveling on weekends to visit friends and having weekly coffee with her oldest friend. Grace similarly talked about how her friends saw a strong "maternal streak" in her that manifested in her care for those around her. She said, "I'm very caring for people that I care about." She mentioned being "very hands-on with people . . . very physically affectionate." Her care also manifested in making sure people had food and being willing to cook for them, or taking people medicine if they are sick, or providing them with a place to stay if needed. She described her reaction when one of her friend's houses burned down: "After establishing she was okay, the first thing I did was go out and go shopping and getting her a bunch of clothes and stuff so she wouldn't not have anything to wear." Like Dianna, she identified specific caring activities that involve sharing space, time, and resources with others she enacts regularly in social relationships. This conception of care is not as socially visible as women's care for children, but interviewees considered it central to their identities.

Some interviewees included care for their friends' children in their practice of nonparenting care. Perhaps the most intense example was Katherine, who lived with her best friend and helped her raise her three children while her friend was going to school and working. Her friend's children still give Katherine Mother's Day gifts although they no longer live together. Katherine said she had to agree with her friend that she was more "nurturing" towards her friend's children than her friend was, referencing how her friend told Katherine she was Katherine's "baby daddy." Katherine said her friend's expectations had made the close relationship possible. As she said, the friend insisted her children "give [Katherine] the same amount of respect that they give her" and listen to her as a parent figure. Katherine gave up her time, energy, and even life to support her friend and her children, but the arrangement was not socially codified because no official partnership existed between her and her friend.

Silvia said that, in a less intense relationship, she likes helping support a friend's children, whom she really loves and likes being there for. She said even though the children had grown up, she was still buying them presents. As she noted, if she had had her own kids, she couldn't have had time for her friend's children. Indeed, she reflected, "I barely have time for them, like I have lots of friends with kids in their lives and I struggle to keep up with them all."

Nicole was less positive about friends' expectations of her because she is childfree. She said, "I had to be careful that I wasn't seen as someone just to buy their kids stuff." She's been invited to children's birthday parties and baby showers, and she has resisted being included only to be "a gift bearer" if she doesn't know their children well. She also described neighbors who want her to babysit, which she does not do. She viewed this boundary setting as important to "not being roped into responsibilities that are not my own and having to really stand firm on that." Her navigation of these relationships demonstrates how the commonplace that women will care for others without complaint and never put themselves first affects childfree women. While some celebrated their excess of resources and their ability to give them to others' children, others resented the assumption they would give these away freely because they do not have their own children.

Social relationships were not easy to nurture long term, especially if any tensions arose about reproductive experiences. Some interviewees spoke about interactions with unsupportive friends that created rifts between them. Cassie is now less close with a friend who told her, " 'Well, I mean, I just, it's not that I don't accept it, I just feel sorry for you.' And I was like, 'Why?' And she's like, 'Cause you'll never understand the love of a child.' And I was like, 'Just because I don't have kids doesn't mean kids won't love me.' And she's like, 'Well no, you'll never understand the joys of being a parent.' " Cassie said it was "hard" because she had been close to the friend and been "bonded with" her a long time. She reflected, "All of a sudden, now that we're growing up a little bit more, and we're making different choices, that empathy is gone." She attributes their rift to a lack of understanding in her weaving a different womanly identity, one her friend doesn't identify with and cannot respect.

Brittany had a similar interaction with a friend who was planning to be a mom. She said her friend thought Brittany was "insane" and insisted, "No, this is what we were built for." Brittany explained her friend "fed into all of that masculinist rhetoric that says that this is woman's pinnacle of her life. And I didn't want to necessarily tell her that I thought she was wrong, because I don't think she is. I mean she knows what decision is gonna be best for her and her life. It's just not the best for me and mine. And I tried to relay that to her and I think she misunderstood a bit and she got a little upset." Similar to Cassie's friend, Brittany's friend struggled to make sense of a woman making the choice not to have children given the happiness scripts in place about women being mothers. Leigh's experiences suggest friends' expectations of sameness play a role: "For a long time my best friend would say, 'Well when you have kids, you'll know. When you have kids.' And then finally, eventually I told her that I wasn't having kids, and I think she is hardcore, I don't want to say offended, but it's like she thinks that we were on track to rush the same sorority." Just as childfree women often gravitate toward the support other childfree women can provide them about their life choices, when friends who are or want to be mothers do not feel validated by their childfree friends, such invalidation can put a strain on the relationship.

Other negative interactions with friends experienced by childfree women point to this difficulty. Dianna talked about one circle of female friends in which she is and will likely continue to be the only single and childless person in the group. This identity can create tension when her friends assume she cannot offer anything to conversations about children. She was unsure whether it is she who feels she cannot offer anything or her friends who do not respect her opinion. On the one hand, she said, "That's not so much them, that's more me, I think, that they have all these shared experiences that I am not entitled to have an opinion on." On the other hand, Dianna is a perinatal epidemiologist, and her friends often ask her to help figure out whether something is wrong with their children. She said, "I definitely know at least one of them feels that way, that I shouldn't be allowed to express any form of opinion, or advice about a child because I don't know what I'm doing, which probably makes sense and is fair enough, but I think it's bollocks because I can still offer a suggestion which they can ignore." Celia does not have a career working with children, so she feels more uniformly left out. She recalled a time when a friend did not want her to hold their baby and implied that she wouldn't understand what they are going through because she doesn't have children of her own. Excluding childfree women from these conversations and connections can create rifts between friends that are difficult to navigate.

Jessica called attention to this complexity when she noted that often it isn't interactions that take place between friends but "tensions and silences and maybe situations that don't happen"; "I feel like there might be a silent judgment, or that friend kind of falls away. So, like these stories, I feel like, a situation as it comes, really just isn't, doesn't really happen. Or, I feel more the consequences of it. Like, oh, I don't really talk to that person anymore, or if they have to, I always talk to her about my sister's kids. But we never really had an explicit, adult conversation about this decision. Instead, it's just like things oscillate in that environment." Jessica's attunement to the unspoken, affectual element of childfree women's friendships also points to the rhetorical limits of dialogue and how happiness scripts are underwritten not only by rhetorical practices but also by affectual moments.

Interviewees demonstrated a lot of care in their social relationships, particularly with friends and friends' children. This care was a primary way many of my interviewees expressed the bonds they had with others and demonstrated the many ways they could care for others that are not as visible as mothering, rearticulating care to childfreedom. Navigating childfreedom in social relationships, however, could be particularly vexed because maintaining these relationships meant having to negotiate how reproductive doxae circulated through their interactions with others and what responses and affectual connections they were or were not willing to respond and try to move forward through.

Talking about Care and the Self as a Strategy

Childfree women are often called selfish and immature if they mention wanting the freedom to indulge their own desires in ways that are difficult for parents. I typically avoid telling people I want to be able to travel or go to the movies whenever I want when they ask why I don't want children. However, Safer (1996) explains many childless women see sleeping in whenever they want as emblematic of their ability to self-regulate: "It's not when they go to bed or get up, or even how much sleep they get, that matters most, but the fact that they're in control" (79). Author Pam Houston (2015) explains,

> Try this on. What if I didn't want to have babies because I loved my job too much to compromise it, or because serious travel makes me feel in relation to the world in an utterly essential way? What if I've always liked the looks of my own life much better than those of the ones I saw around me? What if, given the option, I would prefer to accept an assignment to go trekking for a month in the kingdom of Bhutan than spend that same

month folding onesies? What if I simply like dogs a whole lot better than babies? What if I have become sure that personal freedom is the thing I hold most dear? (170–171)

Many scholars discuss the importance of free time and space in childfree women's lives (Chancey and Dumais 2009; Kemkes-Grottenthaler 2003; Morell 2000; Wager 2000). Grace mentioned how important it was to her to have this kind of freedom.

> I think that's kind of, for me, it's just the freedom of getting up and doing what I want when I feel like it is worth everything to me. Because I . . . sometimes, you know, you wanna do stuff and sometimes you don't. Sometimes you wanna get up early and make breakfast and do that whole Rocky thing, you know, like I feel great. And other days you're like, just slug, you know, watching Netflix [or] *British Baking Show* for ten hours. And I, but whatever I decide, every day when I wake up doesn't affect anyone but me and I think from, like I said, that's worth everything.

Sharon Houseknecht's (1987) review of twenty-nine studies on voluntary childlessness found the reason mentioned the most often was "freedom from child-care responsibility/greater opportunity for self-fulfillment and spontaneous mobility" (377). More recently, Park (2005) found the desire for an adult-oriented lifestyle was one central reason individuals chose to remain childless: "Childlessness allowed the continuation of an adult-centered existence that was currently experienced as satisfying and that respondents wished to continue" (392). Taking time for oneself works against gendered happiness scripts since this ability is often viewed as a masculine privilege (Cloud 1998; O'Grady 2005). Childfree women must deal with accusations of selfishness when they try to claim time to care for themselves, although this freedom forms an important part of the weaving of their identities.

Gail talked about the things she has been able to do in her life in part because she could travel freely: "I'm very clear about why I chose not to [have children] and all the things I've been able to do. Like I have a pretty fucking fabulous life, you know. To move to Scotland for a year-and-a-half degree. I was able to travel all over. I could pick up and move to [the city]. I could go back to school and be an architect." Travel, for her, is not just about travel for leisure but also about free movement to pursue her own goals and dreams. Dianna mentioned how travel helped her maintain social connections that were very important to her: "I went to university in Wales, and so I made friends from all over the country, so my weekends are often spent traveling." Being able to do "whatever [she] wanted, whenever [she] wanted" was very important to her, and travel was part of her ability to exercise this freedom in ways she preferred. Childfree women's reclamation of their time skirts the issues mothers in particular face in trying to embody hegemonic mothering ideologies and not having enough systemic support to care for themselves. Many women, including mothers, may want to have similar freedom, but there is not systemic support in place for them to do so.

In spite of the care many took of others, some interviewees frequently encountered the commonplace that they were selfish (Kelly 2009; Rich et al. 2011). Around half of interviewees mentioned selfishness in some way as informing how they or others thought about childfreedom and parenthood, although some came up against this idea at particular times or in particular places. Alison, for example, was told she was selfish a lot during college, but she felt as if childfreedom was "more normalized" now that she was in her midthirties. Functioning as a discursive shorthand pointing to gendered happiness scripts, selfish points out that these women have failed to have and care for children and, as a result, have rejected typical happiness scripts predicated on this care. Sarah, for example, said people described her as selfish, as refusing to "contribute anything to the world," when she published her article about being childfree. Similarly, Katherine said she finds people "shame [childfree] women" and suggest childfree women "must be really selfish because [they] don't [have children]." Being called "selfish" seems to undermine someone's status as a woman and to question the core of their identities; if they aren't caring for children, then what are they besides selfish? And if they are selfish, what is their value as women? Calling childfree women selfish shuts down dialogue about childfreedom and creates a bind in which childfree women must explain why their not having children is not inherently selfish. For example, they bring up other kinds of care they provide, or agree with that label in some way, while mothers do not have to explain why they have children.

Some childfree women have embraced the *selfish* label. Although it is preposterous to suggest Katherine, who became a live-in parent to her friend's children for a period, is selfish, she said she just responds "Yes, I am" when people accuse her of selfishness. She said she thinks when childfree women, or women trying to figure out whether they want to have children or not, are accused of being selfish, they should "just be super selfish. Super selfish." She pointed out that "at the end of the day, [when it comes to parenting decisions] the buck always stops with women," meaning they give up their bodies and their lives to have children. Similarly, Elizabeth explained she's "okay" with being called selfish: "If it means that I'm a happy person, sure, that's fine. Because I don't want to be guilted into taking care of another human." She sought to rearticulate happiness with selfishness (instead of selflessness) and refused the pressures being called selfish were intended to put on her about not having children.

The label of *selfish* is easily applied to childfree women when they refuse to conform to gendered happiness scripts and try to care for themselves instead of others. Half the interviewees mentioned not wanting to have children due to the lifestyles they wanted to live. While these reasons are most likely to be deemed selfish by others, they represented important ways interviewees sought control over their time, energy, and focal points in their lives and rewove their identities as women.

Some childfree women highlighted their own mental and physical health as part of their reasons for not having children. A radical form of care occurs when childfree women recognize their own health as important, especially given the ways women's health issues, particularly of those women in historically minoritized subject positions, are often minimized even by health professionals (Gochfeld 2010; Sabin et al. 2009; Travis, Howerton, and Szymanski 2012; White and Stubblefield-Tave 2017). For some women, like writer and producer Bonnie Datt (2013), health problems are a reason not to have children. Datt writes she decided as a teenager she didn't want to pass on her multiple allergies to a child. Some interviewees were not certain whether they would have been able to become pregnant without fertility treatments due to their health conditions or their partners'.[11] When Kari's husband had cancer, and the medicine he had to go on "completely kills your sperm motility," they decided "We're not willing to harvest sperm or do any of these things" and in the end were happy with being childfree. Katherine also recognized having a baby was not an easy thing for women's bodies to physically do: "People don't even talk about the effects that it has on women's bodies. . . . Nobody talks about that kind of stuff. It's just . . . and it's a very dangerous . . . it's really dangerous having a baby, it's not as simple as that people act like it's just, oh, listen. Yeah, it is natural, it is a natural process and your body is made to, you know, [it] make[s] you capable of doing it, but it's not an easy, simple thing."[12] Katherine considers how hegemonic mothering ideologies rely on a rhetoric of biological nature in order to try to make women feel as if their bodies are made to become pregnant and have children. Recognizing the possibility of negative outcomes for women during pregnancy and childbirth serves to further underscore these ideologies and opens up potential other challenges to it.

Several interviewees were concerned about mental health and the potential implications it could have on themselves or any children if they had them, which were made even more salient by the mental-health issues some interviewees' mothers had experienced. Pooja Bansil Elena V. Kuklina, Susan F. Meikle, Samuel F. Posner, Athena P. Kourtis, Sascha R. Ellington, and Denise J. Jamieson's (2010) conclusions support the interviewees' instincts: depression in particular can increase adverse health outcomes of birth for women, as well as adverse fetal outcomes (330). Sarah explained that for her, her mental health was "the major thing" that decided her against having children, as she "didn't want to pass that along to another generation." Further, she feels that given her mental health, the pressure of "trying to raise someone to be a healthy, well-rounded, productive member of society" is "too much responsibility for [her]." Similarly, Alicia said that "dealing with some mental health issues" factored into her decision: "I can't imagine having depression or anxiety and raising kids; I just knew that that was not, that didn't feel like a comfortable thing." They recast this decision as one that is actually an act of care for any potential children they might have because it prevents them from being bad mothers. There isn't room in gendered happiness scripts, however, for childfreedom to be framed in this way because the presumption is that children are always good and will bring happiness.

Because a framework of selfishness is often applied to childfree women, explaining how care for themselves is important can be extremely difficult, more difficult even than explaining why the care work they do for others matters. Women have not historically been given the space or time to care for themselves over others or to make choices about how they want to live their lives. In other words, hegemonic mothering ideologies reinforce gendered happiness scripts that revolve around women's care for their own children. Only recently have some women been able to prioritize care for themselves over care for others. While this prioritization is an attempt to rearticulate their relationships with care as women, it is a more subversive approach to reproductive doxae and, as a result, is perhaps the most difficult for others to accept as care.

"FURBABIES" AND (RE)ARTICULATIONS OF CARE

One last way childfree women can try to rearticulate care as part of their identities in ways others can understand is through their relationship with pets, especially for those who describe their pets as their "furbabies"—tantamount to children. While almost three-quarters of US households have a dog and almost half have a cat,[13] some childfree women, like other people with pets, translate their relationships with their pets into human terms, saying pets fill a certain care role in their lives. Some of my interviewees identified pets as one aspect of their lives that challenged gendered happiness scripts and conceptions of family. (Others had no such feelings, such as Cynthia, who said she did not want the work or responsibility of a pet although she had pets in the past.) It is significant that around a third of interviewees mentioned pets even though none of the interview questions explicitly asked about them. Some of their pets also became integrated into larger communities that acknowledged their importance as part of these women's lives.

Shanna referenced the way some women look adoringly at babies: "I look at kittens that way, which is ridiculous," she said. "I'm like, 'I could cover myself in kittens . . . and be the best kitten mom ever.'" Similarly, Brittany said, "[I have] a little doggie who I love more than life itself." Others made more explicit connections between their pets and children. Cassie said, "I have two cats and dogs. I struggle already with all of everything that goes on with them. And I'm one of those people where my animals are always gonna come first." Suzanne explained her and her husband's relationship to their pets: "Our dogs are like our children. We talk more about our dogs on the phone; he's a pilot and he's gone at night so he calls me. And that's, probably 80 percent of our conversation is about our dogs, you gotta guess what [our dog] did. And I'll send him pictures so. Yeah, I love our dogs." Elizabeth said when a colleague pointed out to her that "pets, you know, die," she responded, "'Your kids are gonna die.' And he was just like, (gasp). And I was like, 'I'm sorry, I mean, but it's true. They're gonna die. They're not gonna live forever.'" Of course, Elizabeth was willfully ignoring that given lifespans, it is very common to outlive one's pets but relatively uncommon to outlive one's children. But she was also right to say that knowing a relationship is likely to end is no reason not to invest in it.[14]

A couple of interviewees mentioned ways their families had integrated their pets into the family community. Irene says, "I think my family has learned to back off, they just ask about how my cat's doing." Her family has replaced asking about children with asking about her cat. Cassie said, "[My family has] started to joke a lot more about my dogs being my children. My dad is especially close with him [one dog] and he calls him his granddog." Interviewees not only view their pets as part of their immediate community but also have families who have come to identify interviewees' pets as part of their families. These interactions—asking about the pets, calling pets granddogs—are part of normalizing the close connections some childfree women have with their pets and reweaving new care relationships that are visible and accepted.

Taking these articulations further, some childfree people have used pets to explicitly undermine hegemonic mothering ideologies. In 2015, a photographer, Elisha Collins, and an Australian couple came up with an idea to do a photo shoot of the couple with their groodle (golden retriever and poodle) puppy, Humphry, in poses typical of parents with children (Warren 2015). For example, there are photos of the couple staring at Humphry in a stroller, holding Humphry's front paws and walking with him between them, and of Humphry swaddled in a blanket. The photo shoot was the couple's response to questions from their parents about when they were going to have children. The series of photos is an intervention into the hegemonic belief that heterosexual married couples in particular will have children, asking others to recognize the couple's life is fulfilling even without children, even though others might get mixed messages about who or what is targeted through this intervention. On the one hand, Buzzfeed author Rossalyn Warren (2015) says it was intended as a " 'light-hearted' poke at parents who do similar photo shoots with their newborns." On the other hand, the couple and Collins said the intention was to have fun and not to insult parents who post pictures of themselves with their newborns; Collins explained, "We didn't ever intend to make fun of new parents sharing photos of their newborns. We just wanted to show a different kind of newborn" (Stump 2015). I also post pictures of my "furbabies" on social media, explicitly encouraging people to view them as my children. Similarly, Patricia Scanlon (2013), a childfree writer and actor, wrote about being tempted to send Christmas cards featuring her and her dog Dudley "when the personalized greeting cards begin to pile up" (220). Kristin L. Arola (2011) dissects this phenomenon as being particularly painful when someone is experiencing infertility and feels left out of rhetorics of "the family" encapsulated on personalized holiday cards and letters. Interventions such as Collins's and Scanlon's in genres intended to support happiness scripts predicated on children, genres that are pervasive, as Arola (2011) points out, disrupt these scripts and attempt to make space for others.

Not all childfree women, however, readily embrace the idea that they must take up care work as part of a reweaving of womanhood. Cain (2001) writes, "Another assumption that drives some childless women to distraction is that they will deposit their mothering needs into some other source: their animals or a career such as nursing or teaching. Although some women do this, others recoil at the notion: 'I am tired of being lumped into the nurturer, domestic, craft-loving stereotype just because of my sex. Why do we have to be nurturers of the world just because we're women? What's wrong with just being ourselves?' " (147–48). Nicole identified the ways pets were seen as child substitutes, which reifies reproductive doxae and the correlation between maturity and caring for something seemingly helpless. At her workplace, many colleagues were younger people right out of college; she said, "Most of them had pets and the ones that didn't have pets, they were pressured into getting a pet. One didn't really want a dog so she went out and got a guinea pig. And I'm like, 'That, you know, that shouldn't be it either.' . . . You know, so they had to have some other attachments other than themselves. And I just don't think that's fair." Even as people such as myself encourage others to view pets as our children, by leaving the happiness scripts intact in some way, this orientation can strangely trap people into similar articulations among owning pets, care, selflessness, and happiness and lead to more judgments of those without children and even without pets.

The next chapter more fully takes up alternative tactics childfree women use to counter gendered happiness scripts apart from care. However, as seen in this chapter, childfree women tactically use aspects of reproductive doxae and reclaim negative terms such as *selfishness* to weave identities for themselves that push against hegemonic reproductive beliefs and potentially open space for different women's identities. There are limits, however, to the disruptions childfree women can make to this set of beliefs when rhetorical interventions with others break down and dialogue isn't possible. In these communicative failures, we can see how rhetoric and affect work together to create an environment in which childfree women do not feel accepted and the possibilities of rearticulating reproductive ideologies seem foreclosed. While these failures demonstrate limits to how hegemonic beliefs can be challenged, the next chapter focuses on how different rhetorical and affectual connections open up space for changes that could move childfreedom from social margins to the social center. Considering these two chapters together, then, provides insights into how the complicated interweavings of identity, rhetoric, and affect contribute to the reinforcement or deconstruction of doxae.

5

NEW ARTICULATIONS OF
CHILDFREE WOMEN'S IDENTITIES

Cassie: *I have had many conversations with strangers in the dog park . . . my dog park is kind of like the community. The same people go at the same time every day because they get off work and they take their dog, and they know that they can trust people around them. They found a good set of dog owners that, you know, either don't bring munchkins [children], or don't have rough dogs, or whatever. It's a good cohesive community. And we feel comfortable asking each other to watch our dogs for a second if we need to go to the car or whatever. It's a good group. I'm really happy with that group, but none of them have kids, and it's all varying ages.*

Gail: *I mean, I think a lot of my community is my architecture community. Those are my good, good friends because we actually went through so much. Architecture school is pretty tough.*

Like Cassie and Gail, I have found my own supportive communities that surround me and make me feel as if I belong, despite or sometimes because I don't have children. I have felt integrated into my work communities at various jobs and had plenty of people to connect with on video and phone calls during the COVID-19 pandemic. Crucial people I connect with include family and friends who support my decision not to have children, including both those with and without their own children. There are still many moments when affectual and discursive currents around my not having children influence how I feel and interact with others. However, some of these moments are affirming rather than negating, and in the past decade, I have become better myself at navigating what it means to be a childfree woman.

Many childfree women, like myself, Cassie, and Gail, have constructed supportive communities around them in which they feel as if their identities as childfree women are accepted and even celebrated. Despite the fact that childfree women can be cast as selfish, shallow,

https://doi.org/10.7330/9781646424399.c005

and self-absorbed, to borrow from the title of Megan Daum's (2015) book, many childfree women find ways to weave different patterns for their lives that create space for meaningful relationships with others. Communities in different places both within and outside the nuclear family structure, with friends, colleagues, and even strangers such as Cassie and Gail describe, can be crucial. Support networks may be restricted to the childfree or include those who have children. The crucial thing is to have interactions that allow childfree women to reweave happiness scripts. This chapter complements chapter 4 by discussing how childfree women circulate new ideas about childfreedom to and with the communities around them, disarticulating and (re)articulating gendered happiness scripts built on hegemonic reproductive beliefs.

Childfree women's responses when rhetorically intervening in discourses about motherhood and childfreedom can be strategic or tactical. Spaces of openness and dialogue around childfreedom provide balance to negative interactions. The different spaces in which childfree women find such openness reflect their many unique identities and the different contexts in which they live, which create different threads they use to weave different patterns contesting happiness scripts. In line with Tracy Morison, Catriona Macleod, Ingrid Lynch, Magda Mijas, and Seemanthini Tumkur Shivakumar's (2016) research about how childfree folx in online childfree communities talk about their identities, articulations of care outside motherhood could become a part of new gendered happiness scripts outside motherhood. For example, many interviewees and other childfree women discussed in books about childfreedom articulate the identity of the "aunt" based on their affection for children and their desire to influence children's lives without having their own children, an identity I have found myself taking up with one of my sister's children and friends' children. Often this aunt identity involves different types of care and support, such as physical, emotional, and financial. Websites such as The Savvy Auntie (n.d.) celebrate this role and its impact children's lives, albeit sometimes via rhetorics that reconstruct hegemonic ideologies of motherhood for all women, as I discuss later.

Despite the strength with which childfree women uptake childfreedom as part of their identities, some of my interviewees also noted they found it a type of trap. While motherhood is such an integral part of gendered happiness scripts that it takes conscious work to filter personal desires from reproductive doxae, childfreedom itself could also be a limiting identification. Identifying as childfree can actually create constraints about how women think about reproduction and their own lives. Childfree women thus consider how much their identity as childfree feels authentic and how much its primacy reflects the ways hegemonic ideologies constantly call on women to fuse their identities with their reproductive choices. Overall, this chapter asks what kinds of rhetorical interventions can be made in gendered articulations of reproductive doxae and how new happiness scripts can be articulated that work against these doxae, as well as what kinds of challenges need to be made and in what contexts in order for doxae to change.

RHETORICAL INTERVENTIONS IN GENDERED ARTICULATIONS OF REPRODUCTIVE DOXAE

As the last chapter illustrates, rearticulating even one part of hegemonic ideologies can be very difficult, particularly given how hidden such beliefs often are and how resistant ideologies can be to change, particularly hegemonic gendered ideologies that have been reinforced for millennia. However, there are some rhetorical tactics childfree women use to counter such beliefs that speak to the ways these beliefs can be made visible and challenged. There are also specific relationships or even communities in which reproductive doxae are more visible and open to rearticulation. In these instances, reproductive doxae are malleable and shapeable, although these changes are typically limited to the small groups within which these shifts occur. Here, I explore what it means for reproductive ideologies to become available for critique and evolution as some childfree women disarticulate the happiness scripts around them and identify rhetorical interventions in these scripts that allow them to counter reproductive ideologies that circulate in their larger sociocultural milieu.

Feminist rhetorical scholars have studied different ways women rhetors have disrupted doxae and reshaped expectations of the gendered roles they are supposed to fill (Campbell 1989; Glenn 2004; Goggin 2002; Royster 2000; Royster and Kirsch 2012). Erin A. Frost and Michelle F. Eble's (2020) recent edited collection *Interrogating Gendered Pathologies*, while rooted in a study of medical rhetorics, includes work that demonstrates how women's rhetorical practices can interrogate and disrupt gendered medical practices built on ideologies about women's bodies. One notable example is Novotny and Horn-Walker's (2020) chapter "Arti-I-Facts: A Methodology for Circulating Infertility Counternarratives" discussed in the introduction. As scholar-artists, Novotny and Horn Walker interviewed women who were experiencing infertility and collected art pieces created by these women that spoke to the women's experiences. They then circulated these pieces through their own website and public art galleries as a way to make visible the reproductive ideologies in circulation about women's infertility in hopes this visibility could lead to changes in beliefs about infertility. Although they do not explicitly frame their work around doxae, the project's aim to change "common beliefs" clearly speaks to Novotny and Horn Walker's hope that shared artwork will change reproductive doxae around infertility.

While art is a tactile and visual way of challenging reproductive ideologies, women rhetors countering gendered happiness scripts from different perspectives have developed different strategies for trying to rearticulate these scripts. Scholars have explored what is needed to change doxae, which can be difficult given the embedding of such beliefs in sociocultural systems. A necessary preliminary stage, according to Crowley (2006), is that rhetors and audiences must achieve stasis and be "open to the possibility of exchange" (30). As seen in the previous chapter, when childfree women do not achieve stasis, communication opportunities are shut down rather than opened up. In order for rhetors to take advantage of opportunities to disrupt reproductive doxae, they must be attuned to the affectual, discursive, and material environments that may facilitate such disruption and build bridges with others.

In being open and ready for kairotic moments when rhetorical exchange can occur, the goal for rhetors is to bring doxae that are typically hidden into the open for critique or challenge. McKerrow (1989) argues that those who do this work are typically marginalized "until or unless their heterodoxical rhetoric can successfully supplant that of the ruling elite" (105). Ahmed's (2010) feminist killjoys, as discussed in chapter 3, occupy this marginalized position. She claims feminist killjoys are those who "might kill joy simply by not finding the objects that promise happiness to be quite so promising" (65). Those "objects that promise happiness" are typically underscored or propped up by doxae, and in the case of the gendered happiness scripts Ahmed explores, reproductive doxae typically define happy objects for women as circulated through articulations of motherhood, happiness, selflessness, and care. Feminist killjoys refuse to accept those things taken for granted as the objects of happiness, drawing attention to the problems with such objects. In doing so, they make visible the doxae underlying these objects and their connections with happiness, which marginalizes the killjoys, as McKerrow claims, "until or unless" their alternative perspectives can shift or supplant the doxae already in place.

In order for feminist killjoys or others who challenge doxae to intervene successfully in these beliefs and shift or change larger sociocultural beliefs, identification must be built between a rhetor and others. Muckelbauer (2008) claims individuals experience "a presubjective, affectual response" that becomes *doxa* or opinion, which leads to identification of an individual with a larger group (156). Asking someone to interrogate doxae means a rhetor is asking that person to break an identification with one group and remake an identification with a new group (of which the rhetor is part). Andreea Deciu Ritivoi (2006) claims that to accomplish this change, a difficult one, "rhetorical imagination" can be used to help audiences make a leap from "an existing and a preferred state of affairs" by outlining what is possible if actions are taken to change current ideas or states of being (54). This process of rhetorical imagination challenges doxa by helping people stand outside it to see what is possible through what Ritivoi calls a new, "utopian" doxa (56). As she argues, "If utopias emancipate and distance us from our conventional practices, their function is obviously the reverse of that of ideology: while the latter integrates individuals into an existing social matrix, the former provides the possibility of social subversion, by creating a vantage point from which the seemingly 'given' can be questioned and a replacement considered" (63). Feminist killjoys and others who challenge doxae must, then, create identification with others through affectual, discursive, and material connections and then help others use rhetorical imagination to articulate new doxae that reshape what is possible in a sociocultural milieu.

This process, however, does not necessarily involve assembling completely new and different doxae. Instead, scholars argue rhetors must build on already-existing doxae in order to shift or change doxae in ways their audiences are willing to accept. Crowley (2006), for example, argues that commonplaces can be used "as discursive sites from which to launch arguments that are not so likely to be met with general approval" (71); by starting on common ground, rhetors can try to challenge doxae circulating in a community. In order to accomplish this work, rhetors must first understand what a community believes in order to, as Ritivoi (2006) puts it, "take advantage of its shared assumptions while also being able to challenge them strategically" (51). Out of this process comes invention that allows "new arguments and ideas to be heard" (51). As scholars such as Debra Hawhee (2003), Muckelbauer (2008), and Crowley (2006) claim, this process is affectual as well as discursive, calling on rhetors to take advantage of shifting affectual environments while strategically making rhetorical interventions in doxae. In the case of reproductive doxae, women who are feminist killjoys must intervene in reproductive doxae as one affectual dimension that circulates through happiness scripts. In order to do so, however, they must be affectually attuned to their environments and take advantage of moments when they can discursively disarticulate current happiness scripts with other people or groups.

An interruption of happiness scripts, like many interruptions of doxae, does not immediately occur on a large scale. Instead, reproductive doxae must shift for individuals and smaller communities first and then, eventually, become part of a larger sociocultural shift in ideologies (and eventually hegemony). Attention to a second meaning inherent in doxa helps explain how this shift might occur. Both Robert Hariman (1986) and Muckelbauer (2008) draw attention to this meaning of doxa that emphasizes a speaker's reputation, which Muckelbauer claims is similar to ethos as represented by collective reputation (150). The connection in doxa between belief and reputation points to the ability of some individuals or collectives to change doxae if those individuals or collectives have a reputation or ethos that will garner them respect and a position to posit new beliefs. This process of shifting doxae through a reliance on reputation can work by influencing others to identify with the rhetor and, therefore, to associate with the rhetor and the rhetor's proposed alternative set of beliefs. While a group such as childfree women may not initially have a strong enough collective reputation to influence sociocultural ideologies or hegemony on a broad scale, its members can rearticulate reproductive doxae in their own social circles depending on their positions within those circles. Eventually, these shifting beliefs can lead to larger ideological or hegemonic change if enough childfree women perform this work in their own communities and if the work they do aligns with common goals. While this process can be time consuming, childfree women are starting to have an influence on reproductive ideologies as they become more recognized as a group (as demonstrated through news stories about them) and as they draw more attention to the happiness scripts underlying many women's decisions about their lives and people's judgments about women's reproductive experiences.

Extending this attention to reputation in shifting doxae, the affective cultures at work in a particular context inform the identification felt between a rhetor and those around them, as well as the openness of their audiences to their challenging of doxae. By demonstrating how happiness scripts operate in positive interactions between childfree women and those around them, this chapter illustrates the affectual dimension in shifting doxae and our need to pay greater attention to the affectual currents that shape whether and how doxae can shift in particular communities. The childfree women I interviewed had crafted different rhetorical strategies for speaking back to happiness scripts when confronted with them, including humor, directness, and strategic explanations of their positions. However, they had also formed bonds with others around them that allowed for the critique and challenge of happiness scripts built on reproductive doxae. These changes often took place between themselves and other individuals, but they demonstrate how doxae can shift within smaller groups. Interviewees also identified their role in making reproductive ideologies visible to other women, particularly other women who were thinking about whether or not to have children. They saw themselves as examples of women who had made different choices for themselves, even as they recognized different women's intersectional identities affect the reproductive choices they are able to make. This chapter extends from the previous to illustrate the evolving nature of reproductive doxae while demonstrating the difficulties of challenging ideologies on a broad scale without a group first building a collective ethos or reputation in smaller communities.

One of the ways childfree women unsettle articulations around the identity of mother is by assuming a possible alternative identity for adult women: aunt. Not all childfree women assume this role, but many have taken on an identity as an aunt to some people around them, sometimes children but sometimes adults. The function of rhetorics surrounding aunts has not been extensively studied by rhetorical scholars. Historically, unwed women often engaged in "social mothering," or the work of caring for family members or those in need outside the family (Lisle 1996, 72). This work received great recognition before the mid-nineteenth century; aunts were viewed as able to avoid the problems mothers sometimes suffered from—such as "maternal overidentification and overindulgence," not to mention the possibility of their death—while bringing other strengths to bear upon childrearing, such as energy and affection (73). The title *aunt* has also been used since the eighteenth century as a sign of respect, regardless of a blood connection. Pollet and Dunbar's (2008) analysis of data from 1910 shows that "childless couples [were] much more likely [than couples with children] to have a niece or nephew present" (764) in their household, extending the economic stability they had to the children around them.

More contemporarily, the aunt identity can shift depending on how different communities identify and take up the role of aunt. This type of role has perhaps been most centered in Black communities through the identity of the othermother. Collins (2006) defines othermothers specifically in relation to Black communities as Black women who contribute to "Black women's community work" (206), regardless of whether or not they are biological mothers. Othermothers informally adopt or care for children in the community and can strengthen bonds between biological parents and their children. The network of grandmothers, mothers, and othermothers provides a support system to members of Black communities who do not have systemic support and whom institutions and social structures often threaten, making othermothering a political act against oppression. Other scholars of color such as Cecilia Caballero, Yvette Martínez-Vu, Judith Pérez-Torres, Michele Téllez, and Christine Vega (2019) in *The Chicana Motherwork Anthology* have also taken up this term and Collins's idea of "motherwork" to recognize "Chicana M(other)work as being inclusive to Women of Color (trans and cis), nonbinary Parents of Color, other-mothers, and allies because mothering is not confined to biology or normative family structures" (5). Chapters in their collection explore the connections between m(other)work and political action that intervene in heteropatriarchy, racism, and classism. The term *othermother* thus denotes women's political acts of caring for those around them who typically are not cared for, most notably those in BIPOC communities who have been denied the protections white people socioculturally experience. This type of care work is very different from some of the care work women in more privileged social positions, particularly white women, perform as aunts. Such work is typically less politicized and, instead, revolves around providing for the needs of the children or adults they are mentoring, including material, financial, and emotional needs. Childfree women who take on aunt roles are thus situated somewhat differently depending on their own identities, as well as the communities and sociohistorical contexts in which they perform this care work.

This chapter does not explicitly focus on the differences in the types of aunt roles childfree women assume, although readers should be able to identify some of those in my analysis. Instead, I examine how childfree women discursively articulate the aunt role to speak back to the happiness scripts around them that insist they should be mothers and minimize any other caring work they perform. Farrell (1993) claims that while rhetoric alone may not be enough to disrupt doxae, it does hold "the potential and the promise of using these same ordinary conventions to forge a meaningful reflective consciousness in civic life" (258). Similar to Ahmed's claims, this "reflective consciousness" allows doxae to come to light and be questioned. For childfree women, the aunt identity, while built around an articulation of care typically tied to motherhood, brings to the surface questions about why particular women are expected to be mothers and what other roles might actually support their own and others' lives. For some, it also highlights the problems with presuming that women assume any roles that involve care for others, including the aunt role.

Despite this plethora of strategies and interventions, doxae can still be extremely difficult to undermine, make visible, and contest. Rhetorical scholars must investigate further how different types of doxae operate and how individuals or groups try to challenge them. This research would open up further space for understanding how doxae circulate through people's lives and what kinds of rhetorical and affectual dimensions shape responses to doxae, whether individually or collectively.

STRATEGIES TO CIRCULATE CHILDFREE RHETORICS

In their communities, the rhetorical strategies interviewees used to speak about childfreedom helped cement their childfree identities and circulate childfree rhetorics and new articulations of womanhood to others. While much of this work happened in unique ways depending on who childfree women were, whom they were talking to, what relationship they had with the person they were addressing, and what discourses were already in circulation about reproductive experiences, interviewees noted particular strategies they used in speaking about childfreedom, such as humor, deliberately explaining or not explaining their childfreedom, and directness (for further discussion of rhetorical strategies childfree women use to manage the stigma of being childfree, see Kelly [2009] and Morison et al. [2016]). While some interviewees felt questions about their childfreedom were too personal and did not want to engage with them, other interviewees made it a point to tell others they were childfree, in part because they wanted to be role models for others. Interviewees also recognized that the ways they circulated childfree rhetorics could influence how others wove happiness with childfreedom and what identities others felt empowered to assume.

Using humor could take the edge away from others perceiving childfree women as possibly judgmental. Celia explained,

> I'm never very honest about [not wanting kids]. I think I'm very rhetorical, like I think I told you my two reactions, they're kind of jokey, they're funny, they land a little softer. I'm never like "No, I don't want kids." So I take it out of the realm of want. Doing that, 'cause I think that there's something very harsh in [saying] I don't want children. Well, my context is this and we don't, you know, we're gonna be paying off his [college] loans forever. Or I'm too old, right? You know, and so then the context dictates

rather than the desire, 'cause I think there's something particularly taboo about adding that desire word.

Celia recognizes she is making deliberate and specific choices about how she presents her decision. By avoiding talking about desire, she avoids marking herself as deviant. Using humor is her way to assign blame for the decision to context rather than marking herself as too different from other women who are mothers. Gail uses a similar tactic, although she wished she could be more direct: "I don't want to be cavalier about my answer but I sometimes do, and I'll say, 'Oh, no, I have shoes and stuff. Or I have a Roomba and that's the biggest commitment I should make.' And I wish . . . I'd rather not be cavalier. . . . And I . . . part of me wants to . . . turn the tables and ask them, 'Why do you have kids?' " While using humor allows her to avoid directness and to maintain dialogue with others, Gail recognizes something is lost when she does not directly confront the happiness scripts at work when she is pressed to explain why she doesn't have children.

Deliberately choosing whether or not to engage in explanation of their childfree choice is another way childfree women strategically circulate childfreedom discourses. Nicole talked about not always engaging with strangers about being childfree and explained, "I think people just assume I have kids, and there are times where I feel like, do I feel like having this conversation or no? I just let them think what they want because, again, I don't feel like I should have to justify my decision." Not correcting others' assumptions is a way to avoid a conversation she finds unappealing. Suzanne's approach to interacting with others about childfreedom has evolved over time: "I used to feel a little bit like, I've got to explain myself, you know: 'Well, I was in graduate school and I never got around to [having kids].' But now I don't explain myself. Just like, 'Nope,' and then go on 'cause I'm like, it's not . . . I don't have to explain myself, if you don't like it, too bad, you know. . . . It's not my job to explain to you my reasons for not following your route. I'm not judging you because you do have kids, right?" Just as Suzanne recognizes many mothers do not have to explain why they have kids, she views herself as not needing to explain why she does not want to have kids.[1] Shanna has a different approach, leaving the door open for some questions but limiting how many she is willing to put up with. She said, "My philosophy with these sorts of things is, 'Be nice twice.' So I will say it nicely to you twice, and if you keep pushing, then it's a choice that that person is making that I feel empowered to say, 'You need to back off, because it's inappropriate. I don't ask you about your sex life . . . I would like for you to not ask me about mine.' I've had to say that a couple of times." Shanna is nonconfrontational until she is absolutely confident she has given the person she is speaking to the opportunity to understand she finds certain questions intrusive, at which point she becomes frank.

Other interviewees were more open to having discussions with others that involved explaining why they didn't want children. Alicia said, "If it comes up, I'm happy to have that discussion, and having learned from earlier discussions with my family how to approach it in a way that doesn't make other people feel defensive, which I think is just an interesting thing to have to do. But any time you're in a place where you're not within the social norm or average, that's something you kind of end up doing." As Alicia describes, openly discussing childfreedom can involve being strategic about the ways she approaches others. She describes herself as "happy" to have such discussions even though she recognizes the extra burden she takes on in having them. Like Alicia, Claudia views questions about her childfreedom as opportunities for her to challenge traditional views of family.

> At first, I think my decisions were to challenge sort of the perspective of what it means to be a woman, and what it means to be woman as a Christian particularly. . . . It has become a way for me to say I am able to serve people, or to have the freedom to serve people around me, in a way that people with children aren't able to. And it's a way for us to help people maybe rethink what a family means, and to have a broader perspective, almost like a symbol of not always thinking that a family looks in a particular way.

Claudia is a leader in her church, and she sees her childfreedom as an opportunity to shape how people think about not just her but about what families are. While she doesn't describe this opportunity as a burden, clearly she is taking on a role that would not be thrust upon her if she were not childfree.

Directness was the strategy most often mentioned by interviewees in talking about how they interact with others about their decision. Some mentioned being strategically blunt and direct in order to ward off questions or conversations. Tara said, "I'm very straightforward. I'm like, 'I don't have kids. I don't want them.' If that person has an issue with it, then that's their issue at that point is kind of how I look at it." This strategy does not open up childfreedom for discussion but, instead, presents it as a statement of choice that should not be contested. Other childfree women are even more purposefully blunt. For example, Elizabeth said when people, typically strangers, ask whether she has kids, she says, "Oh, God no," which generally "stops any questions. But I act like I'm offended that they would ask me that." Shutting down questions asserts her right to make her own reproductive decisions without judgment. Elizabeth also mentioned a childfree friend of hers who tries to find "the most outrageous thing" to say to people who push back about her not liking kids: "Her line is, 'I think kids should be used as speed bumps.' She's like, 'And I have to say that to get people off my back.' Cause then they get offended, right?" Similarly, Alicia described childfree friends whose attitudes are intentionally off-putting: "Kids are the worst. I hate them, I don't want anything to do with them." She recognized this as a specific rhetorical tactic rather than necessarily the true attitude her friends have about children: "I know another friend who tends to have that reaction . . . has developed that reaction specifically because she has a family that says, 'But kids are the best.' And so that knee-jerk [answer] is a way of saying, 'No, I disagree with your basic premise.'" Although this rhetorical strategy can be off-putting to others, these childfree women recognize a deliberately abrasive approach can keep them from having to answer questions or explain themselves, which they view as inappropriately invasive. In fact, Devori promoted a direct approach as a way to avoid a lot of pressure from others: "Just own it and just say 'No, I'm not going to have children, I'm not interested' because the more you hem and haw and the more you kind of try to save other people's feelings, or make yourself look like you haven't made the decision you've made, it's going to lead to that pressing, so I feel that because it almost just takes them aback, it knocks them off their feet for a second that a woman is just like 'No.'" Rather than trying to help other people feel better or sugarcoating the decision not to have children, she views directness as a way for childfree women to protect themselves from unnecessary questioning and explaining of their choice and as a way to reinforce their choice-making abilities as women.

Directness could also be a strategy for simply being unapologetic for not having children. Katherine talked about being direct and wanting other childfree women to neither feel as if they must answer for their decision nor hide it. This approach means they must reconcile themselves to potentially disappointing others, which she recognized women are taught not to do: "I feel like the older I get, [the less] I care about what other people think about certain things. . . . And so I just feel like women need to be way more selfish. . . . Listen, the people will get over it. . . . Still people not gonna like it and that's okay. And I think women have to be okay with that, but women are taught to be nice and be liked.

Don't say that because the person, they're not gonna like . . . and well, that's okay." Katherine perceived part of getting over the impulse to be nice and sugarcoat the choice to be childfree as a decision to "stop making excuses about why [women] don't want kids, you know, and 'no' is an answer, is a complete answer. Or 'I don't want them.' End of sentence, bam." Katherine's comments suggest that, like Elizabeth, she was largely referring to strangers who ask about her childfreedom because she said most people accept her "complete answer"; they don't really care why she doesn't have children because she doesn't know them. Similarly, Tasha said "most people are just kind of like, 'Oh, okay.'" Even if there was a "debate," she felt as if people would not keep pushing her after she made her childfree stance clear. She said, however, that she has learned "how to present [her] opinion in a way that refused before they can even say any of those things." Directness as a rhetorical strategy is intended to reinforce the validity of childfreedom and articulate different ways of thinking about women's lives while sometimes pointing to the ways other people's rhetoric can subtly or explicitly rest upon hegemonic mothering ideologies.

Validating childfreedom as a choice women can make was an important part of interviewees' thinking about how they themselves had assumed identities as childfree women and how they could serve as role models for others considering whether or not to have children. Several interviewees mentioned having childless or childfree role models in their lives that showed them the types of lives women could lead apart from motherhood. These ranged from Nicole's aunt to Silvia's graduate school professor to Tasha's older friends at church to Meghan's coworker. Tapping into more public declarations of childfreedom, Devori described podcast interviews with celebrity childfree women who "took ownership of the decision" as "revelatory" to her. She had actually contacted actress and comedian Wendi McLendon-Covey on Twitter after hearing such an interview with her to tell her it was the first time she "had ever heard a woman say that." She reported that McLendon-Covey answered, "That's fine, you do you." Having these role models demonstrated to interviewees the different happiness scripts they could follow beyond motherhood.

Some interviewees also recognized they could be models of alternative happiness scripts for others. Suzanne talked about how "there are other models of adulthood for women [besides motherhood], and I think that we don't see a lot of those models, you know, or either they're framed as the weird aunt who never got married, you know, that trope and like television shows and stuff like that. But I think there are lots of alternative models of adulthood . . . that can lead to a happy, fulfilling life." Interviewees' embodiment of these alternative happiness scripts was one way they demonstrated to others articulations of womanhood outside reproductive norms. Elizabeth was open with her college students about being childfree for this reason: "I tell my students I don't like children." She said that she had no role models for childfreedom when she was a child: "If [I] could be that one person in [her students'] lives who says, 'I don't like kids, I don't have them, and I'm happy,' I will be that person." A friend of Silvia's commended her for playing that role, telling her, "I think it's so cool my daughter has an example of you to grow up to."

Through these affectual, rhetorical, and embodied means, childfree women circulated alternative happiness scripts that undermined reproductive ideologies and created space for others to question these scripts and potentially reweave different models of adulthood. Such strategies help childfree women present their decision not to have children in a variety of deliberate ways depending on who they are talking to, whether or not they want to engage in a discussion, and how they want to position themselves. While these strategies can work in different ways in different contexts, they demonstrate a variety of ways through which reproductive doxae can be resisted and through which a myriad of reproductive experiences can be modelled for others.

CIRCULATING CHILDFREEDOM IN SUPPORTIVE COMMUNITIES

Supportive communities often revolve around positive interactions about childfreedom that seem, in part, to rewrite or simply ignore reproductive doxae. How easily these communities can be constructed depends on many factors, including someone's race/ethnicity, religion, age, geographical location, sexual orientation, and so on (Collins 2006; Martinez and Andreatta 2015; Mezey 2008; Morgan 2018; Rich et al. 2011), and childfree women can have vastly different experiences of support because of these factors. In general, however, my interviewees all found some forms of support that allowed them to weave meaningful identities for themselves that were supported in their interactions with others. This section analyzes the support the interviewees had in interactions with career, family of origin, partner relationships, and social communities. In contrast with my analysis of unsupportive interactions in the previous chapter, this section demonstrates the different ways childfree women are affectually and rhetorically supported in challenging reproductive doxae and articulating new happiness scripts.

Support in Career

Several interviewees mentioned their professional contexts influencing their colleagues' reactions to their not having children. A few specifically mentioned academic workplaces as particularly accepting of their decision to be childfree.[2] Rachel said that not having children is "not really an item" because people in academia make many types of choices. Devori echoed this, pointing out that mothers in academia "aren't only defined by being a mother," which affects how they perceive the childfree choice. Alicia also noted the childfree choice is not particularly unusual in an academic setting; "The friend group I'm around now is a lot of academics and a lot of professionals, including a lot of professional women. And so within that, it's a comfortable fit to be married but choose not to have kids. That's fairly common." Jeanette, who works as staff in higher education, said her workplace is a "very nurturing environment" with "very open acceptance of the varieties of lifestyles that people have here." These experiences echo my own, largely supportive, experiences in academia.

Other workplace environments similarly seemed open to childfreedom. Traci, who works in media, said, "Most people are really, really supportive. Because they know that if you're in this type of line of work, your schedule is not necessarily nine to five, Monday through Friday. . . . And I do have friends that are in this business, that are performers as well, who've had kids. But they're perpetually exhausted, you know, whatever. And so they get it. . . . I can't remember the last time I got serious negativity from a friend about it. It's been many years." Grace mentioned that many people she worked with as a journalist did not have kids and that colleagues asked if people had kids to "see will you be flexible timewise." Sarah said a new coworker of hers mentioned she wasn't going to have children, and "it was a nice little bonding thing that we had a little moment." Colleagues in these workplace contexts understand the sociocultural and material pressures operating on everyone, and they tend to be supportive and accepting of childfree women weaving new patterns for their lives that fit with their expectations of those who work in those fields.

Beyond acceptance, some women said there was simply never conversation about their childfreedom. Tara said that it didn't come up, Brittany that "the topic was never really breached [at work]." Gail said she didn't know what her colleagues thought about her childfreedom, adding, "and [she] never really think[s] about it." This lack of interaction may indicate these women work in contexts where colleagues do not typically share personal information with each other. Sandra mentioned a discussion with a colleague who has a young child during a social interaction outside work. The colleague asked Sandra whether she had children, whether Sandra's partner knew she didn't ever want them, and what that conversation had been like. Sandra saw this not as a judgmental moment but a "tell-me-more moment." She seemed to welcome the questions as an invitation to share her experience. Alicia had a similar experience when a new colleague, who was a mother, asked whether she had kids and Alicia said no; she described "a really interesting and positive conversation" about why she didn't have kids and her colleague's expression that the question of having children had seemed like a choice for her, too. These types of exchanges can help childfree women feel their reproductive choices are reasonable and worth consideration, even if their decision isn't being explicitly affirmed.

Both Elizabeth and Suzanne had more mixed experiences. Elizabeth said her colleagues understand her choice "for the most part" and "nobody hassles [her] about not having kids." Suzanne also said that most of her colleagues were generally supportive but that some told her it wasn't too late to have kids and she could still do it. However, she did not take offense: "It didn't make me feel like they were judging me. I think that they were just trying to be encouraging like . . . it's, you know, it's still possible to have children in your mid- to late thirties when I was in my mid- to late thirties. No one says anything to me about it now [that she is in her forties]. They've given up."

In terms of workplace environment, interviewees were conscious that childfreedom is less an issue for their male colleagues. As Shanna said, whether or not someone has children is "an identity feature for the women" but not for the men. Sandra commented that because she works in a field where men dominate and she exudes a "formal professionalism" at work, she doesn't have many conversations about reproductive choices. Devori and Celia had discussions about reproductive choices with their male colleagues, although these conversations were not necessarily positive or negative and seemed, instead, to come from a place of interest. Mary told a story about a male colleague who still tells the story about how she answered his question as to whether she had children by saying, "I think marriage is a patriarchal institution designed to oppress women." The story has become a part of Mary's reputation as a feminist in her workplace.

Interactions with colleagues around their reproductive decisions can help childfree women feel more supported but can also make them frustrated with the sometimes-sexist assumptions being made about them and other women in the workplace. Many found, though, that their childfree status either wasn't important or was supported by their colleagues, opening space for childfreedom in their workplaces and further normalizing this choice. It may be childfree women have more space not to be care oriented in their workplaces than elsewhere, even though many choose care-oriented professions, as discussed in the previous chapter. More cynically, some childfree women may also find their workplaces less hostile because employers assume they are better able to mimic the habits of ideal workers than are mothers, of whom employers can question availability, commitment, and so forth regardless of their actual work performance.[3]

Support in Family of Origin

While some interviewees had negative interactions with their families of origin about not having children, including interactions that led to ostracization from family members, others experienced levels of support that reinforced their identities as childfree women. Despite the tension between mothers and daughters about reproductive experiences discussed in the last chapter, several interviewees indicated their mothers eventually supported or at least did not question their childfree decision. Jessica described her mother working through the childfree decision in this manner:

> And then, when I probably got into my thirties, I was overseas, and then I came home, I remember my mom saying, "Do you think you're" . . . I remember her really thinking [carefully about] asking this question, "Do you think you're going to have kids?" And I'm like, "I don't think so," and she's like, "Oh, okay." And then, she was very sweet about it. . . . I don't think she was disappointed, like, judgmental disappointed, I think more like, she might secretly cry because I was not like her, and we couldn't bond that way. But she was just very kind of like, "Oh, okay."

Jessica recognizes her mother seems more sad that she can't share the experience of being a mother with her daughter than judgmental of the decision itself. Other interviewees' mothers similarly over time reconciled themselves to their daughters' decisions, even if they did not completely agree with them. Elizabeth talked about how her mother likely doesn't like "the idea that [she's] deciding" but has never pressured her, and Sandra said her mother has "been okay with it" and has never had a judgmental conversation with her. Although perhaps not strongly endorsing their daughters' decisions, these mothers have not imposed gendered happiness scripts on their daughters.

Others mothers more openly supported their daughters not having children. Tasha experienced a high level of support from her mother, as well as her grandmother. She described her grandmother's attitude as "You don't have to do that, girl. Live your best life." She described both her mother and grandmother as accepting: "[They are] super supportive of whatever I wanna do." She said she knew other women had been "ostracized" or "excommunicated" from their families because of being childfree, but she felt it is "not a big deal if you decide not to have kids" in her family. Tasha's mother and grandmother created an environment in which she could flourish as a childfree woman and not question her decision.

In other cases, negative experiences of conforming to happiness scripts played a role in interviewees' mothers' reactions to their reproductive lives. Shanna's mother had three children and five miscarriages, and she feels that's part of the reason her mother's attitude is that "it's every woman's decision whether or not she wants it, and some people don't wanna be moms." Similarly, Christina's mother, who had three children in three years, has acknowledged she "wouldn't have had children" if she had been "given the choice."

Other interviewees' mothers recognize that even though they enjoyed mothering, it does not mean their daughters must become mothers. Bonnie described her mother in this way: "My biological mother also has been incredibly supportive of my decision, and even though she says that her children were the best thing she's ever done in this world, she's never thought that I wasn't doing, you know, I'm not kind or nurturing or a woman if I don't have kids." Bonnie's mother doesn't articulate motherhood with womanhood, kindness, or nurturing as happiness scripts typically do.

In general, fathers were less invested in their daughter's reproductive decisions, which made for less resistance from them. Tara said, "[My] father just doesn't care about anything. So he's never asked me about it. I don't even think he notices that we don't have children." Similarly, Dianna said, "My dad, so there is nothing to be discussed with him. He does not bat an eyelid at anything I throw at him, to be honest. He just says, 'Yes, okay.' And if I turned around to him tomorrow, and said to him, 'Actually I've changed my mind, I do want to have a child, will you support me in this?,' he would just go, 'Yeah, okay.'" This acceptance is in stark contrast to Dianna's mother, who springs tricky discussions about Dianna's childfreedom on her, as discussed in the previous chapter. Nicole's father brought up her childfreedom when she was in her twenties and explained why he was not surprised by it: "Yeah, I know you, I know you're not having kids. . . . You've got a lot of responsibilities as the oldest girl, and then you saw our situation [he and Nicole's mother divorced]." Much like Shanna's and Christina's mothers, he related his own difficulties as a parent to his daughter's decision not to be a parent.

Alicia felt supported by her father in her childfreedom and described "an expectation, particularly from [her] dad, that wanted to be, 'No, get, you know, get degrees, have a job, be professional, be self-sufficient,'" even though her family loved children. Suzanne described only support. She feels very close to her father and specifically supported in her life choices, much as Tasha feels about her mother and grandmother. She said, "My dad was always very supportive of me, and I felt like because of him [and] my brother, I could do anything I wanted to, so as far as making me feel like I had to be a mom or I had to do certain things, my dad and my brother never made [me] feel that way." Suzanne's older brother asked her about whether she wanted children and expressed disappointment that she did not because she would "be such a good mom," but it was clear Suzanne doesn't feel judgment from him about her decision. However, she talked about how her brother supported her playing sports and also going to college, helping her register for classes and even taking two college classes with her. She said, "My brother's super proud of me. He's like, 'Yeah, my sister's a doctor [meaning a PhD], you know.'" It was more typical for interviewees to say their siblings didn't care about whether or not they had children, even as some experienced more judgment from sisters about being childfree, as the previous chapter discusses. Other sisters, though, did not seem to care about the interviewees' reproductive experiences. For example, Dianna said her sister is "pretty laid back" and that they'd never had "a very detailed conversation" about her childfreedom.

Christie described her brother as supportive. Like Shanna's mother, Christina's mother, and Nicole's father, he acknowledged the difficulties of having children. She said, "When I say to him, 'I'm not, you know, I'm never having kids,' he would say, 'Good, because they take up all your time, they take up all your money.' And he says this while they're sitting in the other room. I know, it's awful. I'm like, 'Shut up! You're terrible, you're terrible!' And then he says things like, 'I'm going to write a book.' It's so ridiculous. He's like, 'I'm going to write a book about why you should never have children.'" While Christie is uncomfortable about her brother complaining about the difficulties of having children in front of his own children, she does feel supported in her choice.

In some cases, extended family offered familial support for interviewees' decisions. Jeanette explained that no one in her family had ever questioned her decision: "It was such a natural part of me and nobody really questioned." Celia said, "There hasn't been a lot of engagement with [my childfreedom], and I'm sure that I'm probably unique in, perhaps unique in that, and I'm grateful for [my family]." Similarly, Rachel, Katherine, and Christie said their families did not pressure them and left them to make their own choices. Bonnie said her family seemed to acknowledge reproduction is a personal experience; when people in her family ask her when she will get married and have a baby and she tells them she's not interested, "they back up their line of inquiry and just kind of, they're like, 'Oh yeah, we understand, that's fine, it's personal choice.' "

A few interviewees mentioned that their extended family members slowly normalized the idea that they were childfree, becoming if not supportive then at least silent on the issue. Brittany described her family as having given up on her having children, and Silvia said it had "becom[e] clearer" to her family she wouldn't have children as she approached forty. Tara said her family had acclimated to the fact that she was childfree: "I think it's just like time is making it where it's more normal." Kari said she thinks her family assumes she doesn't have children because of fertility issues and that they therefore don't ask her about it. Devori described "some initial disappointment" among her extended family when she first made it clear she and her husband were not going to have children but said, "Because we don't seem unhappy or unfulfilled in any other aspect of our life, I think that they've come to accept this is just our normal." This normalizing of their childfreedom illustrates an at least partial reweaving of identities and the ability of family members to articulate different versions of womanhood than those represented in happiness scripts.

Although some interviewees did have negative experiences with family members, as discussed in the previous chapter, generally the childfree women I interviewed did not experience challenges from them, with many adopting a stance of openness and support about reproductive choices that allow for the construction of women's happiness scripts apart from motherhood. The long-term relationships interviewees had with their families meant they by and large had roles in their communities besides mother their families respected and accepted.

Support in Partner Relationships

A variety of affectual and rhetorical strategies influence relationships childfree women form with partners, and these interactions influence how childfree women formulate and position their identities as childfree. All but two of my interviewees are heterosexual women, and all my interviewees had been or were in relationships with men, but their relationship status varied considerably: nine were single (two identifying as single by choice), fifteen married, four in long-term partnerships, two divorced, three divorced and remarried, and one widowed. Scholars have frequently noted that some childfree women do not have children because they value maintaining their relationships with their partners more than having children and disrupting these relationships (Basten 2009; Chancey and Dumais 2009; Kemkes-Grottenthaler 2003). The second most frequently appearing motivation in Houseknecht's (1987) review for individuals choosing not to have children was the desire for a "more satisfactory marital relationship," which was reported in 62 percent of the studies (377) and is corroborated by Jean E. Veevers's earlier (1980) study. On the other hand, compulsory heterosexuality perpetuates the belief that married heterosexual couples exist in order to have children. Indeed, as Dykstra and Hagestad (2007) note, "Parenthood has often been construed as the meaning and purpose of being married" (1298–99). In part because of these expectations, negotiating childfreedom in romantic relationships can be difficult, especially if both partners are not completely open about whether or not they want to have children. I did not ask about the interviewees' interactions with partners[4] (something Sandra said she appreciated because my study's "focus is on the woman and not the woman and her partner"), but around half my interviewees talked about their previous or current partners' feelings about children and how these played a role in their relationships with each other. These women negotiated the decision not to have children differently with their partners, depending on how strongly they themselves initially felt about this decision. Especially when interacting with men in dating situations, they sometimes found themselves having to defend their desire to be childfree in terms of the gendered happiness scripts they rejected, even as these interactions reinforced their identities as childfree women.

A couple of the interviewees were able to interact regularly with children through their partners, which they appreciated. Author Henriette Mantel (2013b) describes how her feelings after a breakup with the father of a child she had come to love made her realize how she felt about children: "[I] would rather stick needles in my eyes than ever inflict emotional pain on a child. And most of all, I confirmed once again it's hard to beat the joy I feel when a kid is laughing. But do I *want* or *need* that kid laughing to come out of my own loins? Absolutely not. If there's one thing I learned from Hillary Clinton, it's that I'm part of the village, but I sure don't need to make my own tent full" (12). Such strong identification with children as Mantel expresses is not something people often expect from childfree women, but it is not uncommon. For example, Jessica had married someone who already had two children, and she said she was glad she could "be around kids" without having her own. These moves fit with discourses surrounding women's happiness scripts while deviating from them in the origins of the children they care for.

It seemed others might have preferred not to be stepmothers.[5] They struggled to negotiate their identities as childfree women with the expectations placed on any mothers, including stepmothers. Sarah said she was glad she still had a relationship with her former stepchild but that she was glad she didn't have to be a stepmother anymore. Jeanette had also struggled to establish relationships with her stepchildren as a childfree woman; now widowed, she had been with her husband for twenty-four years, from the time his children were eight and fourteen. Jeanette said she does not have a strong relationship with her stepdaughter and that even with her stepson, she "never, ever played mom. . . . never tried to compete with his parents." Juggling their identities as childfree women with being stepmothers could be difficult for childfree women to navigate, given their own conceptions of themselves apart from motherhood.

For many interviewees, childfreedom had been determinative in their selection of partners. Traci, for example, said that when her current husband told her he never wanted children, she thought, " 'Hello, perfect person.' So I told him then, that I said, 'I've always felt that way. This is amazing.' " Traci's first husband acknowledged when they divorced that he had "always hoped" she would change her mind and want children, demonstrating how reproductive experiences can affectually circulate through relationships with partners even if not explicitly discussed. Similar to Traci's experience with her current husband, Elizabeth said she mentioned to her partner that she hated kids and he said, " 'Oh, good, 'cause [if you wanted to have children] that's a deal breaker.' Okay, thank God, all right, we're on the same track. This is good." Jessica had lost two long-term relationships with partners "because they wanted to have kids and I didn't. And I realized then, oh, this isn't just about finding out what you want, for some people, this is, I've learned, this is not negotiable, this is a deal breaker for some people."

Other interviewees navigated childfreedom with their partners and clarified their own desires through communication with their partners. Tara recalled it was her husband who said, around the time they got married, " 'Hey, we don't have to have kids.' And I was like, 'What? What are you saying?' And I started to, you know, give it some thought and I was like, 'You know, I feel like I don't want to have kids.' . . . And it pretty much solidified, like it slammed the door shut on the idea." Tara's husband opened up motherhood as a choice she could make rather than a script she had to follow. Similarly, Celia said that until she met her husband, she felt she might have children if she "met the right person": "I was still under that impression that maybe something would snap in me hormonally and then you want kids." It materialized that the person she thought was right for her did not want children, and this inclination was not a point of contention, although she had been open to having children.

Childfreedom inevitably affected dating as well. Grace said she felt "interrogat[ed]" by some potential partners who seemed to wonder whether she was "secretly crazy" or "defective somehow" because she didn't want kids: "It was almost like I lacked something that was ground-ing me." She said men she dated seemed to presume children would "bind" a woman to them. Similarly, Jeanette said men she dated engaged in "a simplification that there's something wrong with you" if you don't want children. She recalled a man who felt she should want children: "[He] tried to persuade me he was going to change my mind and I was going to want to have eight kids and he was going to want me to become Catholic." Nicole had also dated men who tried "to convince [her]" that having children would be doable and that they would "help out" with children, which she interpreted as demonstrating they were not interested in being equal parents. Christina said the most "hostile responses" she had received from anyone about being childfree were from men she had dated, including men who had told her, "You're denying your purpose on earth." These confrontational interactions reinforced the marginalization of childfree women and the pathologi-zation of their not having children, but it also clarified these women's childfree identities to themselves.

Other interviewees talked about how they had learned to be upfront about childfreedom with dating partners to avoid wasting time and energy if they were not compatible. As Cassie said, "It saves me so much time . . . if dudes know that they want to be a dad or think that maybe they want to be a dad, they're probably not the dude for me." She said it was "a little awkward to try and bring up the big stuff" early in a relation-ship, but she would do it to try to save everyone's time and feelings. One date asked her why she felt she didn't want children, arguing that "every human has, you know, capabilities to do that." In this instance, Cassie's personal desires not to have children came up against reproductive doxae. Sandra said that opening the discussion had become easier with time, and that she brought it up early on with potential partners. As she said, "It used to be . . . it was just a, you know, don't talk about it, but now it's like, excuse me, I have to let you know something." Interviewees said making such disclosures early on protected them from negative interactions that made them feel abnormal.

Childfree women's romantic relationships, as seen here, can form an integral part of their negotiations of their childfree identities. Sometimes, childfree women must stand up for their decision and be willing to use it as a yardstick by which to measure compatibility with a potential partner. Other times, their childfree identities are formed in part through their affectual and discursive negotiations with romantic partners. These moments allow them to confront and even challenge hegemonic reproductive beliefs, further strengthening their identification as childfree and clarifying their values around childfreedom.

Support in Social Relationships

Friends are an integral part of childfree women's supportive social networks. All but two of my interviewees mentioned having supportive friends in their social communities. Not all these supportive friends were themselves childfree. Supportive interactions with friends who have children validated the decision to be childfree and helped these childfree women determine how to express their childfreedom to others while validating other reproductive decisions. Cassie talked about having gone through cycles with her friends in which unsupportive friends "dropped off" until she had "a good structure around [her] that is mostly positive." By and large these childfree women saw their social relationships as a central way they could find affirmation of their choices and speak back to happiness scripts by reweaving new patterns for themselves, patterns that were supported by others.

Some interviewees observed that logistically having childfree friends sometimes was just easier than having parent friends. Mary said that when she was younger, childfree friends "are more available" and "are similar [to her] that way." Irene said she and her childfree friends have discussed their ability "to hang out so much" because they aren't "busy with kids." A few interviewees specifically mentioned looking for friends who are childfree because they can be particularly supportive and commiserate about life as a childfree woman. Leigh explained, "I think with my childfree friends, we talk a lot about [being childfree] in part because there's so much time that we spend talking with other people who don't get it. It's really nice to be able to have that kind of thing, so that's how it tends to go with those folks." Claudia said, "I remember talking to people who also have had . . . who also don't have kids. A few of the conversations that I have is where other women feel pushed or judged or whatever and we discussed sort of, what do you do when people ask you impertinent questions? And how do you respond? Or how do you, you know, why do you feel the need to feel justified in your decision making?" Strategizing together about how to communicate with others about being childfree can be an integral part of having child-free friends that helps childfree women think about how to rhetorically position childfreedom to others. Elizabeth also talked about having a good friend who is a childfree high-school teacher: "She said, 'You're my only friend without kids. And you're the only one who gets it.' 'Cause all of her friends are also teachers and they all have kids, and she's like, 'It's so hard because it's all they want to talk about. And that's all they want to do, and you're my only friend who I feel like I can just sort of talk about random things with, right?' She feels like she's bothering her friends with kids." The communication possible with childfree friends can make these relationships affirming of childfree women's reproductive decisions.

Alternatively, some interviewees said changes in the lives of women with children could free them up to become available for friendship. Bonnie said that in addition to many childfree friends, she has many older friends who had children later in life. Gail noted that as she has grown older and her friends have gotten divorced and/or become empty nesters, it has been like having an "entire new group of friends." She sees this change as part of friendship cycles that naturally happens as life events occur. Christina described a group of friends in which she is the only one without kids. She said, "We'll get together and their kids are, at this point, teenagers. And I get to be . . . I get to play that quote-unquote role of the cool aunt, and their teenagers generally come to me [with their problems] and, you know. So, [my friends are] real careful not to ruin [that connection] because if something really goes on, I'm the one who knows about it. I'm the one who's usually warning them about it." A consistent statement was that relationships with mothers had to be formed on mutual respect.

Cassie said that one of her best friends "hardcore wants to be a mom," and she and her friend try to support each other's life choices. This balance can be tricky, which Cassie admitted: "It didn't detract from our friendship because we were able to separate it. And she's one of the few people that's been able to do that. That want, that is, personally wants kids herself but doesn't take it out on me that I don't want kids." The sociocultural pitting of mothers and childfree women against each other sometimes has effects at the individual level, and Cassie acknowledged it takes particular people and relationships to avoid this type of conflict. Similarly, Tasha said she has a group of close friends "who even though they might have their own wants and desires they don't necessarily impose it on others." This group accepts everyone, regardless of whether they have children or not: "They also understand my point of view and they also affirm my point of view as well." Such affirmation is an important part of these relationships, which readily makes space for people with many different desires. Tara described how all of her friends have been very supportive, including one of her friends who has a strong mother identity but tells her, "Tara, you know I support you. I just want you to be happy. And I know that you're happy not having kids." This level of support transcends ideas about who women should be and leaves room for many different articulations of womanhood to coexist.

The interviewees also became very aware of the rhetorical choices they made when interacting with friends who were struggling with infertility. In these instances, they and their friends had to work to make sure each was supported while acknowledging the validity of very different reproductive experiences. Sandra described joking with a friend about not wanting children until her friend started doing IVF treatments: "I really had to, kind of, be aware of what I was saying with her or saying around her because I didn't want to be insensitive. So, I would say that is a particular situation that I think was unique in between our relationship. We navigated it and she had her kid two weeks ago. Very happy for her, for sure." Sandra recognized she and her friend had to be cautious around each other and work strategically in order to be supportive of each other. Allison, Mary, and Gail also talked about having friends who were experiencing problems with infertility and finally were able to have children. They characterized these interactions as puzzling at times because they do not really understand having such a strong desire to have a child, but they also saw these periods as an opportunity for them to show support for their friends despite having different reproductive experiences. Gail helped her friend purchase sperm on the internet, and Allison is very close with her friend's daughter. Like Morell (2000), I found that childless women "recogniz[e] that children are a source of unique pleasures as well as a great deal of responsibility and work" (318). Thus the childfree women I interviewed navigated these different conceptions of women's identities together with their friends and figured out ways to support their friends, despite having very different reproductive lives. These strategic interactions and deliberations point to the complexities involved in interactions around reproduction, even between friends, as well as to the ability of these women to find ways to support each other in making different choices.

Interviewees also discussed appreciating some of their mother friends' openness about the difficulties of mothering. Sarah talked about visiting one friend after she had a baby, and during the visit, her friend said,

> "Honestly, there are some days that I wish I didn't have kids." And I was like, "I've never heard a mom say that before." So that was a significant conversation for me. She and I aren't close friends, we're acquaintances at best, but the fact that she was honest and open enough to just be, to just admit that, "Yeah there are some days where I wish I didn't do that." It just made me feel like . . . it endeared her to me . . . at that point, I kind of felt like all moms were like, "Oh motherhood is the best thing ever," and da, da, da. And I was just like sick of it, so that was a good conversation to have.

Sarah found it refreshing that a mother could so openly talk about not always wanting to be a mother, particularly given the expectation that good mothers do not talk about how difficult mothering can be. Silvia had a similar experience with a couple of friends who implied "they weren't totally sure if they would do motherhood again if that was an option, and obviously they love their kids and blah, blah, blah, blah. But just like it was harder than they thought, it wasn't . . . it changed their lives in ways they didn't really know it would, and so those people have kind of almost been like, 'Good, stay that way.'" Nicole has had friends who were parents and responded to her saying she was childfree by saying, "Well, don't [have kids]." Like Christie's brother, they said this teasingly but also as an acknowledgment of the hardships that come with having children. Other childfree women's friends, like Elizabeth's, are less openly questioning of her decisions but completely supportive of the decision not to have children. As Shanna noted, sometimes it is mothers rather than childfree friends who can be particularly supportive: "And it's not always your childfree friends who will be there for you, some . . . because they might not be able to empathize with making a choice. Often it will be your mom friends who will be like, 'Ooh yeah, kids are tough. I can totally understand why.'" The levels of support and open questioning found in these friends validated interviewees' choices and made them feel as if their identities are valued rather than seen as deviant.

In workplaces, families of origin, romantic partnerships, and social relationships, interviewees had some dialogue that supported their identities and formed connections that helped them feel as if their childfree decision was not just acceptable but, sometimes, supported. These exchanges helped normalize their experiences, giving them power to repurpose old rhetorical threads and create new ones as they weave new patterns for themselves. Even though these women also experienced negative interactions, often characterized by a lack of dialogue or empathy, they were able to integrate these experiences into a cohesive vision of themselves as women that helped them undermine reproductive doxae and create new happiness scripts. This work played a role in their identity construction and cemented their work against gendered happiness scripts by using old and new threads to weave new patterns for their lives.

NEW ARTICULATIONS OF WOMANHOOD IN THE AUNT IDENTITY

One of the most recognizable ways childfree women—and other women—articulate different happiness scripts is through identification as an "aunt." While childfree women embrace many of the caregiving roles discussed in the previous chapter, aunt, whether through literal or fictive kin ties, may be the most common. Indeed, Gayle Letherby (1999) found childless women often spoke about their contact with nieces and nephews, godchildren, and friends' children. Childfree women often entangle themselves in the lives of other people's children. This involvement with children expands how we think about bringing up children, making visible the many needs children have and how many people are needed to support them apart from parents. As Mantel (2013a) writes in her introduction to a collection of narratives by childfree women, "Hillary Clinton taught us 'It Takes a Village' to raise the kids of the world" (xiv). She notes that the women in her collection by and large "are extremely proud of their relationships with their nieces, nephews, godchildren, neighbors' kids, students, etc." (xiii).

While most childfree women are not involved with children to the degree mothers are, their labor may be vital to the well-being of young people. Comedian and writer Andrea Carla Michaels (2013) describes serving as a surrogate mother to the "twenty-somethings" in the apartment building where she lives, collecting packages, providing spare keys if needed, and lending out needed items.[6] The aunt identity builds on articulations of care and womanhood, as discussed in the previous chapter, while also weaving a recognizable role—aunt—that solidifies these women's relationships with children apart from motherhood. While this role maintains the ties between care and womanhood, which can make it even more difficult for women who don't like children to say so, it represents a new happiness script that has historically been recognized and has gained more visibility and support contemporarily.

Historically, unwed women often engaged in "social mothering," or the work of caring for family members or those in need outside of family (Lisle 1996, 72). The title aunt has been used since the eighteenth century as a sign of respect, regardless of a blood connection. In a critique of the aunt role that the website *Savvy Auntie* says applies to any women without their own children who are involved in other children's lives, Hayden (2011) points out that the aunt identity can be one way to pull all women into neoliberal constructions of hegemonic motherhood, regardless of whether or not they have their own children. *Savvy Auntie* does have a particularly capitalist slant in that it constructs childless women as consumers who buy products and services for other people's children and includes a gift guide for children broken down by age, category, "auntie's personality," favorite brands, and/or color. Therefore, it does fall into this trap, but childfree women who adopt the aunt or othermother roles in their communities can gain recognition and acceptance through these roles without necessarily conforming to hegemonic mothering practices. Some even explicitly reject the idea that they will participate in consumer models of quasi-motherhood *Savvy Auntie* promotes. Their definitions of being aunts are much broader and capacious, leaving room for the many types of support they provide to the children in their lives apart from simply the financial (although that is part of this support for some).

Many interviewees mentioned liking or loving children in some way, whether in their personal or professional lives. Rachel said she readily serves as caretaker for other people's children when needed: "I like kids. I'm happy to be somebody's go-to local aunt. Had someone drop off their kid for several hours over the weekend, that was fine." Christie tempered her affection for children by focusing on her friends' children: "I have lots of friends who do have kids and I love their kids . . . I don't necessarily love kids, but I love their kids, but I wouldn't wanna keep 'em for more than a few hours." In a similar vein, Sandra expressed deep feeling in particular for the children she tutors at her job—"I love the children that I work with. I think they're amazing"—while also expressing that generally children "are not [her] thing." She demonstrates there are many ways and many contexts in which someone can express love for children. Meghan talked about how her friends seemed to sometimes question her feelings for children, perhaps not understanding why a woman who enjoys children would not have children of their own: "I do feel like my friends with kids, you know. . . . It's funny to me because I'm of course like, 'I work with children, I love children, bring them all to me, I want to squeeze them and hold them and watch them grow up!' And I think that they don't necessarily, maybe they think that's not genuine. But I feel like, I have to say that I feel like there's a little . . . there gets to be a little bit of a barrier." In these types of cases, childfree women can feel as if their interactions with children are scrutinized and judged, circulating affect about their relationships with children. Others often assume childfree women do not like children because, as a default, any woman who likes children is assumed to want to be a mother. Thus it can be difficult for some childfree women to demonstrate or state their love for children without others questioning the genuineness of these feelings. Such tensions demonstrate the types of articulations made between care for children and motherhood and how women can struggle to create new articulations between care for children and other women's roles.

Participants saw the aunt role as allowing for a rearticulation of care and womanhood apart from motherhood. As mentioned in chapter 2, childfree women can find power in this role because it taps into the rhetorical threads associated with motherhood and allows them to claim they are women who care for children. Silvia recognized the rhetorical power of claiming to be an aunt or having an aunt role: "I've claimed kind of like being an aunt. . . . And it gives me this kind of like, it's . . . I feel like that has kind of given this easy way to talk about it with people . . . so I guess that's both actually true and it's been easy for me to think about it, but it's actually also, I guess, like a rhetorical easy thing to say, too, like it's a speech that you can pull out and people kind of seem to understand that versus no thanks." The aunt role, then, is one that not only many childfree women enjoy but also one that has rhetorical power when they interact with others about their decision not to have children. It circulates new articulations of women's identities, contesting happiness scripts through the construction of a caring identity for women that does not revolve around motherhood even as it taps into some of the rhetorical threads of motherhood that can limit how women's roles are seen.

Several interviewees talked about the aunt role they assumed with their biological nieces and nephews. Claudia mentioned having a close relationship with her brother's children and being a parental figure if anything happened to her brother and his wife, emphasizing "that mothering can have many different avenues." Sarah used the gender-neutral term "niblings" to refer to her siblings' children when she spoke about how close she was to them: "And I'm, I, although I never want to be a mom, I'm very, very, very much proud of being an auntie. That's a pretty big thing in my life, and my family is my little niblings." Suzanne also took pride in her relationship with her nieces and nephews: "And I love being an aunt and apparently I'm a very good aunt. They're always like, 'We love Aunt' . . . they call me [nickname] . . . 'we love Aunt [nickname]." In fact, she said that at family gatherings she felt more at ease with the children in the room than with the other adults. These women embrace the connections they have formed with their nieces and nephews, countering assumptions about childfree women always being women who hate children.

Participants also recognize the limits to their role as aunts rather than mothers. Dianna spoke about these limits: "The first time I held him [her nephew], when he was twenty-four hours old, I felt like I adored this child, but I could not wait to give him back to his mother. And I love him very much, and I probably am, in many ways, quite a maternal figure to him. I take him for the night quite often and look after him for a couple days at a time, if my sister needs a break, but I do play quite a maternal role, but it's a maternal role that has a very fixed end point." Dianna definitely prefers the limitations of her aunt role, although she loves her nephew very much. Similarly, Jessica talked about how excited she was when her sister had a baby: "I was like, oh, great, I get to be an aunt, that's perfect, because I get to have . . . I get to hang out with kids, but I don't have to have any." Part of this enjoyment of the aunt role is the flexibility aunts can still maintain when they care for children. Similarly, the comedian Bernadette Luckett (2013) explained, "So I'm the woman who will play with your kids for hours, then be perfectly happy walking away from them and back to 'my life.' That's enough. I don't need to have any of my own" (69). The choice to be childfree reflects a desire to not care for one's own children around the clock. Instead, interviewees appreciated the opportunity to interact with children in a more limited, but still fulfilling, aunt role.

A few women also identified themselves in aunt roles with friends' children or younger people at work, roles they were partially able to take on because they did not have children of their own. Celia described having close friends with kids and being closely connected with them: "I'm Aunt [Celia] to [friend's] kids and I'm very close with my graduate school friend's kids. I send them postcards." Christina and Silvia both have close bonds with their friends' children and appreciate taking up the role of what Christina called "the cool aunt." Silvia also talked about having more time to mentor young people in her job at a university because she doesn't have her own children: "When someone really needed something . . . I had a bit of space to give it, and most of the time I'm selfish with that space and it's my space, but there is kind of something nice about being kinda like, 'Yeah, I can, I can take this on' or 'I can remember to buy this, these kids' birthday presents' or 'You know, we will make this trip out here or do the service sort of thing.' " Gail also mentioned mentoring young women in architecture as discussed in chapter 4. Childfree women often recognize the additional time and attention they have for others because they don't have their own children and the ways this flexibility links into a characterization of themselves as aunts in a variety of contexts, allowing them to create affective relationships that enrich their own lives as well as those around them.[7]

Childfree women who take on aunt identities form part of a cohort of adults who can be meaningful in children's lives, and the aunt identity rearticulates care and happiness associated with womanhood without requiring motherhood. One woman in Carroll's (2000) book about childfree couples, Carole, said of her relationships with her niece and godson, "I want to be a safe place they can always come to, and help give them avenues to express who they are. I want to help them feel valued. Whether we're parents, aunts, uncles, or just people on the street—everyone can do this for children" (138). Making children "feel valued" was Carole's way of expressing the unselfish care children need not just from their parents but from other adult figures around them, including women without children. Carole did not see herself as a replacement parent but as an additional adult who could help children find value in themselves. Contemporary US culture often frames childcare as an individual effort provided primarily by mothers, a belief supported through hegemonic beliefs about family and the gendered roles supported through compulsory heterosexuality. However, Hayden (2010) claims that "when caring for children is framed as a societal responsibility, others, including childless women, fathers, and childless men, are called on to participate in caregiving activities. This, in turn, opens up time and space for mothers to pursue some of their nonmaternal interests and goals" (286). She argues that changes to the construction of childcare from a motherly endeavor to a social endeavor would create more equitable care structures. Like some childfree rhetorics, a more expansive envisioning of familial structures deconstructs ideologies about motherhood and parenting, potentially opening up different happiness scripts for those who want to be involved in children's lives but who, for a variety of reasons, do not have their own children.

The discourses about being aunts childfree women circulate contest the presumption that women must be mothers; instead, these discourses illustrate one possible way childfree women can construct new identities for themselves that are legible to others. They also show how parents can integrate childfree women into their family's lives, providing space for childfree women to build close relationships with their children and recognizing the value of these relationships. Some childfree women even view this articulation of care as central to their identities as women, regardless of whether they are mothers or not. Laurie Lisle (1996) argues that care for children is a central part of her identity, seeking to "enlarge what it means to be a woman" (193) by integrating childless women's perspectives with ideas of womanhood. A childfree woman in Cain's (2001) study spoke to the importance of these relationships: " 'All our nieces, nephews, and godchildren have been important in our lives. I suddenly realized we already have children. A woman I know . . . told me, 'Never underestimate the influence you can have on a child precisely because you are *not* their parents' " (80). Taking such claims further, some childfree women assert they can provide different types of care mothers or parents cannot, creating more space for themselves in gendered happiness scripts. Comedian Tracy Smith (2013) claims she has the opportunity to love all her nieces and nephews and great nieces and nephews equally because she does not compare them to her own children, saying some need that "extra love" because they "feel disenfranchised" (104) or left out through comparisons to others. Aside from these different types of care childfree women can provide, sometimes they view other people's children as their own and assume caretaking duties that support the care children's parents provide, such as Katherine's work to help raise her friend's children as described earlier. Such moves disrupt happiness scripts by asking others to recognize the work childfree women are doing to care for children despite not having children of their own. These women perform their identities in ways others can understand by showcasing their work as care providers, countering the idea that women must be mothers in order to experience happiness, even as one articulation commonly associated with motherhood—care—is part of this challenging of reproductive doxa.

My exploration of childfree women's uptake of the aunt identity and how it provides an alternative happiness script to motherhood demonstrates how reproductive doxae can be articulated in ways that still align care with women. While this realignment opens up space for new identities such as the childfree aunt, it further reifies the ties between women and care that are difficult to contest. Fixmer-Oraiz (2019) points to this paradox: "Cultural discourses aimed at 'savvy aunties' simultaneously disrupt and fuel intensive mothering. They challenge the belief that all women mother, and yet, they work to cast meaningful relationships with children as central to *all* women's lives, including those who do not birth or parent children" (155). Childfree women who do not like children do not have as many options for contesting reproductive doxae and weaving new happiness scripts that do not connect childfreedom with selfishness, as seen in the previous chapter. Thus, the aunt identity demonstrates how there are possibilities and limitations in changing reproductive doxae and articulating different happiness scripts.

WHEN NEW SCRIPTS CREATE NEW CONSTRAINTS

Although the childfree women interviewed found communities that helped them circulate new happiness scripts, social pressures often complicated their understandings of their identities. As discussed in chapter 3, these pressures could vary quite a bit depending upon a woman's race or ethnicity, sexual orientation, socioeconomic class, and even geographic location. In fact, in the final interview question when I asked childfree women what advice they had for other childfree women or women thinking about whether or not to have children, some focused on the need for women to filter out other voices and pressures—from society and those around them—to make certain the decision they were making was right for them. These pieces of advice represent their suggesting other women should focus on their own desires rather than social pressures as much as possible in taking up or refusing reproductive doxae.

Some interviewees directly spoke about the sociocultural pressures women can feel about reproductive decisions and the need to try to filter these out so they can focus on their own desires. Christina framed this around the need to ignore accusations of selfishness: "I feel like [motherhood] is an all-in experience, and if you are not willing to be all-in, and if you're on the fence about it, please don't let anybody else talk you into that. So the biggest advice is ignore people. There's . . . people will have you thinking that you're selfish and self-centered or, you know, anti natural order of things 'cause you don't want children, but you're the one who's gonna have to deal with them if you have them, so, no, ignore people is usually my biggest thing." Kari put it bluntly: "Just to make your own decision. Cut out the noise and the pressure, negative or positive, that people give you and the social pressure, negative or positive. And just make the decision that's best for you and your circumstances." In giving this advice, however, interviewees seemed to acknowledge that ignoring happiness scripts is difficult and requires conscious effort.

Participants also suggested women consider their own circumstances. Traci offered, "Well, I would say definitely think about it hard. . . . And, you know, just gather information, think about how it would affect your life. . . . I can take satisfaction in knowing that I didn't bow to family pressure or cultural pressure or whatever. So definitely tell people to think about it. But don't give in because somebody is pushing you really hard to make one decision or the other." Grace similarly said the decision needed to be made carefully and with a lot of thought: "What I would tell childfree women or any woman that's at that crossroads in her life is to really, really, really think it through. Don't make an emotional decision. You have to look at the financial repercussions; you have to look at the health repercussions for you. You have to really assess where you are truthfully in life." She and a couple of other interviewees pointed out that even though other people may say they will support a woman if she has a child, ultimately such promises are unenforceable, and mothers bear a heavy burden even if they have significant support. This means it's important for women to think carefully about what they want rather than give into pressure from others that they should have children.

Tasha suggested women should recognize they could be "a mother figure" without being mothers, including by helping "children in need." Paralleling the ways childfree women discussed the ways they cared for others apart from motherhood, Tasha recognized the desire to nurture others could be accomplished in multiple ways. Beyond expanding how mother might be defined, several interviewees also emphasized that women who wanted children should be open about this decision as well. Tara explained, "If you have doubts [about being childfree], and you think maybe you do [want to have children], then you know, maybe you should . . . give it some consideration. But I would say, you know, try not to be swayed or bothered too much by what other people say." Also emphasizing being open to any choice right for women, Claudia said she would tell women, "Just to talk it through, not to put pressure. But if you do wanna have children, not to be afraid to say, 'Yes, I wanna have children.' " In providing this advice, interviewees directly recognized how reproductive doxae circulate around women and tried to make this visible so other women could grapple with it more explicitly.

Sometimes, a woman who identifies as childfree can feel trapped into this identity. For example, when I presented part of this work at a professional conference a few years ago, a young woman in the audience (who was much more articulate and thoughtful than I was at that age!) said she identified as childfree. However, she expressed uncertainty about what to do if she changed her mind and decided she wanted to have children because she was stubborn and didn't want to justify the position of those people who had told her she would eventually change her mind. Although this book has argued that motherhood is a tightly woven cloth for many women, an interesting line of research could be whether some women who identify as childfree, particularly earlier in their lives, struggle to escape those new strands they have created if they decide later they want to become mothers. In other words, does identifying as childfree create its own set of constraints in the ways women think about, experience, and communicate their identities? A study by Julia Moore (2018) in which she interviewed thirty-two mothers who had previously identified as childfree suggests childfree women who later decided to become mothers used silence "to maintain face during their shift in childbearing identity" (10) by withholding information about this change until they were well into their pregnancies, even though they "overwhelmingly" received "support from family and friends who expressed excitement about participants' pregnancies" once they were announced (13). The women in Moore's study sometimes still felt ambivalent about their roles as mothers but felt they could not voice these concerns because they had to perform as "good (future) mothers" (14). Their identification with being first childfree and then mothers was complex, drawing on different strands that pushed them into totalizing identities of mother or childfree they did not feel they could easily unravel.

A few of my interviewees emphasized the need for women to be open to whatever reproductive choices they wanted to make and to be open to their minds changing. Jessica perhaps spoke the most about this: "But you don't have to make a very strong decision, upset people in the process, and then find yourself one day being like, my needs and wants have changed. My life expectations have changed. I feel differently biologically, and emotionally, and my work's different, whatever it is. That you just . . . that choice, no matter how adamantly you expressed it, you have the right to change it. . . . You can actually change that decision. And some people don't feel comfortable going there because it was such a hard time in the first place"—that is, because they experienced so much pushback from their earlier decision to be childfree. Recognizing deciding to be childfree and telling others about this decision can be difficult, Jessica claims it is important for women to be open to changing their minds depending on their needs and wants, as they may shift over time. As the audience member at my presentation and Moore's research shows, however, women who identify as childfree may feel increasing pressure to maintain this identity as different happiness scripts are created around it, just as many women feel pressure to become mothers and, then, to present as perfect mothers.

The spaces interviewees opened up for women to consider reproduction on their own terms rather than anyone else's is valuable. However, the challenges childfree women have made to reproductive doxae, and the supportive communities they have formed in which doxae can be challenged, may be limited and not influence the happiness scripts circulating in larger cultural ways. The communities in which reproductive doxae are contested and new happiness scripts constructed are small. While these communities can form bubbles in which childfree women feel supported, they do not necessarily affect how those outside these communities circulate reproductive ideologies, as seen in the previous chapter. However, Fixmer-Oraiz (2019) argues that childfree identities can more broadly challenge compulsory motherhood, which "is decidedly not about devaluing motherhood, but rather it is fundamentally concerned with rendering its quotidian labor visible. As such, it stands to value the labor of caregiving and nurturance *more* in terms of structural support while, simultaneously, resisting attempts to fashion it requisite of femininity" (155). In circulating affectual and discursive alternatives to gendered happiness scripts such as those seen in this chapter, childfree women can circulate new ideas about womanhood and reproduction and, in the process, construct new happiness scripts for women's lives. In this work, though, childfree women also recognize that happiness scripts—whether aligning with or against reproductive doxae—ultimately constrain someone's choices and lived experiences. Understanding the ways happiness scripts are constructed allows scholars to consider what happens when arguments about people's identities become so tightly wound they threaten to trap them, even if they chose those identities and arguments at one time. It also allows scholars to think about the broader sociocultural investment in happiness scripts that pulls affects and rhetorics together in solidifying these scripts, ideas I explore further in the concluding chapter.

Conclusion

NO REGRETS?
Happiness and Reproductive Doxae

Irene: *"I just talk every day about how happy we are to not have [kids]"*

Meghan: *"So of course there's part of me that worries that someday I'll regret it, but again, that's not really enough of a motivating factor, so I feel like I'm happy with how things have turned out and I'm not . . . I don't ever question it."*

Jessica: *"If there's anything I would want [other childfree women] to feel, I would say, feel comfortable with your decision and be happy, be comfortable with it. Own that."*

Suzanne: *"I think there are lots of alternative models of adulthood that can lead to a happy, fulfilling life."*

Challenging gendered happiness scripts, as childfree women do, is not easy since the reproductive doxae tying motherhood with womanhood invisibly underscore these scripts. Childfree women dig into and contend with hegemonic reproductive ideologies while rewriting happiness scripts and seeking out communities that will support this work. Because of the articulation weaving together motherhood and happiness, childfree women are often presumed to be unhappy. A 2020 survey of a representative sample of one thousand Michigan adults found, however, that 27 percent were childfree and that "their life-satisfaction ratings were no different from those of parents or people who planned to have children" (Norton 2021). Sociological research over the past several decades has also shown childfree people generally tend to be happy (Ramu 1984; Somers 1993; Weiss 1993; Wu and Musick 2008). In fact, in Marsha D. Somers's 1993 study of seventy-four voluntarily childfree men and women, only one did not say they were "happy about their parenting decision," and that one was neutral.

https://doi.org/10.7330/9781646424399.c006

As this book demonstrates, despite such evidence, childfree women can struggle to make legible their happy identities apart from motherhood, in part because identifying other locations of happiness undermines gendered happiness scripts predicated on motherhood. Claire Cain Miller, in the July 5, 2018, issue of the *New York Times*, reported that a survey of 1,858 people ages twenty to forty-five who said they didn't want or were not certain they wanted children revealed the top reasons were that the person wanted leisure time, had not found a partner, couldn't afford child care, and had no desire for children. As I have described, many of the participants in this study, as well as current research, report similar reasons for childfreedom revolving around independence, economics, and personal feelings. As childfree women, we have been able to locate happiness in things other than children. We have done so by channeling our time and energy into other avenues that bring us happiness—other family members, friends, careers, hobbies, travel, or other things. Our lives counter conceptions of childfree women as unhappy. But many childfree women still feel left on the margins of broader society because their reproductive experiences do not align with hegemonic mothering ideologies and their lives do not follow gendered happiness scripts.

Building out from the ways childfree women have been shown to navigate reproductive ideologies in their own lives, I conclude this book with attention to some of the new avenues it offers scholars to reconsider doxae, particularly reproductive doxae in relation to gendered happiness scripts, and the methods by which we explore how doxae are circulated, reified, and challenged. As I hope is clear throughout this project, reproductive doxae in particular articulate women's happiness very particularly in relation to motherhood and have historically operated by shutting down space for women's identities outside motherhood. Examining the affectual and rhetorical circulations of reproductive doxae in childfree rhetorics offers insights into how they exert sociocultural pressures on women and how childfree women respond to these pressures. My research also demonstrates how scholars can examine the ways other types of doxae are circulated through different happiness scripts and how different groups respond to these in ways that are shaped by their own identities and that shape how others view their identities.

NEW DIRECTIONS IN RHETORICAL STUDIES: ANALYZING AFFECT AND DOXAE

Affect theory helps rhetorical scholars analyze the ways unverbalized yet consequential ideas, or doxae, influence discourse. While other scholars have connected affect and rhetoric (Blankenship 2019; Bratta 2018; Crowley 2006; Hariman 1986; Muckelbauer 2008; Santos and Browning 2014; Simonson 2014), this book demonstrates how focusing on the affectual and discursive circulations of reproductive doxae through gendered happiness scripts can help us better understand the rhetorical strategies childfree women and other groups take up in responding to these doxae. In the process, connecting happiness with reproductive doxae illustrates the ways affect can be made visible and, perhaps, evolve from affect to argument. This study also highlights the process and slippage between affect and rhetoric as doxae influence people's lived experiences and the ways they communicate about these with others and themselves.

As legal and political structures create some space that accounts for the diversity of the population in the United States and other countries, affective circulations of hegemonic beliefs become a primary means by which people can socioculturally reinforce racism, patriarchy, xenophobia, homophobia, and other oppressive ideological systems. Reproductive doxae, as chapter 1 particularly points to and as scholars such as Collins (2000), Roberts (2017), Fixmer-Oraiz (2019), and Harper (2020) argue, is often at the nexus of colonialist, white-supremacist, heteronormative power. This means reproductive rhetorics, including childfree rhetorics, are often entangled in discourses that reinforce oppressive power structures and maintain the status quo, even in the absence of explicit laws that do so.[1] However, similar doxae circulate through many other rhetorics, such as immigration rhetorics, policing rhetorics, housing rhetorics, and so on. This book offers rhetorical scholars one way to examine how affect circulates through doxae and shows up in rhetorics around people, by people, and about people that can straighten bodies into particular subject positions or open space for new, imagined subjectivities.

For feminist rhetorical scholars, doxae underlying gender identities are particularly important to analyze because they, like all doxae, constrain the ways people interact with and communicate with others and how they relate to themselves and their worlds at a fundamental level. Feminist rhetorical scholars are also interested in how gendered doxae shift or can be changed over time, and studies such as mine show how some groups are trying to shift reproductive ideologies at a broad sociocultural level by articulating new happiness scripts, even as those moves do not always contribute to this type of change. Childfree women are in a unique position to unravel the interwoven threads of motherhood, care, selflessness, and happiness even as they continue to contend with commonplaces that position them as unhappy. As the childfree women in my study show, what often makes them unhappy is not necessarily their reproductive experiences themselves but having their reproductive experiences questioned because they do not align with hegemonic reproductive beliefs. The childfree women in my study also reveal how their intersectional identities and backgrounds shape their experiences of childfreedom, calling for further attention to the ways doxae evolve and morph based on the particular communities within which they circulate.

Beyond considerations of gendered reproductive doxae in particular, rhetorical scholars can further develop theories of how people rhetorically position their lived experiences in relation to doxae. What rhetorical strategies do people use to align with doxae? To contradict or counter them? For example, how do different immigrant groups align themselves in relation to nationalist doxae that often position them as "outsiders"? Further exploration is also needed of how doxae operate by examining other groups who disrupt doxae at local and broader levels. How might disruptions to doxae among smaller groups and/or in smaller communities lead to the evolution of ideologies and hegemony at broader levels? When and why do doxae morph, particularly to the extent that they lead to sociocultural evolution as reflected in laws, policies, and practices? For instance, how have the Black Lives Matter protests contributed to changes in policing laws, and what kinds of resistance to the Black Lives Matter protests have highlighted racist doxae underscoring policing practices? Finally, rhetorical scholars must investigate what people or groups have the agency and power, whether in local communities or national conversations, to shift doxae. Where does power lie in the way doxae circulate? How can this power shift through strategic rhetorical strategies? What rhetorical strategies bolster a person's ability to assume power and challenge doxae? What are the limits to shifting power dynamics? In community activism about gentrification, for example, in what people or groups does power reside and how can these power dynamics shift through particular rhetorical strategies? Better understanding what doxae circulate around and through people's lives, how people can challenge them, and what rhetorical strategies are used to reinforce and challenge these doxae can allow rhetorical scholars to contribute to an understanding of the constraints people live under and how they can resist those constraints.

NEW METHODS IN RHETORICAL STUDIES: RESEARCHING AFFECT AND DOXAE

In pursuing this project, a central question has come up for me that rhetorical scholars should pursue further: Does affect stop being affect when it rises to consciousness/language? Affect scholars typically identify affect as a preemotional, preverbal state that influences people's lives but is outside their control (Gregg and Seigworth 2010). As can be seen in this project, however, because affect influences people's lives, it shapes rhetoric, sometimes on a subconscious level and sometimes on a conscious level. When a childfree woman senses changes in the atmosphere after she says she doesn't want children, this affectual response shapes how she then rhetorically positions herself. For instance, Jessica said that when talking about children with strangers, she has a choice about whether to just tell them she doesn't have kids or to "play the 'but my husband has daughters' card"; whenever she does the latter, she sees "a reconnection . . . that somehow bridges a situation . . . [and] makes them feel comfortable." In these moments, affect influences the rhetorical responses Jessica gives to others and, as a result, influences how she thinks about and positions her childfree identity. In situations such as these, the delineation between affect and rhetoric can become slippery and circular: affect influencing rhetoric feeding back into affect. What happens when affect—and in the case of this study, affective circulations of doxae—is part of rhetoric? In short, can affect be rhetorical?

Answering this type of question may call for rhetorical scholars to take up commonly used methodologies in new ways or to explore less typical methodologies. For example, more direct observations of people such as childfree women as they interact with others would allow a researcher to gain a better understanding—and a felt, if subjective, sense themselves—of the affectual currents undergirding the rhetoric used in these situations. This type of ethnographic or case-study methodology could also involve a participatory interview process in which researchers meet with participants afterward to gather their affectual or felt sense of what was happening in those particular situations, especially as participants' responses will likely differ from the affectual understanding the researcher develops. This approach would help the researcher craft a more nuanced understanding of how affect and rhetoric are interconnected and how doxae circulate through these.

Researching affect and doxae could also entail more personal and less common but fruitful methodologies, such as personal narratives, that connect a person's felt sense of being in a place with the rhetorics (spoken, written, auditory, visual, bodily, etc.) they experience in that space. I envision this approach being similar to work done by Berlant and Stewart (2019) in *The Hundreds*, a book in which the authors experiment with how affect, emotions, and impressions can be communicated through language, creating "exercises in following out the impact of things (words, thoughts, people, objects, ideas, worlds) in hundred-word units or units of hundred multiples" (ix). While many of the "hundreds" reference ideas from other scholars, thus situating these personal impressions in larger bodies of work, they are integrated into the poems indirectly, and the scholarship is only referred to at the end of each hundred in parenthetical citations. Rhetorical scholars embracing and supporting this type of personal, affectual methodology would allow for further explorations of affect and rhetoric that mirror what it means for felt senses to circulate through and around people's lives and rhetorics.

Beyond opening up space for new research methods, a methodological conundrum I and other scholars researching childfree women and similar kinds of groups across disciplines have run into is how to recruit a more diverse, representative research population when the group being studied—in this case, childfree women—has less visible and public gathering grounds. Childfree women do not necessarily congregate together, and the childfree women who choose to join social media groups or meetup groups for childfree women might create selection bias. Unlike mothers who often congregate around play groups, daycares, or schools, childfree women—like women dealing with infertility—live among and around us but are not always visible or open about their choice to be childfree. This invisibility means researchers such as myself often must rely on snowball sampling, which has limitations based on our own social networks, and contact with interest groups that might attract particular sorts of childfree women as members to recruit participants. As Novotny and Givhan (2020) note about support groups for women with infertility, women of color in particular can feel isolated if such groups seem to only include the perspectives of white women. This limitation can mean researchers must be cautious in how they approach participant recruitment and who is included and excluded in this process.

As a white woman researching childfree women, I experienced this barrier in recruiting interviewees. I recruited childfree women of color largely through a social media group specifically for this population, with the moderator's permission and help; however, I was aware that I was, in many ways, an intruder into this group because of my whiteness. Alexandria L. Lockett, Iris D. Ruiz, James Chase Sanchez, and Christopher Carter (2021) argue in *Race, Rhetoric, and Research Methods* that researchers who want to practice antiracism and challenge "White hetero-normative epistemologies" must "acknowledge their identity and privilege," "articulate the continuity between historical practices of exclusion and their contemporary relationship to structures of power and oppression," and "concede the limitations of their cultural knowledge as an outsider" (26). Throughout this book, I try to demonstrate my awareness of my own white identity and the privileges that come with being a white woman; to demonstrate how reproductive doxae are built on racist, colonialist, heteronormative ideologies that continue to inform the ways childfree women are situated depending on their intersectional identities; and to be open about the ways my identity as a white woman necessarily impacted the interviews I did and my analysis of those interviews, especially when trying to account for the perspectives of women of color, whose experiences I cannot and will never be able to fully understand. Such moves, however, can never replace the perspectives of women of color themselves, and white scholars in our field such as myself must be extremely cautious about the claims we make about the experiences people of color have and how we talk about those experiences in our own work. I have tried to uphold that standard.

CODA: DISCARDING RHETORICS OF REGRET

People need spaces in which many different identities can be imagined, lived, and supported. Despite the sociocultural strength of gendered happiness scripts that tie women to motherhood, Ireland (1993) argues childless women potentially have the power to break these bonds by creating "a space in which alternative female identities might be imagined" (118). Much as Butler (1990) calls for a proliferation of gender identities to deconstruct the binary between men and women, Ireland (1993) recognizes the potential power of childless women to disrupt what she views as "two opposing models of female sexuality: the nonsexual mother or the sexual nymphomaniac" (9). Citing the emphasis on childless women's "lack" that precludes the construction of woman's identity apart from motherhood, Ireland explains childless women must redefine " 'absence' as 'potential space' " to permit "an interpretation of female identity development in which nonmaternal identities are equivalent alternatives to, and not substitutions for, maternal identities" (127). Similarly, Kelly (2009) argues distancing women's identities from motherhood can support not only childless women but all women, including mothers. Creating this space would have to be supported through changes to reproductive doxae as discussed in this project, that would then change "the policies and practices that shape mothering practices" (Kelly 2009, 171). In other words, this change would involve taking up a reproductive justice stance, as Ross and Solinger (2017) argue, that provides paths that support people's ability to have children, to not have children, and/or to nurture their children in healthy and safe environments. These paths do not mean there would be no regrets about what people miss in having different reproductive experiences, but it does mean each person would have more freedom and opportunity to articulate happiness scripts for themself.

In concluding this project, I hope to show how it opens up more avenues to better understanding how doxae circulate through attention to affect and rhetoric, to further research about doxae and gendered happiness scripts as they surface through rhetorics, and to explorations of more questions about the methodologies taken up in conducting this type of research. However, I also find myself wanting to keep an eye on not asserting conclusions that prevent further questions and spaces being opened up for exploration, questions and spaces some of my interviewees gestured toward embracing. As this project demonstrates, many different factors affect how different women experience child-freedom and how they weave happiness scripts for themselves. Some interviewees, such as Meghan in the epigraph to this chapter, have also been vulnerable about reproductive decisions not being completely knowable. Arguments about knowability can trap people into thinking they must make one decision or another, with the end goal of never regretting anything. Regret, though, as some interviewees recognized, can be an inevitable part of life. Feeling regret does not necessarily mean a decision was wrong; instead, it is a recognition that something is missed. Both mothers and childfree women have reproductive lives limited, in part, by the experiences they do and do not have. Happiness does not necessarily imply a lack of regret, and both mothers and child-free women may be happy and/or regretful. The question is how to open up rhetorical space that recognizes the ways happiness and regret can live alongside each other.

What we can do as feminist rhetorical scholars is better account for how the undercurrents of affect circulate through reproductive rhetorics and offer insights into the ways people can intervene in these rhetorics to make space for any reproductive experiences people may have, regardless of the outcome of those experiences. As interviewees' reproductive experiences demonstrate, we must open spaces to explore affective and discursive circulations of doxae through rhetorics and deconstruct how affectual-emotional terms such as *happiness* and *regret* have been leveraged to center some reproductive experiences and push others to the social margins. Rhetorical explorations of reproductive rhetorics can make visible—both literally and figuratively—the grounds through which people's reproductive experiences are judged and the rhetorical strategies that can bring these experiences to public attention. Such work provides pathways through which more people's reproductive experiences are valued and centered in public rhetorics and individual interactions and, as my interviewees show, opens space for new imaginings of adult life.

APPENDIX A

INTERVIEW SCRIPT

1. Can you state your name, age, educational background, and any other demographic information you think could be helpful for others to know about you?

2. Can you describe your family's background?

3. How do you situate yourself within your family, friend, or work groups as an individual?

4. What were some formative events, people, etc. that influenced your decision not to have children?

5. Can you describe a particular situation in which you spoke with your family about not wanting to have children?

6. In general, what have been your family's reactions to your decision not to have children?

7. Can you describe a particular situation in which you spoke with friends about not wanting to have children?

8. In general, what have been your friends' reactions to your decision not to have children?

9. Where do you work and what have been your colleagues' reactions to your decision not to have children?

10. Can you describe a particular situation in which you spoke with colleagues about not wanting to have children?

11. Can you describe a particular situation in which you spoke with strangers about not wanting to have children?

12. In general, do you often end up talking to strangers about your decision not to have children? When or how does this happen?

13. Is there anyone you haven't told or don't generally tell about not wanting children? Why?

14. What would you want to tell other childless-by-choice [or childfree] women or women who are thinking about not having children?

https://doi.org/10.7330/9781646424399.c007

NOTES

INTRODUCTION: NORMALIZING CHILDFREEDOM

1. Following Loretta Ross and Rickie Solinger (2017) and Fixmer-Oraiz (2019), I use "woman" deliberately to highlight how cisgender misogyny is often embedded in reproductive rhetorics while using more broad, inclusive language in moments when the analysis I conduct reflects how reproductive *doxae* situates all people in relation to their bodily experiences.

2. For an in-depth analysis of the ties between motherhood and US nationalism, see Fixmer-Oraiz (2019).

3. I use *deviant* in this book to denote taking an alternative path from gendered happiness scripts, which is a form of heterodoxy.

4. Research and books about childfree people, my interviews, and popular discourse about the childfree all repeat these assumptions.

5. However, the numbers of women having children in their forties and later is rising. Of the 3.8 million babies born in 2017, 114,730 were born to women ages forty to forty-four, and 9,325 were born to women forty-five and older (Livingston 2018). Such pregnancies, though, often require medical intervention through artificial reproductive technologies (ART).

6. This includes, in the forty-five- to fifty-year-old age category, 18.8 percent of white women, 15.1 percent of Black women, 10.9 percent of Hispanic women, and 19.3 percent of Asian women.

7. This is the term used when researchers were gathering this data, although I prefer the term "Latinx" elsewhere in this book.

8. These figures slightly shift when looking at involuntary childlessness, typically due to infertility; 69.8 percent of women who are infertile are white, 13.8 percent Black, 9 percent Hispanic, and 1.6 percent Asian. The numbers also shift when looking at temporary childlessness, which is assumed to account for women who do not currently have children but plan on having them at some future point: 63.5 percent are white, 11.6 percent Black, 14.6 percent Hispanic, and 5.1 percent Asian (US Census Bureau 2017).

9. While *intersectionality* is a contested term (Carastathis 2016; Tomlinson 2019), I follow Kimberlé Crenshaw (1991) here in using the term to refer to the differing power dynamics at work in the "identity politics [that] tak[e] place at the site where categories intersect" (1299). As Natasha N. Jones, Kristen R. Moore, and Rebecca Walton (2016) suggest, intersectional identities include "gender, sexuality, ableness . . . and . . . other factors such as body size" (220). These varying privileges cohere uniquely for different women. Power then operates upon those with different positionalities depending upon the privilege(s) associated with them. They write, "If privilege is positionality that confers unearned advantages, it follows that privilege by definition involves relative amounts of power. And relative is an important modifier, indicating that occupying a position of privilege means not just having power but having more power than certain other groups of people have" (220–21).

10. Rich et al. (2011), for instance, note that in Australia "not all women . . . are encouraged to be mothers. Lesbian women, teenage mothers, and single women,

are often deemed as inappropriate to mother" (235). Fixmer-Oraiz (2019) similarly argues that white, wealthy heterosexual women are positioned in an affirmative relationship with the nation-state while "pathology and criminality [are] assigned to 'other' mothers—those who dare to parent while poor or undocumented or ill or addicted" (13).

11.   I asked interviewees if they wanted to be identified by their real names or not. In the text when I talk about interviewees, I do not distinguish between pseudonyms and actual names.

12.   Many mothers also resist the idea that motherhood requires strict adherence to particular standards of responsible adulthood, as evidenced in a growing genre of "bad" (meaning inadequate) mother movies, blogs, books, and so on. Although "bad" mothers is a related population worthy of closer study, I maintain attention here on childfree women because their interventions differ from those of mothers. For interested readers, see Janelle Hanchett's blog *Renegade Mothering* (n.d.) and her memoir *I'm Just Happy to Be Here* (2018), Kate Long's (2007) novel *The Bad Mother's Handbook*, and Susan Martínez Guillem and Christopher C. Barnes's (2018) article about the "bad mother" trope as it particularly plays out in the television show *Mad Men*.

CHAPTER 1: HEGEMONIC MOTHERING IDEOLOGIES AND GENDERED HAPPINESS SCRIPTS

1.   See Marica C. Inhorn and Frank Van Balen's (2002) *Infertility Around the Globe* for work on how infertility is contemporaneously experienced in various sociocultural contexts, particularly non-Western contexts.

2.   For examples of how some women's subjectivities prevent them from experiencing motherhood in state-sanctioned ways, see Hong's (2011) analysis of Cherríe Moraga's experiences of lesbian motherhood and Fixmer-Oraiz's (2019) analysis of responses to (Octomom) Natalie Suleman's birth of octuplets.

3.   This binary has existed for a long time in our cultural consciousness. The biblical valuing of the Virgin Mary, the purest of mothers, as contrasted with sinful women such as Eve, reflects an ongoing judgment of women based on their perceived character.

4.   See Elaine Tyler May's (1995) book *Barren in the Promised Land* for a discussion of the historical lineages of tropes such as the childless career woman who selfishly compromises the nation for her own desires.

5.   Women who are called selfish are often seen as less than fully women. However, those women who have publicly failed at motherhood can be just as harshly judged as those who choose not to be mothers, although the force of the judgment comes from different places. Society views "failed" mothers as "unfit" and may punish them by removing their children from their care, a judgment most likely to happen when women from historically minoritized groups try to mother (see Fixmer-Oraiz 2019).

6.   See Koerber's (2018) book for a discussion of the development of the wandering womb theory.

7.   As a rhetorical scholar whose approach is similar to Koerber's and Reilly's, I am not here invested in the psychological ramifications of such theories, although feminist scholars have tread and retread that ground (see Chodorow [1978] and Bernheimer and Kahane 1990 for early examinations of Freud's theories in a feminist context). Instead, my attention is on the *arguments* these theories make about women, particularly childless women.

8.   His exploration of the male reproductive system, including the testicles, was less successful.

9. Anna O. was the pseudonym of Bertha Pappenheim, whom both Breuer and Freud treated.

10. Dora's real name was Ida Bauer.

11. See Buchanan's (2013) *Rhetorics of Motherhood* for an analysis of Margaret Sanger's strategies, including as they relate to eugenics, to argue for women's access to birth control.

CHAPTER 2: REPRODUCTIVE COMMONPLACES AND RHETORICAL ROADBLOCKS

1. Kimya L. Dennis has started this work by studying childfree people in the African diaspora, although her work largely remains unpublished. Other work includes Candace Vinson, Debra Mollen, and Nathan Grant Smith (2010); Alejandra Martinez and Maria Marta Andreatta (2015); Melda Sibel Uzun (2018); Emily Kazyak, Nicholas Park, Julia McQuillan, and Arthur L. Greil (2016); Aaronette White (2017); and Keturah Kendrick (2019).

2. This approach is in keeping with the feminist interviewing methods outlined by Marjorie L. DeVault and Glenda Gross (2012), which draw attention to the importance of accounting for differences among women: "We need to be cognizant of the differences that exist among women and be sure that, when we speak on behalf of women, we are not really speaking only on behalf of some women" (n.p.).

3. See also the next section about childfree women's interactions with medical professionals for further exploration of how choice is constrained.

4. In chapter 3, I discuss how several of my interviewees felt varying levels of support and pressure from their religious communities about reproduction.

5. Ironically, Western cultures often value women's physical beauty and appearance while denying women space to physically work on and demonstrate their fitness as they may wish (Banister 2017; Fulton-Babicke 2021; Shellenberger 2021).

6. For scholarship about the rhetorics of nonbiological motherhood/parenthood, see Kirsti Cole and Valerie R. Renegar 2016; Jennifer Potter 2013; Anindita Majumdar 2014.

7. See chapter 1 in this book for a discussion of how sterilization has been used as a tool of reproductive control in historically minoritized communities. For more on childfree women being denied sterilization procedures, see Campbell (1989), Cristina Richie (2013), Nina Bahadur (2018), and Elizabeth A. Hintz and Clinton L. Brown (2019).

8. Studies have shown that female sterilization procedures are overall safe and complications are rare; only around 1–5 percent of women experience any complications (Antoun, Smith, Gupta, and Clark 2017; Stuart and Ramesh 2018).

CHAPTER 3: REPRODUCTIVE ARGUMENTS AND IDENTITY WORK

1. Myra Hird (2003) identifies an ontological crisis in childfree women's decision not to have children, which she claims disrupts the idea that women's identities are based on their reproductive decisions.

2. For work about queer motherhood and queer childfree women, see Amy Hequembourg (2007) and Kazyak et al. (2016).

3. She refers here to 1 Corinthians chapter 7, in which Paul writes it is better for people not to marry unless they cannot control their sexual desires.

4.   According to the US Census Bureau (2017), in 2017 more than 2.8 million grand-parents reported being responsible for their grandchildren, and 1.6 million were women.

CHAPTER 4: THE LIMITS OF RE-ARTICULATING
HEGEMONIC REPRODUCTIVE BELIEFS

1.   This idea persists today, despite the availability of paternity testing, as seen, for example, in rhetorics around childcare and child support.

2.   This view also ignores the many women who are mothers but whose bodies did not biologically produce a child, such as adoptive mothers, some queer mothers, those women who employ surrogates, and stepmothers.

3.   Similarly, rhetorics used to disparage marriage equality sometimes claim to be based on some queer couples' inability to biologically (or "naturally") reproduce through procreation with each other (see NeJaime 2013).

4.   See Courtney Adams Wooten's (2021) "'I Get Some Discrimination They Don't Get; They Get Discrimination I Don't Get': Childfree Reproductive Experiences in English Studies" for a more in-depth analysis of the reproductive experiences of childfree women in English departments.

5.   See also Madelyn Cain (2001) for more description of childfree women in religious contexts. She talks with two former nuns who now work as teachers about their childfreedom in relation to their spiritual lives.

6.   Laura Carroll's (2000) study of childfree couples similarly describes a woman par-ticipant who considered it important to talk with her students, especially women students of color, openly about her decision not to have children to serve as an example of the options available to women (65).

7.   Although Nicole does not mention this, her colleague here denigrates the skills this job candidate brought with them, focusing on their family status rather than their being the best candidate for the position.

8.   Alternatively, Nicole's parents made a point when she was growing up that she should not have children "unless [she was] prepared to take care of them," insisting they would not be primary caretakers for their grandchildren.

9.   The labor differential between fathers and mothers, as well as the very different expectations for parents, has been well documented (Barstad 2014; Douglas and Michaels 2004; Hochschild 1989; Offer and Schneider 2011).

10.   For an exploration of ways queer women and women of color have challenged definitions of family, see Patricia Hill Collins (2000, 2006); Carolyn Morell (2000); Julie Thompson (2002); Laura Mamo (2007); Mezey (2008); Roísín Ryan-Flood (2009); Patterson and Riskind (2010); Taylor (2011); Delvoye and Tasker (2016); Kazyak et al. (2016); and Nishta Mehra (2019). Feminist scholars such as Donna J. Haraway (2016) reject the idea of the nuclear family from a different perspective: the need for the human species to bond with other species in a col-lective movement against impending environmental breakdown. Her imagining of a new kind of kinship includes children being born at a much lower rate and having three parent figures instead of two, much as Thomas V. Pollet and Robin I.M. Dunbar (2008) suggest other species have already expanded caretaking functions.

11.   See Novotny and Horn-Walker (2020) for work about infertility rhetorics and how some women struggling with infertility push back against common narratives about infertility.

12. See Harper (2020) for more about how women of color in particular can experience negative childbirth experiences because doctors and other medical professionals do not adequately care for them.

13. According to the *2021–2022 APPA National Pet Owners Survey* (American Pet Products n.d.), approximately 69 percent of US households own a dog, and 45 percent own a cat.

14. For instance, some parents know they will outlive their children and still dedicate themselves to those relationships, such as memoirist Emily Rapp Black (2021), whose son had a genetic disorder, Tay-Sachs disease, and died when he was only two (almost three) years old.

CHAPTER 5: NEW ARTICULATIONS OF CHILDFREE WOMEN'S IDENTITIES

1. It is important to note, however, that society may actually expect some historically minoritized women—including poor, teenage, disabled, or queer women and/or women of color—to defend their desire to be mothers.

2. See Elrena Evans and Caroline Grant (2008); Kelly Ward and Lisa Wolf-Wendel (2012); Mari Castañeda and Kirsten Isgro (2013); Mary Ann Mason, Nicholas H. Wolfinger, and Marc Goulden (2013); Rachel Connelly and Kristen Ghodsee (2014); and Adams Wooten (2021) for more about motherhood and childfreedom in academic settings.

3. For more about workplace disparities between childless women and mothers, see Shelley J. Correll, Stephen Benard, and In Paik (2007); Jennifer L. Hook and Becky Pettit (2016); and Adams Wooten (2021).

4. Carroll's (2000) book *Families of Two* focuses on childfree heterosexual couples specifically.

5. See Cole and Renegar (2016) for more about the construction of the "wicked stepmother" identity in social media.

6. The August 19, 2018, *San Francisco Chronicle* also ran a story by Kevin Fagan about Andrea handing out pizza to homeless people in San Francisco, resulting in her nickname "Pizza Lady."

7. Amy Stiller (2013), sister of actor Ben Stiller, comments about her own childfree life, "I love kids. I'm a fabulous aunt. I like the idea of being a mother, but as a day-to-day thing . . . it's not for me" (145). She tells a story of acting for her niece, Ella, when Ella was five years old and concludes, "We laugh[ed] hysterically. To be appreciated by a child—that's the thing that makes my adulthood magical" (145).

CONCLUSION: NO REGRETS?

1. This is not to ignore the fact that sometimes laws are explicit, and as of this writing, given the configuration of the US Supreme Court and the events of the early 2020s, the number of laws that threaten women's reproductive rights in the United States seems likely to increase.

REFERENCES

Adams Wooten, Courtney. 2015. "Dottie and Me: Constructing Childless-by-Choice Alternative Rhetorics." *Harlot* 13. http://harlotofthearts.org/index.php/harlot/article/view/238/163.

Adams Wooten, Courtney. 2021. " 'I Get Some Discrimination They Don't Get, They Get Discrimination I Don't Get': Childfree Reproductive Experiences in English Studies." *College English* 83 (5): 379–402.

Ahmed, Sara. 2006. *Queer Phenomenology*. Durham, NC: Duke University Press.

Ahmed, Sara. 2010. *The Promise of Happiness*. Durham, NC: Duke University Press.

Ahmed, Sara. 2015. *The Cultural Politics of Emotion*. New York: Routledge.

Alexander, Jonathan, and Jacqueline Rhodes. 2015. *Sexual Rhetorics: Methods, Identities, Publics*. New York: Routledge.

Alford, Caddie. 2016. "Creating with the 'Universe of the Undiscussed': Hashtags, Doxa, and Choric Invention." *Enculturation* 23. https://www.enculturation.net/creating-with-the-universe-of-the-undiscussed.

American Pet Products Association. n.d. "2021–2022 APPA National Pet Owners Survey." https://www.americanpetproducts.org/press_industrytrends.asp/.

Anagnost, Ann. 2000. "Scenes of Misrecognition: Maternal Citizenship in the Age of Transnational Adoption." *Positions* 8 (2): 389–421.

Anderson, Dana. 2007. *Identity's Strategy: Rhetorical Selves in Conversion*. Columbia: University of South Carolina Press.

Anderson, Deborah J., Melissa Binder, and Kate Krause. 2003. "The Motherhood Wage Penalty Revisited: Experience, Heterogeneity, Work Effort, and Work-Schedule Flexibility." *Industrial and Labor Relations Review* 56 (2): 273–94.

Antoun, Lisa, Paul Smith, Janesh K. Gupta, T. Justin Clark. 2017. "The Feasibility, Safety, and Effectiveness of Hysteroscopic Sterilization Compared with Laparoscopic Sterilization." *American Journal of Obstetrics and Gynecology* 2017 (5): 570.e1–570.e6.

Arola, Kristin L. 2011. "Rhetoric, Christmas Cards, and Infertility." *Harlot* 6. http://harlotofthearts.org/index.php/harlot/article/view/83/73.

Ashburn-Nardo, Leslie. 2017. "Parenthood as a Moral Imperative? Moral Outrage and the Stigmatization of Voluntarily Childfree Women and Men." *Sex Roles* 76 (5–6): 393–401.

Bachu, Amara. 1999. "Is Childlessness Among American Woman on the Rise?" United States Census Bureau. Working Paper Number POP-WP037. https://www.census.gov/population/www/documentation/twps0037/twps0037.html.

Bahadur, Nina. 2018. "Child-free by Choice: When You Don't Want Kids—But Your Doctor Won't Listen." *SELF*, March 1. https://www.self.com/story/childfree-by-choice.

Baldwin, Kylie. 2019. *Egg Freezing, Fertility, and Reproductive Choice: Negotiating Responsibility, Hope and Modern Motherhood*. Bingley: Emerald.

Balsam, Rosemary. 2000. "Integrating Male and Female Elements in a Woman's Gender Identity." *Journal of the American Psychoanalytic Association* 49 (4): 1335–60.

Banister, Lindsey. 2017. "Sporting Bodies: The Rhetorics of Professional Female Athletes." PhD diss., Syracuse University.

Bansil, Pooja, Elena V. Kuklina, Susan F. Meikle, Samuel F. Posner, Athena P. Kourtis, Sascha R. Ellington, and Denise J. Jamieson. 2010. "Maternal and Fetal Outcomes Among Women with Depression." *Journal of Women's Health* 19 (2): 329–34.

https://doi.org/10.7330/9781646424399.c008

Barstad, Anders. 2014. "Equality Is Bliss? Relationship Quality and the Gender Division of Household Labor." *Journal of Family Issues* 35 (7): 972–92.

Basten, Stuart. 2009. "Voluntary Childlessness and Being Childfree." Future of Human Reproduction: Working Paper 5: 1–23. https://scholar.google.com.hk/citations?view_op=list_works&hl=zh-CN&hl=zh-CN&user=jh_Fm7oAAAAJ.

Battersby, Christine. 1998. *The Phenomenal Woman: Feminist Metaphysics and the Patterns of Identity.* New York: Routledge.

Ben-Yehuda, Nachman. 1980. "The European Witch Craze of the Fourteenth to Seventeenth Centuries: A Sociologist's Perspective." *American Journal of Sociology* 86 (2): 1–31.

Berlant, Lauren. 2011. *Cruel Optimism.* Durham, NC: Duke University Press.

Berlant, Lauren, and Kathleen Stewart. 2019. *The Hundreds.* Durham, NC: Duke University Press.

Bernheimer, Charles, and Claire Kahane. 1990. *In Dora's Case: Freud, Hysteria, Feminism*, 2nd ed. New York: Columbia University Press.

Bessette, Jean. 2017. *Retroactivism in the Lesbian Archives: Composing Pasts and Futures.* Carbondale: Southern Illinois University Press.

Bivens, Kristin Marie, Kristi Cole, and Amy Koerber. 2019. "Activism by Accuracy: Women's Health and Hormonal Birth Control." In *Women's Health Advocacy: Rhetorical Ingenuity for the Twenty-First Century*, edited by Jaime White-Farnham, Bryna Siegel Finer, and Cathryn Molloy, 163–76. New York: Routledge.

Black, Emily Rapp. 2021. *Sanctuary: A Memoir.* New York: Random House.

Blackstone, Amy. 2019. *Childfree by Choice: The Movement Redefining Family and Creating a New Age of Independence.* New York: Dutton.

Blankenship, Lisa. 2019. *Changing the Subject: A Theory of Rhetorical Empathy.* Logan: Utah State University Press.

Booher, Amanda K., and Julie Jung. 2018. *Feminist Rhetorical Science Studies: Human Bodies, Posthumanist Worlds.* Carbondale: Southern Illinois University Press.

Bourdieu, Pierre. 1977. *Outline of a Theory of Practice.* Cambridge: Cambridge University Press.

Bratta, Phil. 2018. "They Believe Their Belief." In *Affect, Emotion, and Rhetorical Persuasion in Mass Communication*, edited by Lei Zhang and Carlton Clark, 93–105. New York: Routledge.

Breuer, Josef, and Sigmund Freud. 2000. *Studies in Hysteria.* Translated by James Strachey. New York: Basic Books.

Britt, Elizabeth C. 2014. *Conceiving Normalcy: Rhetoric, Law, and the Double Binds of Infertility.* Tuscaloosa: University of Alabama Press.

Broedel, Hans Peter. 2003. "Witchcraft as an Expression of Female Sexuality." In *Malleus Maleficarum and the Construction of Witchcraft*, 167–88. Manchester: Manchester University Press.

Buchanan, Lindal. 2005. *Regendering Delivery: The Fifth Canon and Antebellum Women Rhetors.* Carbondale: Southern Illinois University Press.

Buchanan, Lindal. 2013. *The Rhetoric of Motherhood.* Carbondale: Southern Illinois University Press.

Bute, Jennifer J., Lynn M. Harter, Erika L. Kirby, and Marie Thompson. 2010. "Politicizing Personal Choices? The Storying of Age-Related Infertility in Public Discourses." In *Contemplating Maternity in an Era of Choice*, edited by Sara Hayden and D. Lynn O'Brien Hallstein, 49–69. Lexington: Lanham.

Butler, Judith. 1990. *Gender Trouble.* New York: Routledge.

Butler, Judith. 1993. *Bodies That Matter: On the Discursive Limits of "Sex."* New York: Routledge.

Caballero, Cecilia, Yvette Martínez-Vu, Judith Pérez-Torres, Michele Téllez, and Christine Vega. 2019. "Introduction." In *The Chicana Motherwork Anthology*, 3–25. Tucson: University of Arizona Press.

Cain, Madelyn. 2001. *The Childless Revolution: What It Means to Be Childless Today.* Cambridge, MA: Perseus.

Campbell, Annily. 1999. *Childfree and Sterilized: Women's Decisions and Medical Responses.* London: Cassell.

Campbell, Karlyn Kohrs. 1989. *Man Cannot Speak for Her: A Critical Study of Early Feminist Rhetoric.* Vol. 1. New York: Praeger.

Carastathis, Anna. 2016. *Intersectionality: Origins, Contestations, Horizons.* Lincoln: University of Nebraska Press.

Carroll, Laura. 2000. *Families of Two: Interviews with Happily Marries Couples without Children by Choice.* Bloomington, IN: Xlibris.

Cary, Tamika. 2020. "Necessary Adjustments: Black Women's Rhetorical Impatience." *Rhetoric Review* 39 (3): 269–86.

Castañeda, Mari, and Kirsten Isgro. 2013. *Mothers in Academia.* New York: Columbia University Press.

Centers for Disease Control and Prevention, National Center for Health Statistics. n.d. National Survey of Family Growth. Last reviewed March 30, 2021.https://www.cdc.gov /nchs/nsfg/nsfg_2015_2017_puf.htm.

Chancey, Laurie, and Susan A. Dumais. 2009. "Voluntary Childlessness in Marriage and Family Textbooks, 1950–2000." *Journal of Family History* 34 (2): 206–23.

Chodorow, Nancy J. 1978. *The Reproduction of Mothering.* Berkeley: University of California Press.

Cloud, Dana L. 1998. *Control and Consolation in American Culture and Politics: Rhetoric of Therapy.* Thousand Oaks, CA: SAGE.

Cole, Kirsti, and Valerie R. Renegar. 2016. "The 'Wicked Stepmother' Online: Maternal Identity and Personal Narrative in Social Media." In *Taking the Village Online: Mothers, Motherhood, and Social Media,* edited by Lorin Basden Arnold and Bettyann Martin. Bradford: Demeter.

Coles, Gregory. 2016. "The Exorcism of Language: Reclaimed Derogatory Terms and Their Limits." *College English* 78 (5): 424–46.

Collins, Patricia Hill. 2000. *Black Feminist Thought.* New York: Routledge.

Collins, Patricia Hill. 2006. *From Black Power to Hip Hop: Racism, Nationalism, and Feminism.* Philadelphia: Temple University Press.

Collins, Vicki Tolar. 1999. "The Speaker Respoken." *College English* 61 (5): 545–73.

Connelly, Rachel, and Kristen Ghodsee. 2014. *Professor Mommy: Finding Work-Family Balance in Academia.* Lanham, MD: Rowman & Littlefield Publishers.

Correll, Shelley J., Stephen Benard, and In Paik. 2007. "Getting a Job: Is There a Motherhood Penalty?" *American Journal of Sociology* 112 (5):1297–1338.

Crenshaw, Kimberlé. 1991. "Mapping the Margins: Intersectionality, Identity Politics, and Violence Against Women of Color." *Stanford Law Review* 43 (6): 1241–99.

Crowley, Sharon. 2006. *Toward a Civil Discourse: Rhetoric and Fundamentalism.* Pittsburgh: University of Pittsburgh Press.

Datt, Bonnie. 2013. "What to Expect When You're Never Expecting." In *No Kidding: Women Writers on Bypassing Parenthood,* edited by Henriette Mandel, 16–21. Berkeley: Seal Press.

Daum, Meghan. 2015. *Selfish, Shallow, and Self-Absorbed: Sixteen Writers on the Decision Not to Have Kids.* New York: Picador.

Davidson, Maria del Guadalupe. 2017. *Black Women, Agency, and the New Black Feminism.* New York: Routledge.

Davis, Angela Y. 1983. *Women, Race, and Class.* New York: Vintage Books.

De Hertogh, Lori Beth. 2020. "Interrogating Race-Based Health Disparities in the Online Community Black Women Do Breastfeed." In *Interrogating Gendered Pathologies,* edited by Michelle Eble and Erin Frost, 188–204. Logan: Utah State University Press.

Deleuze, Gilles, and Felix Guattari. 1987. *A Thousand Plateaus.* Translated by Brian Massumi. London: Continuum.

Delvoye, Marie, and Fiona Tasker. 2016. "Narrating Self-Identity in Bisexual Motherhood." *Journal of GLBT Family Studies* 12 (1): 5–23.

DeVault, Marjorie L., and Glenda Gross. 2012. "Feminist Qualitative Interviewing: Experience, Talk, and Knowledge." In *Handbook of Feminist Research: Theory and Praxis*, edited by Sharlene Nagy Hesse-Bieber. Los Angeles: SAGE. https://dx.doi.org/10.4135/9781483384740.

DiQuinzio, Patrice. 1999. *The Impossibility of Motherhood: Feminism, Individualism, and the Problem of Mothering.* New York: Routledge.

Douglas, Susan, and Meredith Michaels. 2004. *The Mommy Myth: The Idealization of Motherhood and How It Has Undermined Women.* New York: Free Press.

Dubriwny, Tasha N. 2013. *The Vulnerable Empowered Woman: Feminism, Postfeminism, and Women's Health.* New Brunswick, NJ: Rutgers University Press.

Dykstra, Pearl A., and Gunhild O. Hagestad. 2007. "Roads Less Taken: Developing a Nuanced View of Older Adults Without Children." *Journal of Family Issues* 28 (10): 1275–1310.

Dykstra, Pearl A., and Michael Wagner. 2007. "Pathways to Childlessness and Late-Life Outcomes." *Journal of Family Issues* 28 (11): 1487–1517.

Eble, Michelle, and Erin A. Frost. 2020. *Interrogating Gendered Pathologies.* Logan: Utah State University Press.

Evans, Elrena, and Caroline Grant, eds. 2008. *Mama, PhD: Women Write about Motherhood and Academic Life.* New Brunswick, NJ: Rutgers University Press.

Evans, Ruth. 2013. "Children as Caregivers." In *Handbook of Child Wellbeing*, edited by Asher Ben-Arieh, Ferran Casas, Ivar Frønes, and Jill E. Korbin. Dordrecht: Springer.

Fanon, Frantz. 2005. *The Wretched of the Earth.* Translation by Richard Philcox. New York: Grove.

Farrell, Thomas B. 1993. *Norms of Rhetorical Culture.* New Haven, CT: Yale University Press.

Firestone, Shulamith. 1971. *The Dialectic of Sex: The Case for Feminist Revolution.* New York: Bantam.

Fischer, Clara. 2018. "Special Issue on Gender and the Politics of Shame." *Hypatia* 33 (3): 371–577.

Fixmer-Oraiz, Natalie. 2019. *Homeland Maternity: US Security Culture and the New Reproductive Regime.* Urbana: University of Illinois Press.

Foucault, Michel. 1988. *The Care of the Self.* Translated by Robert Hurley. New York: Random House.

Frank, Adam. 2007a. "Some Affective Bases for Guilt." *English Studies in Canada* 32 (1): 11–25.

Frank, Adam. 2007b. "Phantoms Limn: Silvan Tomkins and Affective Prosthetics." *Theory and Psychology* 17 (4): 515–28.

Freud, Sigmund. 1993. *Dora: An Analysis of a Case of Hysteria.* New York: Scribner.

Freud, Sigmund. 1962. "The Aetiology of Hysteria." In *The Standard Edition of the Complete Psychological Works of Sigmund Freud.* Vol. 3. Edited and translated by James Strachey. London: Hogarth.

Fulton-Babicke, Holly. 2021. "Ripped Goddess: New Ways of Making Women's Fitness." In *Women's Ways of Making*, edited by Maureen Daly Goggin and Shirley K. Rose, 57–72. Logan: Utah State University Press.

Gaines, Janet Howe. 2001. "Lilith: Seductress, Heroine, or Murderer?" *Bible Review* 17 (5). https://www.biblicalarchaeology.org/daily/people-cultures-in-the-bible/people-in-the-bible/lilith/.

Garcia-Rojas, Claudia. 2017. "(Un)Disciplined Futures: Women of Color Feminism as a Disruptive to White Affect Studies." *Journal of Lesbian Studies* 21 (3): 254–71.

Geiger, T J, II. 2013. "Unpredictable Encounters: Religious Discourse, Sexuality, and the Free Exercise of Rhetoric." *College English* 75 (3): 248–69.

Gillespie, Rosemary. 2000. "When No Means No: Disbelief, Disregard, and Deviance as Discourses of Voluntary Childlessness." *Women's Studies International Forum* 23 (2): 223–34.

Gilligan, Carol. 1993. *In a Different Voice: Psychological Theory and Women's Development.* Cambridge, MA: Harvard University Press.

Glenn, Cheryl. 1997. *Rhetoric Retold: Regendering the Tradition from Antiquity Through the Renaissance.* Carbondale: Southern Illinois University Press.

Glenn, Cheryl. 2004. *Unspoken: A Rhetoric of Silence.* Carbondale: Southern Illinois University Press.

Glenn, Cheryl. 2018. *Rhetorical Feminism and This Thing Called Hope.* Carbondale: Southern Illinois University Press.

Gochfeld, Michael. 2010. "Sex-Gender Research Sensitivity and Healthcare Disparities." *Journal of Women's Health* 19 (2): 189–94.

Gold, David. 2020. "Creating Space for Black Women's Citizenship: African American Suffrage Arguments in the *Crisis*." *Rhetoric Society Quarterly* 50 (5): 335–51.

Goggin, Maureen Daly. 2002. "An Essemplaire Essai on the Rhetoricity of Needlework Sampler-Making: A Contribution to Theorizing and Historicizing Rhetorical Praxis." *Rhetoric Review* 21 (4): 309–38.

Gregg, Melissa, and Gregory J. Seigworth. 2010. "An Inventory of Shimmers." In *The Affect Theory Reader*, edited by Melissa Gregg and Gregory J. Seigworth, 1–25. Durham, NC: Duke University Press.

Gries, Laurie, and Phil Bratta. 2019. "The Racial Politics of Circulation: Trumpicons and White Supremacist *Doxai*." *Rhetoric Review* 38 (4): 417–31.

Griffin, Cindy L., and Sonja K. Foss. 2020. *Inviting Understanding: A Portrait of Invitational Rhetoric.* New York: Rowman and Littlefield.

Gross, Daniel M. 2007. *The Secret History of Emotion: From Aristotle's Rhetoric to Modern Brain Science.* Chicago: University of Chicago Press.

Guglielmo, Letizia. 2013. *MTV and Teen Pregnancy: Critical Essays on 16 and Pregnant and Teen Mom.* Lanham, MD: Rowman and Littlefield.

Guillem, Susana Martínez, and Christopher C. Barnes. 2018. "Am I a Good [White] Mother? *Mad Men*, Bad Mothers, and Post(Racial)Feminism." *Critical Studies in Media Communication* 35 (3): 286–99.

Hanchett, Janelle. 2018. *I'm Just Happy to Be Here.* New York: Hachette Books.

Haraway, Donna J. 2016. *Staying with the Trouble: Making Kin in the Chthulucene.* Durham, NC: Duke University Press.

Hariman, Robert. 1986. "Status, Marginality, and Rhetorical Theory." *Quarterly Journal of Speech* 72 (1): 38–54.

Harper, Kimberly C. 2020. *The Ethos of Black Motherhood in America: Only White Women Get Pregnant.* Lanham, MD: Lexington Books.

Harris, Tamara Winfrey. 2015. *The Sisters Are Alright: Changing the Broken Narrative of Black Women in America.* Oakland, CA: Berrett-Koehler.

Hawhee, Debra. 2003. "Kairotic Encounters." In *Perspectives on Rhetorical Invention*, edited by Janet M. Atwill and Janice M. Lauer, 16–35. Knoxville: University of Tennessee Press.

Hayden, Sara. 2010. "Purposefully Childless Good Women." In *Contemplating Maternity in an Era of Choice*, edited by Sara Hayden and D. Lynn O'Brien Hallstein, 269–90. Lexington, KY: Lanham.

Hayden, Sara. 2011. "Constituting Savvy Aunties: From Childless Women to Child-Focused Consumers." *Women's Studies in Communication* 34 (1): 1–19.

Henderson, Danielle. 2015. "Save Yourself." In *Selfish, Shallow, and Self-Absorbed: Sixteen Writers on the Decision Not to Have Kids*, edited by Meghan Daum, 147–62. New York: Picador.

Hequembourg, Amy L. 2007. *Lesbian Motherhood: Stories of Becoming.* Binghamton, NY: Harrington Park.

Hintz, Elizabeth A., and Clinton L. Brown. 2019. "Childfree by Choice: Stigma in Medical Consultations for Voluntary Sterilization." *Women's Reproductive Health* 6 (1): 62–75.

Hird, Myra J. 2003. "Vacant Wombs: Feminist Challenges to Psychoanalytic Theories of Childless Women." *Feminist Review* 75: 5–19.

Hochschild, Arlie. 1989. *The Second Shift: Working Parents and the Revolution at Home*. New York: Viking.

Holiday, Judy. 2009. "In[ter]vention: Locating Rhetoric's *Ethos*." *Rhetoric Review* 28 (4): 388–405.

Hong, Grace Kyungwon. 2012. "Existentially Surplus: Women of Color Feminism and the New Crises of Capitalism." *GLQ: A Journal of Lesbian and Gay Studies* 18 (1): 87–106.

Hook, Jennifer L., and Becky Pettit. 2016. "Reproducing Occupational Inequality: Motherhood and Occupational Segregation." *Social Politics* 23 (3): 329–62.

hooks, bell. 1989. *Talking Back: Thinking Feminist, Thinking Black*. Cambridge, MA: South End.

hooks, bell. 1990. *Yearning: Race, Gender, and Cultural Politics*. Boston: South End.

Houseknecht, Sharon K. 1987. "Voluntary Childlessness." In *Handbook of Marriage and the Family*, edited by Marvin B. Sussman and Suzanne K. Steinmetz, 369–95. New York: Springer.

Houston, Pam. 2015. "The Trouble with Having It All." In *Selfish, Shallow, and Self-Absorbed: Sixteen Writers on the Decision Not to Have Kids*, edited by Meghan Daum, 163–83. New York: Picador.

Inhorn, Marcia C., and Frank Van Balen, eds. 2002. *Infertility around the Globe: New Thinking on Childlessness, Gender, and Reproductive Technologies*. Berkeley: University of California Press.

Ireland, Mardy S. 1993. *Reconceiving Women: Separating Motherhood from Female Identity*. New York: Guilford.

Jarratt, Susan. 2009. "Rhetoric and Feminism: Together Again." *College English* 62 (3): 390–93.

Jensen, Robin. 2016. *Infertility: Tracing the History of a Transformative Term*. University Park: Pennsylvania State University Press.

Johnson, Nan. 2002. *Gender and Rhetorical Space in American Life, 1866–1910*. Carbondale: Southern Illinois University Press.

Jones, Natasha N., Kristen R. Moore, and Rebecca Walton. 2016. "Disrupting the Past to Disrupt the Future: An Antenarrative of Technical Communication." *Technical Communication Quarterly* 25 (4): 211–29.

Kahn, Joan R., Javier Garcia-Manglano, and Suzanne M. Bianchi. 2014. "The Motherhood Penalty at Midlife: Long-Term Effects of Children on Women's Careers." *Journal of Marriage and Family* 76 (1): 56–72.

Kazyak, Emily, Nicholas Park, Julia McQuillan, and Arthur L. Greil. 2016. "Attitudes Toward Motherhood Among Sexual Minority Women in the United States." *Journal of Family Issues* 37 (13): 1771–96.

Kelly, Maura. 2009. "Women's Voluntary Childlessness: A Radical Rejection of Motherhood?" *Women's Studies Quarterly* 37 (3/4): 157–72.

Kemkes-Grottenthaler, Ariane. 2003. "Postponing or Rejecting Parenthood? Results of a Survey among Female Academic Professionals." *Journal of Biosocial Science* 35 (2): 213–26.

Kendrick, Keturah. 2019. *No Thanks: Black, Female, and Living in the Martyr-Free Zone*. Berkeley, CA: She Writes.

Koerber, Amy. 2018. *From Hysteria to Hormones: A Rhetorical History*. University Park: Pennsylvania State University Press.

Kopper, Beverly A., and M. Shelton Smith. 2001. "Knowledge and Attitudes toward Infertility and Childless Couples." *Journal of Applied Social Psychology* 31 (11): 2275–91.

Langan, Maureen. 2013. "Sitting on the Fence." In *No Kidding: Women Writers on Bypassing Parenthood*, edited by Henriette Mandel, 112–18. Berkeley: Seal Press.

LeFevre, Karen Burke. 1986. *Invention as a Social Act*. Carbondale: Southern Illinois University Press.

Letherby, Gayle. 1999. "Other Than Mother and Mothers as Others: The Experience of Motherhood and Non-Motherhood in Relation to 'Infertility' and 'Involuntary Childlessness.'" *Women's Studies International Forum* 22 (3): 359–72.

Lindlof, Thomas R., and Bryan C. Taylor. 2017. *Qualitative Communication Research Methods*. Los Angeles: SAGE.

Lisle, Laurie. 1996. *Without Child: Challenging the Stigma of Childlessness*. New York: Ballantine Books.

Livingston, Gretchen. 2018. "They're Waiting Longer, but U.S. Women Today More Likely to Have Children Than a Decade Ago." Pew Research Center, January 18. https://www.pewresearch.org/social-trends/2018/01/18/theyre-waiting-longer-but-u-s-women-today-more-likely-to-have-children-than-a-decade-ago/.

Lockett, Alexandria L., Iris D. Ruiz, James Chase Sanchez, and Christopher Carter. 2021. *Race, Rhetoric, and Research Methods*. Fort Collins, CO: WAC Clearinghouse. https://wac.colostate.edu/books/perspectives/race/.

Logan, Shirley Wilson. 1999. *We Are Coming: The Persuasive Discourse of Nineteenth-Century Black Women*. Carbondale: Southern Illinois University Press.

Long, Kate. 2007. *The Bad Mother's Handbook*. New York: Ballantine Books.

Lopez, Iris. 2008. *Matters of Choice: Puerto Rican Women's Struggle for Reproductive Freedom*. New Brunswick, NJ: Rutgers University Press.

Lorber, Judith. 1994. *Paradoxes of Gender*. New Haven, CT: Yale University Press.

Luckett, Bernadette. 2013. "Without Issue." In *No Kidding: Women Writers on Bypassing Parenthood*, edited by Henriette Mandel, 63–69. Berkeley: Seal Press.

Lunsford, Andrea. 1995. *Reclaiming Rhetorica: Women in the Rhetorical Tradition*. Pittsburgh: University of Pittsburgh Press.

Majumdar, Anindita. 2014. "The Rhetoric of Choice: The Feminist Debates on Reproductive Choice in the Commercial Surrogacy Arrangement in India." *Gender, Technology, and Development* 18 (2): 275–301.

Mamo, Laura. 2007. *Queering Reproduction: Achieving Pregnancy in the Age of Technoscience*. Durham, NC: Duke University Press.

Mantel, Henriette. 2013a. Introduction. *No Kidding: Women Writers on Bypassing Parenthood*, xiii–xiv. Berkeley: Seal Press.

Mantel, Henriette. 2013b. "The Morning Dance." In *No Kidding: Women Writers on Bypassing Parenthood*, 1–12. Berkeley: Seal Press.

Marinelli, Kevin. 2016. "Revisiting Edwin Black: Exhortation as a Prelude to Emotional-Material Rhetoric." *Rhetoric Society Quarterly* 46 (5): 465–85.

Martinez, Alejandra, and Maria Marta Andreatta. 2015. "'It's My Body and My Life': A Dialogued Collaborative Autoethnography." *Cultural Studies—Critical Methodologies* 15 (3): 224–32.

Martinez, Gladys, Kimberly Daniels, and Anjani Chandra. 2012. "Fertility of Men and Women Aged 15–44 Years in the United States: National Survey of Family Growth, 2006–2010." *National Health Statistics Reports* 51: 1–28.

Mason, Mary Ann, Nicholas H. Wolfinger, and Marc Goulden. 2013. *Do Babies Matter? Gender and Family in the Ivory Tower*. New Brunswick, NJ: Rutgers University Press.

Massumi, Brian. 2002. *Parables for the Virtual: Movement, Affect, Sensation*. Durham. NC: Duke University Press.

Mastrangelo, Lisa. 2017. "Changing Ideographs of Motherhood: Defining and Conscribing Women's Rhetorical Practices During World War I." *Rhetoric Review* 36 (3): 214–31.

May, Elaine Tyler. 1995. *Barren in the Promised Land: Childless Americans and the Pursuit of Happiness*. Cambridge, MA: Harvard University Press.

McDermott, Lydia M. 2019. *Liminal Bodies, Reproductive Health, and Feminist Rhetoric: Searching the Negative Spaces in Histories of Rhetoric.* Lanham, MD: Lexington Books.

McFarlane, Megan D. 2021. *Militarized Maternity: Experiencing Pregnancy in the U.S. Armed Forces.* Oakland: University of California Press.

McKerrow, Raymie E. 1989. "Critical Rhetoric: Theory and Praxis." *Communication Monographs* 56 (2): 91–111.

McOmber, James B. 1996. "Silencing the Patient: Freud, Sexual Abuse, and 'The Etiology of Hysteria.'" *Quarterly Journal of Speech* 82 (4): 343–63.

McQuillan, Julia, Arthur L. Greil, Karina M. Shreffler, Patricia A. Wonch-Hill, Kari C. Gentzler, and John D. Hathcoat. 2012. "Does the Reason Matter? Variations in Childlessness Concerns Among U.S. Women." *Journal of Marriage and Family* 74 (5): 1166–81.

Mehra, Nishta J. 2019. *Brown White Black: An American Family at the Intersection of Race, Gender, Sexuality, and Religion.* New York: Picador.

Mezey, Nancy J. 2008. *New Choices, New Families: How Lesbians Decide about Motherhood.* Baltimore: Johns Hopkins University Press.

Miller, Pavla. 2005. "Useful and Priceless Children in Contemporary Welfare States." *Social Politics: International Studies in Gender, State and Society* 12 (1): 3–41.

Michaels, Andrea Carla. 2013. "Mother to No One." In *No Kidding: Women Writers on Bypassing Parenthood,* edited by Henriette Mandel, 87–96. Berkeley: Seal Press.

Molloy, Cathryn, Cristy Beemer, Jeffrey Bennett, Ann Green, Jenell Jonson, Molly Kessler, Maria Novotny, and Bryna Siegel-Finer. 2018. "A Dialogue on Possibilities for Embodied Methodologies in the Rhetoric of Health and Medicine." *Rhetoric of Health and Medicine* 1 (3/4): 349–71.

Monagle, Clare. 2020. *Scholastic Affect: Gender, Maternity and the History of Emotions.* Cambridge: Cambridge University Press.

Moore, Julia. 2018. "From 'I'm Never Having Children' to Motherhood: A Critical Analysis of Silence and Voice in Negotiations of Childbearing Face." *Women's Studies in Communication* 41 (1): 1–21.

Morell, Carolyn. 2000. "Saying No: Women's Experiences with Reproductive Refusal." *Feminism and Psychology* 10 (3): 313–22.

Morgan, Danielle Fuentes. 2018. "Visible Black Motherhood Is a Revolution." *Biography* 41 (4): 856–75.

Morison, Tracy, Catriona Macleod, Ingrid Lynch, Magda Mijas, and Seemanthini Tumkur Shivakumar. 2016. "Stigma Resistance in Online Childfree Communities: The Limitations of Choice Rhetoric." *Psychology of Women Quarterly* 40 (2): 184–98.

Muckelbauer, John. 2008. *The Future of Invention: Rhetoric, Postmodernism, and the Problem of Change.* Albany: SUNY Press.

Mueller, Karla A., and Janice D. Yoder. 1999. "Stigmatization of Non-Normative Family Size Status." *Sex Roles* 41 (11–12): 901–19.

NeJaime, Douglas. 2013. "Marriage, Biology, and Gender." *Iowa Law Review Bulletin* 98 (83): 83–96.

Norton, Amy. 2021. "Survey Finds Many Adults Don't Want Kids—And They're Happy." *U.S. News and World Report,* June 21. https://www.usnews.com/news/health-news/articles/2021-06-21/survey-finds-many-adults-dont-want-kids-and-theyre-happy.

The Not Mom. n.d. Accessed May 24, 2016. https://www.thenotmom.com.

Novotny, Maria, Lori Beth De Hertogh, and Erin A. Frost, eds. 2020. *Reflections: Rhetorics of Reproductive Justice in Public and Civic Contexts* 20 (2): 7–244.

Novotny, Maria, with Juliette Givhan. 2020. "'You Google *Infertility* and You Don't See Me': Towards an Intersectional Framework Resisting the Rhetorical Slippages of Reproductive Activism." In *Failure Pedagogies: Learning and Unlearning What It Means to Fail,* edited by Allison D. Carr and Laura R. Micciche, 191–200. New York: Peter Lang.

Novotny, Maria, and Elizabeth Horn-Walker. 2020. "Art-i-facts: A Methodology for Circulating Infertility Counternarratives." In *Interrogating Gendered Pathologies*, edited by Michelle Eble and Erin Frost, 43–63. Logan: Utah State University Press.

O'Brien, Mary. 1978. "The Dialectics of Reproduction." *Women's Studies International Quarterly* 1 (3): 233–39. https://doi.org/10.1016/S0148-0685(78)90158-6.

O'Grady, Helen. 2005. *Woman's Relationship with Herself: Gender, Foucault and Therapy.* London: Routledge.

Offer, Shira, and Barbara Schneider. 2011. "Revisiting the Gender Gap in Time-Use Patterns: Multitasking and Well-Being among Mothers and Fathers in Dual-Earner Families." *American Sociological Review* 76 (6): 809–33.

Owens, Kim Hensley. 2015. *Writing Childbirth: Women's Rhetorical Agency in Labor and Online.* Carbondale: Southern Illinois University Press.

Park, Kristin. 2005. "Choosing Childlessness: Weber's Typology of Action and Motives of the Voluntarily Childless." *Sociological Inquiry* 75 (3): 372–402.

Patterson, Charlotte J., and Rachel G. Riskind. 2010. "To Be a Parent: Issues in Family Formation among Gay and Lesbian Adults." *Journal of GLBT Family Studies* 6 (3): 326–340.

Pollet, Thomas V., and Robin I.M. Dunbar. 2008. "Childlessness Predicts Helping of Nieces and Nephews in United States, 1910." *Journal of Biosocial Science* 40 (5): 761–70.

Potter, Jennifer E. 2013. "Adopting Communities: A Burkean Cluster Analysis of Adoption Rhetoric." *Adoption Quarterly* 16 (2): 108–27.

Probyn, Elspeth. 1993. "Choosing Choice: Images of Sexuality and 'Choiseosie' in Popular Culture." In *Negotiating at the Margins: The Gendered Discourses of Power and Resistance*, edited by Sue Fisher and Kathy Davis, 278–94. New Brunswick, NJ: Rutgers University Press.

Protevi, John. 2009. *Political Affect: Connecting the Social and the Somatic.* Minneapolis: University of Minnesota Press.

Protevi, John. 2013. *Life, War, Earth: Deleuze and the Sciences.* Minneapolis: University of Minnesota Press.

Pruchnic, Jeff. 2017. "The Priority of Form: Kenneth Burke and the Rediscovery of Affect and Rhetoric." In *The Palgrave Handbook of Affect Studies and Textual Criticism*, edited by Donald R. Wehrs and Thomas Blake, 371–90. Cham: Palgrave Macmillan.

Ramu, G. N. 1984. "Family Background and Perceived Marital Happiness: A Comparison of Voluntary Childless Couples and Parents." *The Canadian Journal of Sociology* 9 (1): 47–67.

Ratcliffe, Krista. 2006. *Rhetorical Listening: Identification, Gender, Whiteness.* Carbondale: Southern Illinois University Press.

Reilly, Collen A. 2020. "Orgasmic Inequalities and Pathologies of Pleasure." In *Interrogating Gendered Pathologies*, edited by Michelle Eble and Erin Frost, 121–37. Logan: Utah State University Press.

Restaino, Jessica. 2019. *Surrender: Feminist Rhetoric and Ethics in Love and Illness.* Carbondale: Southern Illinois University Press.

Rich, Stephanie, Ann Taket, Melissa Graham, and Julia Shelley. 2011. "'Unnatural,' 'Unwomanly,' 'Uncreditable' and 'Undervalued': The Significance of Being a Childless Women in Australian Society." *Gender Issues* 28 (4): 226–47.

Richards, Rebecca S. 2017. *Transnational Feminist Rhetorics and Gendered Leadership in Global Politics: From Daughters of Destiny to Iron Ladies.* Lanham, MD: Lexington Books.

Richie, Cristina. 2013. "Voluntary Sterilization for Childfree Women: Understanding Patient Profiles, Evaluating Accessibility, Examining Legislation." *Hastings Center Report* 43 (6): 36–44.

Ritivoi, Andreea Deciu. 2006. *Paul Ricoeur: Tradition and Innovation in Rhetorical Theory.* Carbondale: Southern Illinois University Press.

Roberts, Dorothy. 2017. *Killing the Black Body: Race, Reproduction, and the Meaning of Liberty.* 2nd ed. New York: Vintage Books.

Rocheleau, Matt. 2017. "Chart: The Percentage of Women and Men in Each Profession." *Boston Globe*, March 7. https://www.bostonglobe.com/metro/2017/03/06/chart-the-per centagewomen-and-men-each-profession/GBX22YsWloXaeHghwXfE4H/story.html.

Ross, Loretta J. 2006. "The Color of Choice: White Supremacy and Reproductive Justice." In *Color of Violence: The Incite! Anthology*, 53–65. Cambridge, MA: South End Press.

Ross, Loretta J. 2017. "Trust Black Women: Reproductive Justice and Eugenics." In *Radical Reproductive Justice*, edited by Loretta J. Ross, Lynn Roberts, Erika Derkas, Whitney Peoples, and Pamela Bridgewater Toure, 58–85. New York City: Feminist Press.

Ross, Loretta J., and Rickie Solinger. 2017. *Reproductive Justice: An Introduction.* Oakland: University of California Press.

Royster, Jacqueline Jones. 2000. *Traces of a Stream: Literacy and Social Change among African American Women.* Pittsburgh: University of Pittsburgh Press.

Royster, Jacqueline Jones, and Gesa E. Kirsch. 2012. *Feminist Rhetorical Practices: New Horizons for Rhetoric, Composition, and Literacy Studies.* Carbondale: Southern Illinois University Press.

Ruppanner, Leah, Xiao Tan, Andrea Carson, and Shaun Ratcliff. 2021. "Emotional and Financial Health During COVID-19: The Role of Housework, Employment and Childcare in Australia and the United States." *Gender, Work, and Organization* 28 (5): 1937–55.

Ryan-Flood, Roísín. 2009. *Lesbian Motherhood: Gender, Families, and Sexual Citizenship.* London: Palgrave Macmillan.

Sabin, Janice A., Brian A. Nosek, Anthony G. Greenwald, and Frederick P. Rivara. 2009. "Physicians' Implicit and Explicit Attitudes About Race by MD Race, Ethnicity, and Gender." *Journal of Health Care for the Poor and Underserved* 20 (3): 896–913.

Safer, Jeanne. 1996. *Beyond Motherhood: Choosing a Life Without Children.* New York: Pocket Books.

Saldaña, Johnny. 2016. *The Coding Manual for Qualitative Researchers.* 3rd ed. Los Angeles: SAGE.

Sandler, Lauren. 2013. "The Childfree Life." *Time*, August 12. http://content.time.com/time /subscriber/article/0,33009,2148636,00.html.

Santos, Marc C., and Ella R. Browning. 2014. "Maira Kalyan and/as Choric Invention." *Enculturation* 18. https://www.enculturation.net/kalman-choric-invention.

Savvy Auntie. n.d. Accessed May 24, 2016. http://Savvyauntie.com.

Scanlon, Patricia. 2013. "What's It All About, Dudley?" In *No Kidding: Women Writers on Bypassing Parenthood*, edited by Henriette Mandel, 212–20. Berkeley: Seal Press.

Schell, Eileen E., and K. J. Rawson. 2010. *Rhetorica in Motion: Feminist Rhetorical Methods and Methodologies.* Pittsburgh: University of Pittsburgh Press.

Sedgwick, Eve Kosofsky. 2003. *Touching Feeling: Affect, Performativity, Pedagogy.* Durham, NC: Duke University Press.

Seigel, Marika. 2014. *The Rhetoric of Pregnancy.* Chicago: University of Chicago Press.

Settle, Braelin, and Krista Brumley. 2014. " 'It's the Choices You Make That Get You There': Decision-Making Pathways of Childfree Women." *Michigan Family Review* 18 (1): 1–22.

Sharer, Wendy B. 2004. *Vote and Voice: Women's Organizations and Political Literacy, 1915–1930.* Carbondale: Southern Illinois University Press.

Shellenberger, Lorin. 2021. "Building Embodied Ethe: Brandi Chastain's Goal Celebration and the Problem of Situated Ethos." In *Women's Ways of Making*, edited by Maureen Daly Goggin and Shirley K. Rose, 73–94. Logan: Utah State University Press.

Showalter, Elaine. 1997. *Hystories: Hysterical Epidemics and Modern Media.* New York: Columbia University Press.

Simonson, Peter. 2014. "Reinventing Invention, Again." *Rhetoric Society Quarterly* 44 (4): 299–322.

Smith, Tracy. 2013. "The Flying None." In *No Kidding: Women Writers on Bypassing Parenthood*, edited by Henriette Mandel, 101–4. Berkeley: Seal Press.

Solinger, Rickie. 2005. *Pregnancy and Power: A Short History of Reproductive Politics in America.* New York: New York University Press.

Somers, Marsha D. 1993. "A Comparison of Voluntarily Childfree Adults and Parents." *Journal of Marriage and Family* 55 (3): 643–50.

Stern, Alexandra. 2020. "Forced Sterilization Policies in the US Targeted Minorities and Those with Disabilities—And Lasted into the Twenty-First Century." Michigan Institute for Healthcare Policy and Innovation, September 23. https://ihpi.umich.edu/news/forced-sterilization-policies-us-targeted-minorities-and-those-disabilities-and-lasted-21st.

Stiller, Amy. 2013. "Mommy Boo-Boo." In *No Kidding: Women Writers on Bypassing Parenthood*, edited by Henriette Mandel, 142–45. Berkeley: Seal Press.

Story, Kaila Adia, ed. 2014. *Patricia Hill Collins: Reconceiving Motherhood.* Bradford: Demeter.

Stuart, Gretchen S., and Shanthi S. Ramesh. 2018. "Interval Female Sterilization." *Obstetrics and Gynecology* 131 (1): 117–24.

Stump, Scott. 2015. "Couple Shares 'Newborn' Puppy Photo Shoot Responding to Baby Questions." Today, August 27. https://www.today.com/parents/couple-shares-newborn-puppy-photo-shoot-responding-baby-questions-t41011.

Taylor, Hannah. 2021. "Complicating Reproductive Agents: Material Feminist Challenges to Reproductive Rhetorics." *College English* 83 (6): 463–72.

Taylor, Tiffany. 2011. "Re-examining Cultural Contradictions: Mothering Ideology and the Intersections of Class, Gender, and Race." *Sociology Compass* 5 (10): 898–907.

Thimsen, A. Freya. 2015. "The People Against Corporate Personhood: *Doxa* and Dissensual Democracy." *Quarterly Journal of Speech* 101 (3): 485–508.

Thompson, Julie M. 2002. *Mommy Queerest: Contemporary Rhetorics of Lesbian Maternal Identity.* Amherst: University of Massachusetts Press.

Thompson, Lana. 1999. *The Wandering Womb: A Cultural History of Outrageous Beliefs about Woman.* Amherst: Prometheus Books.

Throsby, Karen. 2004. *When IVF Fails: Feminism, Infertility, and the Negotiation of Normality.* New York: Palgrave Macmillan.

Tomkins, Silvan. 1962. *Affect, Imagery, and Consciousness: The Positive Affects.* New York: Springer.

Tomlinson, Barbara MacMichael. 2019. *Undermining Intersectionality: The Perils of Powerblind Feminism.* Philadelphia: Temple University Press.

Travis, Cheryl B., Dawn M. Howerton, and Dawn M. Szymanski. 2012. "Risk, Uncertainty, and Gender Stereotypes in Healthcare Decisions." *Women and Therapy* 35 (3–4): 207–20.

Tronto, Joan C. 2013. *Caring Democracy: Markets, Equality, and Justice.* New York: New York University Press.

Tronto, Joan, and Berenice Fisher. (1990). "Toward a Feminist Theory of Caring." In *Circles of Care: Work and Identity in Women's Lives*, edited by Emily K. Abel and Margaret K. Nelson, 36–54. Albany: SUNY Press.

United States Census Bureau. 2017. "Fertility of Women in the United States: 2016." Washington: US Census Bureau. https://www.census.gov/data/tables/2016/demo/fertility/women-fertility.html#par_list_57.

US Congress. 1875. *The Page Act.* 43rd Congress, 2nd sess., ch. 141.

Uzun, Melda Sibel. 2018. "Choosing to Be Childfree: Exploring the Experiences of Black, Hispanic, and Latina Women." PhD diss., Fordham University.

Veevers, Jean E. 1980. *Childless by Choice.* Toronto: Butterworths.

Vinson, Candice, Debra Mollen, and Nathan Grant Smith. 2010. "Perceptions of Childfree Women: The Role of Perceivers' and Targets' Ethnicity." *Journal of Community and Applied Social Psychology* 20 (5): 426–32.

Wager, Maaret. 2000. "Childless by Choice? Ambivalence and the Female Identity." *Feminism and Psychology* 10 (3): 389–95.

Ward, Kelly, and Lisa Wolf-Wendel. 2012. *Academic Motherhood: How Faculty Manage Work and Family.* New Brunswick, NJ: Rutgers University Press.

Warren, Rossalyn. 2015. "A Couple Did a Newborn Photo Shoot with Their Dog to Stop People Asking About Babies." BuzzFeed News, August 21. https://www.buzzfeed.com/rossalynwarren/this-is-the-only-parenting-goal-i-have.

Weiss, Rick. 1993. "The Kidless Culture." *Health* 7 (4): 40–43.

White, Aaronette. 2017. "Tubes Tied, Truly Child-Free at Last!" In *Radical Reproductive Justice*, edited by Loretta J. Ross, Lynn Roberts, Erika Derkas, Whitney Peoples, and Pamela Bridgewater Toure, 404–12. New York: Feminist Press.

White, Augustus, and Beauregard Stubblefield-Tave. 2017. "Some Advice for Physicians and Other Clinicians Treating Minorities, Women, and Other Patients at Risk of Receiving Health Care Disparities." *Journal of Racial and Ethnic Health Disparities* 4 (3): 472–79.

Wilde, Elizabeth Ty, Lily Batchelder, and David T. Ellwood. 2010. "The Mommy Track Divides: The Impact of Childbearing on Wages of Women of Differing Skill Levels." National Bureau of Economic Research. https://www.nber.org/papers/w16582.

Wilson, Julie, and Emily Chivers Yochim. 2015. "Pinning Happiness: Affect, Social Media, and the Works of Mothers." In *Cupcakes, Pinterest, and Ladyporn: Feminized Popular Culture in the Early Twenty-First Century*, edited by Elana Levine, 232–48. Urbana: University of Illinois Press.

Wilson, Kristin J. 2014. *Not Trying: Infertility, Childlessness, and Ambivalence.* Nashville: Vanderbilt University Press.

Wu, Lawrence L., and Kelly Musick. 2008. "Stability of Marital and Cohabiting Unions Following a First Birth." *Population Research and Policy Review* 27: 713–27.

Yomoah, Doreen Akiyo. 2019. *Childfree African.* https://childfreeafrican.com.

Zavodny, Madeline. 2021. "Immigration's Contribution to Population Growth and Economic Vitality." National Foundation for American Policy. https://nfap.com/wp-content/uploads/2021/02/Immigrations-Contribution-to-Population-Growth-and-Economic-Vitality.NFAP-Policy-Brief.February-2021.pdf.

INDEX

Page numbers followed by *n* indicate notes; followed by *t* indicate tables

ABOUT THE AUTHOR

Courtney Adams Wooten is associate chair of composition and assistant professor of writing and rhetoric at George Mason University. She coedited the collections *WPAs in Transition* and *The Things We Carry: Strategies for Recognizing and Negotiating Emotional Labor in Writing Program Administration*. Her coauthored article "Rethinking SETs: Retuning Student Evaluations of Teaching for Student Agency" won the CWPA Outstanding Scholarship Award in 2020. Her previous work has focused on feminist rhetorics and writing program administration and has been published in *College English, WPA: Writing Program Administration, Academic Labor: Research and Artistry, Composition Studies, Peitho*, and *Harlot*, as well as several edited collections.